Race Against Evil

RACE AGAINST EVIL

The Secret Missions of the Interpol Agent Who
Tracked the World's Most Sinister Criminals
— A Real-life Drama

David Race Bannon

New Horizon Press
Far Hills, New Jersey

David Race Bannon
    Race Against Evil: The Secret Missions of the Interpol Agent Who
    Tracked the World's Most Sinister Criminals—A Real-life Drama

Letters written by Toni G. Brynes, Jacques Defferre and "Annie's" father that appear on pages 305, 306 and 310 are printed with permission of *Kungfu Qigong Magazine* and kungfumagazine.com.

Cover Design: Robert Aulicino
Interior Design: Susan M. Sanderson

Library of Congress Control Number: 2002103022
ISBN: 0-88282-231-4
New Horizon Press

Manufactured in the U.S.A.

2007   2006   2005   2004   2003 / 5   4   3

This book is for Sid, Seungho, Jessica, Lane and the children.

The question of good and evil remains in irremediable chaos for those who seek to fathom it in reality.
— Voltaire

You have taken my companions and loved ones from me; the darkness is my closest friend.
— Psalms 88:18

There are times when even justice brings harm with it.
— Sophocles

Where's that Rock of Ages
When I need it most?
— Jude Johnstone, "Unchained"
(Johnny Cash: *Unchained*, Universal 2002)

v

Author's Note

This book is based on my experiences in Interpol. The personalities, events, actions and conversations portrayed within the story have been largely taken from my memories, personal papers and documents, some confidential and others obtained under the Freedom of Information Act, other participants' memories and personal papers.

Some of the dialogue represented in this book was reconstructed from my memories, documents and/or the memories of others. The reconstructed dialogue represents my best recollection of these events and conversations and I believe more accurately reflects reality than paraphrase would. The presumed thoughts and imagined words of the participants were written in consonance with the true actions of the people involved. When I was unable to determine precise dates, the relevant scenes were placed at the points in the narrative that are most consistent with the timing in other documents and interviews.

In order to protect their privacy, some characters have been given fictitious names and descriptions, and identifying details have been altered. All of the events in this book are real; the people in this book are actual. There are no composites.

I understand the need for documentation, because it is so important to my book. I also recognize that some documentation is hard to come by for any book like mine which exposes secret programs of an intelligence agency like Interpol. And some, as I've learned in recent months, is almost impossible to get.

Although it has been difficult to obtain evidence about Archangel, all the facts set forth in this book are based on my personal observations as confirmed by all available documentation. It's no surprise that in all the decades, not one exposé of Interpol has been published. Until now...

TABLE OF CONTENTS

	Acknowledgements	xi
	Introduction	xiii
	Prologue	1
Chapter 1	Hello Kitty	3
Chapter 2	Riots in Korea	15
Chapter 3	Peanut Butter Crime	29
Chapter 4	Doing Time	43
Chapter 5	Hidden Talents	55
Chapter 6	Spy Guy	69
Chapter 7	Close Quarters	83
Chapter 8	Walking the Path That's Given	99
Chapter 9	Trick or Treat	111
Chapter 10	Terror in Marseilles	123
Chapter 11	How to "Clean" Practically Everything	135
Chapter 12	Dracula by Daylight	149
Chapter 13	Bug Hunt	163
Chapter 14	Seoul Man	179
Chapter 15	Free Market	191
Chapter 16	Padlocks	205
Chapter 17	Masks	215
Chapter 18	Communion	227
Chapter 19	Forgotten Season	241
Chapter 20	Captive in North Korea	253

Chapter 21	Reverence	267
Chapter 22	Homecoming	283
Chapter 23	The Wonderland Club	289
	Epilogue	305
	Appendix A	313
	Appendix B	315
	Glossary	323

ACKNOWLEDGEMENTS

This book has its origin in 2000 when my daughter, then age eleven, asked about a particularly nasty scar on my back. I weaved and dodged until she finally blurted out, "You work for the government. I know it!" I denied it in true Archangel fashion, but she kept asking until the spring of 2001 (then age 12), when I told her about my years with Interpol. She shrugged, "I figured it was something like that."

"Would you like to hear a little about it?" I asked.

"Write a book," she said, hoping to avoid a long story. "I'll read it when I'm thirty or something."

Nobody has inspired me more to create an accurate, vivid picture of my life than my daughter so she may read it when she's "thirty or something." If she's interested before that mature age, I'll scribble an abridgement for young readers.

For graciously summoning memories and providing bits of information, my sincere thanks to Kim Seungho, Ph.D., Toni Brynes, Ph.D., M.D., E. Phillip Johnson, Captain Henri Wolper and Commissaire Jacques Defferre. Deep gratitude also goes to Claude Rimbaud for his valuable time and insights into the life of his daughter, the heroine Sidelle Rimbaud. On such a difficult subject, he warned me, "I really don't think I have much to say about it all," and then spent three hours one long afternoon talking about our favorite person.

Special thanks to the readers and staff of *Kungfu/Qigong Magazine* for years of support, friendship and advice, in particular: Risk Castinado, Gigi & Thomas Oh, Martha Burr, Gene Ching, Patrick

Lugo, Kevin Ho and Jason Chang. *Kungfu's* publication of my Interpol article directly led to the writing of this book.

Appreciation is due to Paul Crehan (FilmRoos, Inc.) and producer/director Jim Grapek (Rising Sun Productions) for pulling truth out of me; Scott Simmons and Chris Foss (*Heroes and Dragons*) for supporting volunteer efforts; and the entire crew of Starbucks at Morrocroft for providing essential fuel—especially Jillian, Faith, Ryan, Joshua and Krissy.

I must thank the long-suffering Susan for putting up with me though I didn't deserve it; Shibata Mariko for believing in me through the worst; and my parents for unconditional acceptance. I am deeply grateful to my wife, Elaine, for her relentless verification and generous support.

Rebecca Sheil of New Horizon Press deserves heartfelt thanks for her professionalism, grace and hard work. Acknowledgement is due to publisher Joan Dunphy who, with an iron hand wrapped in brass knuckles, slapped this manuscript and any support documentation we could ferret out from reliable sources out of me when I wasn't sure it could ever be completed.

I enthusiastically thank you all!

INTRODUCTION

A Look at Interpol's History

Interpol's beginning grew out of a 1914 incident in the life of Prince Albert I of Monaco. At age sixty-six, the Prince became enamored of a young German woman. Unbeknownst to the Prince, while he and his new friend dallied on the beach, the woman's boyfriend stole into the Prince's chambers, robbing precious jewels. Then, the two thieves ran away to Italy where they could not be prosecuted.

Angry, not only at being bamboozled but at having no recourse, the prince invited leading jurists, police officers and lawyers from twenty-four countries to the "First International Criminal Police Congress at Monaco." At the congress, it was suggested that an international agency be set up to stop the exploitation of the relative freedom of borders by criminals who used them to escape prosecution in one country by fleeing to another. However, World War I intervened and the idea wasn't picked up again until 1923, when Dr. Johannes Schober reconvened the Congress in Vienna.

There the idea for Interpol, an agency to combat crime around the world through the mutual cooperation of its members, was born. Its name was derived from its telegraphic address, but today its image, like such fictional counterparts depicted in *Men in Black*, *Mission Impossible* and the James Bond movies, has grown to embody a larger-than-life international organization which fights the most heinous of crimes by criminals who thwart all laws.

The modern history of Interpol from 1972 onward, as well as much of the operations of its individual member units, still is cloaked in secrecy. Due to its murky past, including a domination for some years by presidents with Nazi ties such as: Gestapo Colonel Otto Steinhaust, Ernst Kaltenbrunner, who was hanged at Nuremburg for war crimes, and Paul Dickopf, some have raised fears that these leaders may have left a permanent imprint on the ethos of the organization. Nevertheless, much of Interpol's work has been heralded by nations around the world. Still, some of its clandestine dealings have been the subject of controversy and given rise to the rumor that it may have a vigilante arm. And there are some critics: In the 1970s, when Interpol was the target of a number of lawsuits for invasion of privacy and investigations of its intelligence activities by a United States Senate panel chaired by Senator Joseph Montoya, the organization began negotiations to gain complete immunity for itself and its officers in France, where its headquarters were moved. In addition, it would have the right to keep its files private and for the Interpol General Secretariat to be "inviolate." In June 1983, United States President Ronald Reagan issued Executive Order 12425 giving Interpol not only U.S. headquarters but also complete immunity from any lawsuit in the United States. On February 14, 1984, the Interpol Headquarters or "Seat Agreement" giving Interpol immunity and almost everything else for which it asked went into effect in France.

Noted French attorney and Interpol expert Mourad Oussedik later observed, "Interpol cannot be sued in any court in the world. As a result, the organization is completely above the law and answerable to no one."

One case which was heard despite the edicts was Steinberg vs. International Criminal Police Organization in the Washington D.C. Circuit Court in 1985. The court commented, "Interpol appears to occupy a rather ambiguous and shadowy existence in this country."

The charter of Interpol holds it to narrow bounds which are clearly set out. Headquartered in Lyon, France, Interpol is supposed to deal only with international crimes in the areas of human trafficking, high-tech crime, crimes against children, arms dealing, drug trafficking, money laundering, terrorism and organized crime. The charter expressly forbids engaging in military, political or racial matters. Some claim Interpol also engages in intelligence work, yet because such activity is political by its very nature, it would be a violation of Interpol's charter. In fact, when Interpol Secretary General, Jean Nepote, was questioned in 1975 by a U.S. Senate panel, he said, "We have never had any reason to suspect any employee of being an intelligence agent."

Interpol is the second largest organization internationally, next in line behind the United Nations. One hundred and seventy-nine countries from five continents have joined Interpol. The organization is financed according to the individual country's ability to pay, taking into account their Gross National Product. The published annual budget is twenty million U.S. dollars (twenty million Euros).

Every member country has its own Interpol division, called a National Central Bureau or NCB, usually run by a national police organization and not bound by the tenets set in Interpol's charter. In the United Kingdom, Interpol is part of the National Criminal Intelligence Service, housed within its International Division. In the United States, the U.S. National Central Bureau of Interpol was authorized by the State Department and operates within the guidelines prescribed by the Department of Justice in conjunction with the Department of Treasury. In a 1989 letter clarifying Interpol's relationship with its NCBs, Interpol Secretary General at the time, Raymond Kendall, wrote, "The National Central Bureau in each Interpol member country is not part of the legal entity known as 'ICPO-Interpol.' An NCB is a body designated by the appropriate authorities in each member country as its correspondent with ICPO-Interpol and other NCBs." Later in this same memorandum, Kendall denied all responsibility for the actions of the NCBs.

"Only the member country concerned is responsible for the actions of the NCB, not the organization."

William Walsh, a Washington D.C. attorney, wrote back to the Interpol Secretary General in 1989 and later related his letter to the public. Among his points: "Interpol's rules and regulations must be adhered to whenever an NCB initiates an investigation... Interpol headquarters cannot simply hide its head in the sand when NCBs are infringing rights and the Interpol constitution is being violated. Otherwise Interpol's constitution and guiding principals are not worth the paper they are printed on."

The same year, the Council of Europe, a twenty-three member group of European countries, moved on July 4, 1989, to begin an extensive investigation of Interpol. Among their complaints: "Interpol was organized as a private organization by police officers, never submitted its constitution for ratification by any government and has located its headquarters in France where it has been granted immunity from the legal process by the government of the French Republic, thereby placing the organization above the laws of any land, not being legally accountable for its acts."

Though the actions of the members of the quasi police group are not subject to the direction, review or authority of any government and are often secretive, some of the members' actions have come to the public's, critics' and political leaders' attention and raised criticisms. Among these questionable acts:

Jolly Bugarin, Interpol president from 1980-1984, was Chief of the Philippines National Bureau of Investigation and head of the Filipino Interpol office under President Ferdinand Marcos. Marcos' political opponent, Benigno Aquino, who Bugarin was supposed to protect, was assassinated by known killers. It was learned that one assassin had been a thirteen-year member of Bugarin's police force.

Bugarin excused the man's actions by stating, "In the fight against crime, we also use criminals." (Associated Press, February 7, 1984). According to Reuters (July 4, 1988), Bugarin also ordered evidence suppressed in the Aquino murder case.

Another criticized member is Miguel Aldana Ibarra, the Interpol Chief in Mexico who United States agents revealed had taken a bribe. On January 30, 1990, Aldana was indicted in Los Angeles on charges of participating in the murder of U.S. Drug Enforcement Agent Enrique Camarena Salazar.

However, many countries around the world have come to value Interpol's expertise. It has been pointed out by G. Wayne (Duke) Smith, of the U.S. Marshals, formerly Associate Director for operations and Chief of the IOB (International Branch of the Enforcement Division), that from 1987 to 1991, U.S. Marshals opened almost 14,000 cases with Interpol and Interpol closed 867 of those cases. And, as Fenton Bresler observed in his book, *Interpol*, "The organization has proved its worth. It has survived a troubled and sometimes murky history. Of course, it has its failings and its limitations. But what would the prospects for fighting international crime be without it?"

Bresler also notes on the subject of contemporary slavery and child abuse, that nearly every civilized country has laws but the reality is that prosecutions in international child abuse cases are a rarity. One of Interpol's major stated objectives since 1996 is to work on and coordinate "the international fight to eradicate the exploitation of, and crimes against, children." Today, Interpol uses its own officers and the Internet to help find tens of thousands of children who are being exploited and sexually abused. Yet even if you catch this brand of criminal, there is no guarantee that he (or she) will receive appropriate punishment. In its overt posture on this issue, Bresler feels "the organization's usefulness is extremely limited." However, in this book, David Bannon describes his and others' hitherto unknown roles in ridding the world of this scourge.

On December 11, 2001, the United States Treasury Undersecretary James Gurule and Interpol's Secretary General Ronald K. Noble met at Interpol Headquarters in Lyon, France to confer on the organization creating a terrorist financing database to hinder money being funneled into terrorist organizations. "Interpol is committed to both the fight against terrorism and the funds that make such heinous acts possible," said Ronald K. Noble. To this end, a new joint United States Treasury - Interpol partnership to crack down on terrorist financing was announced.

Once a year, the general assembly which governs Interpol meets and makes decisions regarding policy and strategy. It also elects the organization's executive committee. One vote is given to each member country and the delegates are appointed by their own country's government. Jesus Espigares Mira of the Spanish National Police was elected President to serve from 2000 to 2004. American Ronald K. Noble, the current Secretary General, is the first non-European to hold that position.

Interpol's vision, articulated on its website, is to "help create a safer world. Our aim is to provide a unique range of essential services for the law enforcement community to optimize the international effort to combat crime," which synchronizes perfectly with Interpol's stated mission to be "the world's pre-eminent police organization, in support of all organizations, authorities and services whose mission is preventing, detecting and suppressing crime."

In order to meet the challenge of ever-changing forms of international crime, the organization states that it seeks to "employ men and women with the highest ability and integrity."

PROLOGUE

Last night I dreamed about Sid again. I watched her shoot her SIG Sauer pistol and heard her beg me to leave Interpol "to grow fat together." This is a story of valor, loss, redemption and crimes so unthinkable it's still hard to wrap my mind around it. Like all good stories, it's also about love.

Even now, years later, I can't believe that even for a moment I forgot her. As you read this book, pages will fly by without a mention of Sidelle Rimbaud. Years of Interpol tactics, weapons, crimes and grim punishment will all unfold without a hint of her. But she will be there, beneath the surface, because everything that happened from the day I met her until the day I was able to make peace with her memory is about that one woman.

This story is true but sometimes I wish it were not.

My scars and flaws are painfully obvious. I have revealed what happened, because this story deserves telling. You will read of humanity at its worst and best; powerful secrets and organizations that work without public knowledge. You will read of evil that must see the light of day and good that transcends it.

I've pieced together my life from memories, documents and facts. It is a grim and terrifying world. If I misremember, I accept blame. If I seem vague at times, especially in relating instances of crimes against children, please consider that the few children who lived are still enduring unimaginable, unforgettable horrors. I wish to spare them public scrutiny.

In writing this I've stumbled through the dimly lit caverns of my own memory. I beg the indulgence of friends and ask only one small boon of my readers: please acknowledge as cold reality the international underground that fosters child molestation, enslavement and trafficking, and encourages the resulting pornography.

The hell inflicted on these children is real. We, who are citizens of the world, must band together to protect the innocent.

Some of what you read will be repulsive and grotesque; other pages may inspire you at the quiet valor of those who remain unsung. Every page is real. It is my life.

I invite you into the truth of this world.

one

HELLO KITTY

Suites at the Byron Hotel in the Bayswater section of London weren't cheap. Exquisite taste went hand-in-hand with an air of opulence and refinement. After a stroll in Kensington Gardens, I crossed Queensborough Terrace, straightened my tie, buttoned my gray suit and entered the country house hotel atmosphere of the Byron. I felt classier and better behaved just stepping into the Victorian-style lobby. I was in London because of a conversation I'd had with my boss in Brussels a few days before.

"At last we've got Jergens, *mon ami*. The skell in Thailand rolled and gave up some tapes." Commissaire Jacques Defferre, Interpol, French, was a great fan of Humphrey Bogart to the point of slicking his hair back like the famous actor. He had always teased me about my fiancée, Sidelle Rimbaud, a French *Direction de Surveillance du Territoire* (DST) agent whose smoldering beauty would probably have broken decency rules at the Moulin Rouge. "She's my Bacall," he would laugh, sipping port. "You just got her before she fell for my rugged elegance."

We had sat at the tiny *Moeder Lambic* café on rue de Savoie, St-Gilles—one of many such places in Brussels where people minded their own business. The neighborhood had seen better days and the décor was tatty, but Defferre liked it for the nearly thousand varieties of beer. I plucked a comic from the shelves. We ordered a platter of Belgian cheese and set to work.

We had tagged Jergens months earlier. He was the primary supplier in a ring of kiddie porn that fed to London and New York—then went out globally from there. Jergens was once a Catholic priest who had been arrested for exposing himself to two youngsters in Romania. He was a tall Brit with an overhanging belly. No longer a man of the cloth, he bragged to his contacts that he was "a sensualist, a modern Herrick."

Seventeenth-century cavalier poet and Episcopal minister Robert Herrick may have been a sensualist, but he preferred grown women who said no as often as yes. Jergens had a darker fetish.

"You won't believe where he's staying this week," Defferre had said. "The Byron Hotel in the heart of London." The "skell" Defferre mentioned was a Thai informant, Narit Chaiyasut, who had given exact locations and some video samples. Commissaire Defferre handed me the tape enclosed in a sealed manila envelope. "Jergens used the suite in at least two tapes."

Later, in my room in Brussels, we had watched the tape, confirming that Jergens was "with child"—a euphemism for the primary condition placed on every assignment. The subject had to be either caught performing an act of direct molestation with a child or we had to possess absolute photographic evidence of same. The photos and tapes passed careful scrutiny by tech experts before being released to the Archangel team.

Archangel was founded in 1979, an offshoot of an earlier program that dated to the early 1960s that had been designed specifically to hunt those who traffic in children.

The idea of parents selling their children is not a new one in the world. Even though there are countries that ignore the traffic, such as Thailand or Pakistan, other countries don't want the sold children being imported into their borders. Within the 170-plus member countries participating in Interpol—and the many others that did so without official membership—there was unanimous condemnation of this traffic. The practice not only included buying children as young as one year from willing parents, but also kidnapping others and trading them around the world.

Invariably this traffic included unspeakable sexual abuse, murder of the victims and the resulting pornography which recorded these acts. This "kiddie porn" as it was termed, commanded huge amounts of money on the international market. Photos and movies recovered by the Interpol teams included sexual acts with infants, bloody torture and the screaming deaths of too many children to record in a book this small—even if we dedicated every page to lists of names.

Not all children in these dark pictures were bought and sold, however. Many images and tapes were made by individuals abusing their relatives or children in their care and then sold on the market. The overwhelming, global nature of child molestation and pornography forced the creation of a team dedicated to hunting those who produced and traded these materials.

Team Archangel's mission: Identify child porn producers who danced around the laws of multiple nations and eliminate— or "clean"—them.

Watching the tape, I assessed the layout of the room
behind the three-year-old girl being tortured on screen. Her plain-
tive cries for her mother were too common a part of this skell's
game. I committed the room to memory. I also tagged the method
of Jergen's torture of the child. Defferre passed me a badge. "You're
Belgian gendarmerie again, Major Bannon."

I nodded at the familiar association, which included a rank
and traceable position with a known organization. I had only worn
the gendarme uniform twice. Defferre slid one hand back across
the Bogie hairstyle. "The Met knows nothing," he said, referring
to the Metropolitan Police—Scotland Yard. "But the inspector
most likely to investigate the case is aware of us. He's worked with
MI6 before."

I took the badge and the ID for my Interpol rank as a major
in the Belgian Gendarmerie. I had lived in Marseilles before, but
after I began working full-time with Defferre and Archangel, my
semi-permanent, low-rent rooms were in Brussels, Washington
state, USA, and Pusan, South Korea. Mostly, I just traveled from
assignment to assignment.

Defferre passed me a hand-towel with a pink *Hello Kitty*
motif embroidered on the blue cloth. It was a carry-over from the
first time we worked together on this type of assignment—and a
sign between us that this job was a go. "Clean," he said.

I took the towel. "Will do."

I left for England the next day.

Having arrived in London, I waited in the elegant hotel
lobby for the elevator to take me to Jergen's room, then I walked
down the tenth floor corridor.

The door was easy. Although I owned a lock-pick case, I always found a simple knock did wonders. Jergens answered the door in shorts and an over-sized V neck shirt. Comfort clothes that barely covered his tool shed gut. He carried it well in what was probably six feet and change. His left hand was behind his back.

"Narit Chaiyasut said you needed a man in Miami," I said with an obliging shrug and smile.

Jergens nodded. "He said you'd be coming. You got it?"

I laid out the buy in jack: five thousand American dollars. Jergens stepped back, motioning me in. I laid the cash on a desk by the window, scoping the room. Yeah, it was the place in the tape. Yeah, it needed cleaning.

Jergens sat opposite me on a luxurious Queen-Anne style chair. A low glass table was between us, covered with magazines and tapes. The window drapes were tightly closed to our left. To the right I caught the bedroom suite. Seemed empty.

"Here's the way I do things," he said, laying both hands on the table, spreading out his fat fingers nimbly over the tapes. "I supply the product; you copy and reproduce. Anything you produce you send to me and I decide what gets to our customers. They have particular tastes and I aim to satisfy them with quality product." It all sounded so legitimate in his standard, south-of-London tones. A British accent could make anything sound respectable. "You earn half of what you sell. Any extra manpower or expenses come from your percentage."

I stretched, leaning back to get a better view of the bedroom. Reasonable chance it was empty. "Sounds good, like Narit said it would." I smiled, eager to please and make some cash. I saw what looked like a German Walther P5 peeking from between the seat cushions next to Jergens. Not quite James Bond's famous Walther PP7, but close enough for this guy. That's what he held behind his back when he answered the door. "How about special requests?" I asked. "Infants, boys, girls, black, Asian, like that." Call me Mr. Customer Service.

Jergens went over the pricing and deliverables, just like any business. I nodded and smiled and acted like I enjoyed talking about the kids almost as much as the money. His hands waved over the pictures and videos, occasionally twisting his ear—a distracting habit that caused his ear to redden the more excited he became.

"These kids," he said, "they are all eager to please once you train them."

I nodded. I'd heard it before: The kids really wanted it. They asked for it. Guys like Jergens were teaching them things that they would learn later as bumbling teenagers—without the guidance of a "loving" adult mentor. "We pedophiles are misunderstood," he concluded, using a term that took the sting out of raping little kids.

"Mind if I use the restroom?" I asked politely. He graciously pointed out the bathroom through the master bedroom. As I walked through I confirmed that the place was empty. A tripod with video camera attachment stood by the bed. I snagged a hand towel and walked back, wiping my hands and a few things my fingers had touched.

Jergens was warming to his business and had popped in a tape of himself and an infant of maybe eighteen months. "This is my best seller." He giggled lightly.

I figured it was a mistake to let this guy live a minute longer.

"Souvenir," I said as I tossed a video tape on Commissaire Defferre's desk at Interpol headquarters. I'd been back in Lyon, France about two hours.

He frowned. "What's this?"

I shrugged and sat down.

He pushed the cassette aside and bore down on me. "He's clean?"

"Yep." Jergens was dead.

"You left the tapes untouched for the homicide inspector to find?"

"Yep." Kiddie porn starring the corpse found on the scene sometimes made for an investigation that was, at best, half-hearted if not just plain unconcerned with catching whoever did the world a favor by offing the skell. Forensic work was expensive and required signatures that might be hard to come by with an inspector who knew about the Archangel team looking into the death. Investigators would be more interested in matching the images to missing children reported worldwide. One of Interpol's contributions in curtailing the traffic of human beings was its vast database of missing child cases. The painstaking task of matching child pornography with known reports often took years—and just as often provided few tangible results.

"Then what's this?" asked Defferre, pointing at the video tape.

"Jacques, he had hundreds of pictures and tapes," I said, leaning forward. "Easily thirty or forty different kids. And that was just the stuff lying around. He had a video camera set up in his bedroom. He was fat and he smelled bad and was bragging about how many kids he'd had. Like I want to listen to that. I figured, maybe he wanted a slice of his own pie. Maybe he liked making movies enough to be in one last scene."

Defferre sighed, lifting the video gingerly. "*C'est mal.* What have you done?"

"I did what you trained me to do, Defferre. You and Archangel and this whole place. You want me to clean the mess? Great. Here's a taste of what I do. You don't like it? How about you kiss my entire ass." I ran the tape of me using the same ropes and knife and cigars on Jergens that he used on that three-year-old girl in the video Defferre had shown me. Defferre leaned back, staring at the ceiling. I paused, surprised that I was short of breath, angry, unable to stop. "Oh yeah, it's all there, but you only see and hear him. Nothing traceable. At the end he begged to tell me the name of every distributor. He begged me to send him to hell. It should make for interesting viewing—if anyone has the stomach. Me, I'd do it again just to to be sure he was dead."

Jacques' eyes glistened. He raked his fingers through his hair and picked imaginary dust from his lapel. "*Cher ami,* what have we done to you?"

I was never a precocious child—never brilliant—just the usual pack of friends and participation in school sports. Swimming, track and a little drama club tossed in with some student government and decent grades. I did manage to complete my ninth grade algebra coursework six months prior to the end of my freshman year in school, which led to taking classes at the local community college my last two years of high school. I still laugh at how intimidating the eighteen-year-old girls in the college classes seemed. I'll spare you all my crushes.

It was in my personal relationships that the attributes Interpol found most useful reared their ugly heads. One example involved my sister, a decent, ethical and completely creative soul with a unique perspective on the world. Plenty of brains and an artistic flair to which I aspire. One day, when she was fourteen and I was eleven, we were enduring the end-of-summer, back-to-school shopping trip. She trotted out of the dressing room in size 3 pants—a bit snug and revealing in the 1970s' style. My mother strongly voiced her opinion, which caused me to step out of harm's way and my sister to storm back to the dressing room in search of size 5, or better yet, size 7. Mom stormed in a different direction.

Moments later, my sister emerged in size 7 pants, pouting.

"Hey, goofball," I said, calling her over in my most charming little brother manner. "Why not think it through and get the size you want?"

Eyeroll from sister. I swear, it wasn't until I had my own daughter that I saw an eyeroll that equaled my sister's complete bodily/verbal disgust all in one motion. "How?" she asked, turning in front of the mirror, frowning at her image in the baggy pants.

"Take size 3 and size 7 into the dressing room," I said, miming the action. "Try on the 7s, show them to Mom. She's all pleased, right? Then when you take the 7s off, carry out the 3s and hand them to her. She thinks she's buying the right size."

"What about later?" My sister usually didn't care much about consequences—being only fourteen—but that was a good question.

I shrugged. "They shrunk. Darn cheap pants."

I have no idea if my sister ever took my completely unethical advice. At age eleven ethics weren't my strong suit. Later, when

I came to think of myself—in my own small way—as having an ethical standard to which I adhered, I shook my head regretfully that I had so casually tossed out such bad wisdom to my friends and siblings. I realized it wasn't the unethical act I so ardently encouraged—it was the concept of making things simpler with a new approach that ignored conventional thinking. As a child this concept reflected itself in embarrassing little scams.

Interpol would find a far more potent use for these traits. Dr. Kim Cholkyu, who would one day give me a psychiatric exam as part of my training with Interpol, officially was the director of the South Korean National Medical Center. I later learned that he received his directorship with the assistance of Interpol, the organization for which he often did work ups via the Korean National Central Bureau of Interpol (KNCB). He gave me the exam long before I began cleaning work full-time. His report included these characteristics:

"Subject considers violence as a solution to difficult situations on the same scale as negotiation… Subject expressed strong ethical convictions."

Violence may have once been a viable solution for me until I learned better in the eighth grade. When we returned to school after summer break, I swaggered over to the class scapegoat and gave him the usual smartass treatment. He challenged me to a fight after school, at which time he beat me to a gasping pulp. Turns out he had spent summer school at boxing camp. Later, he was regional golden gloves champ for our high school. As a class officer at a pep rally, I was pleased to announce, "I was the first in a long string of suckers to get his butt beat by our own champion." After my eighth grade whopping, I was less inclined to consider violence as a solution equal to negotiation. At least until I got better training.

The ethical convictions I learned were reflections of my first foray into the outside world. At age eighteen (nearly nineteen), I was a member of The Church of Jesus Christ of Latter-Day Saints, whose missionary activities encourage young men and women to spend two years sharing the Word of the Bible and performing other religious activities—often far from home. I accepted this challenge and was sent to South Korea, where I learned the language and worked with many fine and altruistic people. The activities were what one might expect in such an endeavor: working with the deaf, participating in church functions, assisting the sick or unemployed and inviting people to attend services and consider joining the church.

That was not all I did.

two

RIOTS IN KOREA

After arriving in South Korea for my missionary work, I decided to improve my martial art skills. I trained under Hapkido masters in Pusan, Chunju, Chinhae and Seoul. My first teacher, Kim Changsik, is the one who remains the most vivid in my memory.

His school was austere but warm, brightly lit and filled with the smells of sweat, leather and effort. It was located in the posh Namchon District of Pusan. We trained on weekdays from 6 A.M. to 7:30 A.M., usually beginning with simple calisthenics followed by one hour of *hyung* (forms) practice or attack/defense techniques. The final half-hour was for each student's exercise of choice. Frequently, my friends and I focused on heavy bag work and weight training. Every Saturday was reserved for free sparring.

The heavy bag was an important part of Kim's training. A great believer in physical strength, he refused to instruct any students who fell on the "technique over exercise" method of study, which he flatly dismissed as lazy. The bag and the mat became close companions, primarily due to my temper.

Within a short time, I spoke Korean fluently—a combination of my missionary training and complete immersion in the culture. Although my instructor and I spoke almost exclusively in his native tongue, he never failed to reprimand me in awkward English.

"You bad temper!" he cried continually. "Twenty push-up!" Or just as frequently, ten full minutes on the bag. Anyone familiar with heavy bag work knows that ten minutes winds even the toughest boxers.

Once, during Saturday sparring, my opponent employed a Kuk Sool Won *bang jok* counterattack against my roundhouse kick from a left offensive stance. He had assumed a right Kuk Sool Won defensive stance. Blocking my roundhouse kick with both arms, left inside and right wrapping, he advanced forward, grabbed my lapel and brought his right foot behind my left knee. His right foot swept back, sending me sailing backward onto the mat.

Although it was a well-timed and effective defense, the danger of injury by applying techniques from other martial styles during a Hapkido sparring session is high and was strictly forbidden by the instructor. I lost my temper. Again.

Employing the Hapkido *Sun 6 Sool* attack, I stepped forward on my left foot, slamming my opponent with a right front kick to his *dan jun hyul* pressure point on the lower abdomen, followed immediately by a crescent kick to his ribs. The move was executed with speed, strength and anger, for which my opponent was unprepared. He fell, gasping.

"Bannon! You bad temper!" yelled Kim. "Twenty push-up!"

Switching to Korean, I explained lamely about the Kuk Sool Won defense. Kim responded in curt Korean, a language filled with nuances of high- and low-level speech. "You think I didn't see that? Sparring discipline is my job, not yours." Though easily five inches shorter than my six feet, he seemed to tower over me in his gray T-shirt, loose sweat pants and perpetually messy black hair. He added in English, "Twenty push-up!"

After the push-ups, Kim judged correctly that my mood had not been tamed, so he pointed at the heavy bag. "Five minute!"

Groaning, I considered the wisdom of controlling my temper in the future.

Kim's gym, called a *dojang* in Korean, required no extra fees. We paid monthly, in advance, and were free to leave the dojang at any time if dissatisfied. *Dobok*, the standard Taoist martial arts uniform worn throughout Asia, was entirely optional and could be purchased at any shop in town. Patches representing the dojang were distributed at Kim's discretion as gifts for merit. He insisted on choosing those who would represent the school by wearing his patch.

Belt ranking was simple. After years of training, experience and earned knowledge, particularly adept students were awarded black belts by the instructor. There were no intermediary belts. Tests to gauge the students' competence in forms and techniques were applied often at no charge. In the years I studied with Kim— while living in Korea and later when my trips to the peninsula allowed—no student ever paid to test or paid for the cherished black belt. When, and if, sufficient knowledge of the Hapkido system was achieved, a black belt was awarded. The advanced black belt degrees were attained in similar fashion.

Students referred to Kim alternately as Master (*Sabu*) or Teacher (*Sensaeng*), depending on the student's personality, inclination and the social setting. Kim did not demand any particular title, nor did any of the instructors under whom I studied in Korea. Without fail, I followed the lead of fellow students and referred to my instructors as Teacher, reserving Master for formal gatherings and tournaments.

Hapkido does not have any tournaments. It is a violent art designed to maim and kill. However, many Hapkido schools participated in other martial arts tournaments for the social benefits to the students. At tournaments, Kim's students wore traditional dobok. Almost all of the students simply wore sweats during daily training and sparring. I spent six months training under Kim before I ever saw a dobok. The newspaper, *Pusan Ilbo*, was doing a feature on Kim's school and for the photo shoot the students were required to dress in the more traditional outfits. I had to buy one from a local clothing store and—like my fellow students—I did not wear it again until a regional tournament.

With considerable pleasure and warmth, I occasionally take out a Korean newspaper clipping from that tournament. On the local sports page, amid blaring Chinese and Korean characters, is a picture of a much-too-serious young man throwing a sidekick. My intense gaze is almost laughable, particularly for such a relatively unremarkable regional tournament. After all, the picture was commenting on the novelty of an American winning the forms competition and not for that sidekick, which was thrown in a bout that I lost!

My reason for studying Hapkido was not lofty. I didn't care about mental and physical discipline at first. I had no concept or foreknowledge of how Hapkido's lethal skills would soon save my life or how quickly they would become a necessary part of my career. I went to Hapkido class because in Korea everyone goes to class. It's like the company softball team in the United States. If one desires the companionship of new friends, martial arts training is a popular and socially accepted means to that end.

Fortunately, Kim's instruction was imbued with the deeper disciplines that martial artists across the globe respect. From him, I learned not only to control that temper (eventually, no more push-ups), but also the value of preparation, perseverance and hard physical work. No doubt my father was relieved to have someone else assume the burden! And I met some wonderful people who remain friends to this day.

One, Lee Hyung-Jin, has been my closest friend through many good and some horrific times across borders and years. We studied Hapkido together in Pusan. Hyung-Jin summarized our feelings toward training and our instructor: "Hapkido taught me so much about inner strength," he said. "Not just how to train my body and fight, which is great, but also how to make and keep friends. Back then it was just fun."

Physical training of any type requires focusing on inner strength. Discipline and perseverance prepare us to act as we hope we will act, to realize the heroism of our inner vision when life requires it.

That spring, South Korea was tormented by mass student demonstrations against the repressive government. An emergency decree banned all political activities and dissolved all political parties. For four days from May 19 to 22, nearly 200,000 citizens and students clashed with military forces in Kwangju City. The students took over government offices and seized police stations and armories. On the same dates in 1980, an almost identical demonstration was staged. As if to commemorate the 1980 uprising, the bloody student riots were repeated in Kwangju in 1981. I was there.

When I first realized the danger, I was walking just south of downtown Kwangju, a few blocks away from the National Kwangju Museum in Maegok district. I had spent the morning in the museum. As I got closer to the center of the city, I saw an old man slumped in the street, blood seeping from a cut on his head. The smell of tear gas was thick in the air. At the same time, I heard shots—heavy, thudding sounds that I later learned came from a large gun positioned on the roof of the museum.

I rushed to the man, kneeling beside him, speaking in Korean. "Grandfather, what has happened?" I lifted his head. Blood ran. He moaned. Behind me I could hear shouting from just two blocks away. More shots. And a voice.

"May I help?"

A boy of fifteen or so stood beside me, looking intently at the old man. His name was Moon Jongjin, he quickly told me.

"He's hurt," I whispered.

"So are they," he said, pointing at a group of people huddled in front of the grade school. Moon's eyes lifted, trying to determine if I meant good or ill.

"Yes." I stood, not knowing what else to say. We lifted the old man and carried him across the street. A girl was there, a ferociously competent seventeen-year-old named Yoon Myungju. She insisted that the school must have medical supplies in the building.

Here my martial arts' training was truly needed. Not to fight, but to serve. Kim's words from the dojang echoed in my mind: "Your body is nature's gift to shape and grow, your heart the energy that binds it… but it is the virtue within that defines you as a person."

Looking about, I went to the door of the school. We needed to get in. Smoke wafted down the street. The shots seemed to be getting closer. All I could see was the blood on these people. I shook the firmly locked door, then turned to find a rock.

But Moon was faster. With a heavy strike that belied his youth, he slammed his fist through the glass and unfastened the door. His hand was only superficially cut.

"How did you do that without seriously cutting yourself?" I said, gaping.

"Tae kwon do." He shrugged, grinning.

"Hapkido for me."

He nodded. He taught me the technique later.

For three days we sat in the school, nursing the seemingly endless stream of wounded Kwangju citizens who came to our makeshift relief center. How word spread throughout the city that we were there, caring and offering shelter, I didn't know. Even today, I have no idea how the people knew.

It was bloody work. We made bandages of any material we could find. No power (the government forces shut down the power plant to hinder the students), but plenty of water. Moon, Yoon and myself felt a sort of unified clarity. We knew only sleepless service that bound us to the hearts of each other and the people we helped. By the third day, I wondered if I would ever sleep again.

Moon was passed out, sleeping for the first time since he broke the glass door in what seemed forever ago. Yoon sat beside me, weak and exhausted. The school was filled with more than

200 wounded, hurt, desperate people. A few arrived to help; most came because they had no other place to go as their homes were burned or taken by the students. Gas, guns and shrapnel from the students' homemade bombs wounded them.

"Sleep," I said to Yoon, trying to remember what the term meant.

She shook her head.

"Please, if not for me, then for my Hapkido teacher."

She raised an eyebrow, half-smiling. "For whom?"

I nodded. "It's true. If he finds out that I let my *yodongseng* go for three days without sleep, he'll make me do push-ups." I smiled quietly. "I do a lot of push-ups."

She warmed to the appellation *yodongseng*, meaning "younger sister," a Korean term of kindness that reassured her. She lay down and slept immediately. After three days of heat, blood and effort, we all could have used a little reassurance.

"Remember, we each have within us a hidden *dokjang*," Kim said, referring to the Korean term for a person of high virtue. One Saturday, after a particularly vigorous and satisfying sparring session, he called us to sit around him on the mat. He rarely spoke at length, but when he did, the words always touched me deeply. "A dokjang refines himself, finds inner virtue, strength, wisdom and courage. There are many paths to becoming a dokjang. I hope Hapkido helps you find one."

As Moon and Yoon slept, I walked through the school, collecting trash in a rolling container we had found for the purpose. It was dark outside, perhaps around 8 P.M., and those who weren't sleeping were working on it. I rolled the can behind the gym, through the kitchen and out an exit door that led to an alley behind the school. I lifted the plastic sack, tied it and turned my back to the alley as I dropped it into a large bin.

Suddenly, unbelievable pain pierced my lower back, just to the left of my spine. My whole body went rigid with agony and, looking down, I saw a sharp point pressing against the skin of my stomach from the inside. I turned my head. A Korean student, no older than myself, had driven a long blade deep into my back. His eyes were filled with fear and triumph.

Training and luck saved my life.

Spinning counter-clockwise, I swung my left arm up and brought it down on the hinge of the student's right arm. He jerked his hand away at my unexpected attack, dropping the knife as it pulled out of my back. I pressed my right palm into his chin, pushing his head far back, then stepped forward and grabbed the back of his head with my left arm, still pushing with my right. I shoved his chin to my left, pulling the back of his head toward me and down at the same time. I felt a dull, sickening snap as I twisted his head around and down, to my left, forcing him to the ground.

I couldn't move. Pain radiated through my body and I felt blood flowing from my back. I swayed on my feet, almost fainting. My bladder released involuntarily and the acrid stench worked like smelling salts. I looked up and saw Moon standing in the doorway.

"He stabbed you," Moon said. I nodded. Moon stood over the student. "You killed him."

I felt dizzy. Dead? Of course, Hapkido is designed for just that, but even so. To have killed him. Moon pressed his hand against my back, calling out. In a haze I saw Yoon, felt her hands dragging me inside. I felt my clothes removed, bandages and cold.

Yoon and Moon found a place for the body, they said, where there were so many others. I kept wondering how old the boy was, his name, how and why he was in that alley ramming a knife into me.

Over the years I have participated in numerous physical confrontations and have used Hapkido in ways I never imagined when I first began training. Yet, through the hatred and manipulation and impossible evils, I have witnessed rare kindness and loyalty.

Fighting, maiming and overcoming were physical realities of Hapkido training. But that day in Kwangju, I was the man my instructor hoped I would be. In service lay my path to becoming a dokjang. Because of Hapkido, my body was strong enough to endure the three days of ceaseless effort. Because of my instructor, my soul was prepared to offer what little I could to others in need.

Later that night, on May 22, paratroopers stormed the city and restored order at the cost of hundreds of deaths and thousands of wounded. I received expert medical attention, but I owe my life to Moon and Yoon. They were the first of many to do me that favor. They have both become my lifelong friends.

Though not as terrible as the 1980 tragedy that saw the slaughter of nearly 2,500 students—and which is commemorated each year in South Korea—that bloody spring was violent enough. Our small part in the incident was just a footnote in Korea's military affairs. Still, I spent a little over a month in Chonju Presbyterian Hospital and carry the scar on my back even now.

After the riots, I knew what it was to kill another human being. It altered my perspective. It wasn't a question of bad dreams or even regret. I knew then that my act was in self-defense and an aggravated response to what seemed a state of war within the borders of Kwangju. However, a young man on a Christian mission isn't trained for combat and its consequences and I attempted to deal with the strong visceral feelings I felt on my own.

About a month after my release from the hospital, the United States Consulate and the International Cultural Society of Korea co-hosted an event to encourage international amity. The reception was held at the United States Consulate offices in the Taechong District, Pusan. I was on the large invitation list due to some small attention for my participation in the riots. I didn't know until later in the evening the real reason for my invitation.

A charming Frenchman ingratiated himself with me early in the evening. He admired my language skill, my acumen, my other things in a long list of flattery. He had thick dark hair, a Bogey haircut, a white blazer reminiscent of *Casablanca* and a demeanor that was both suave and manly in the finest European tradition. He tossed in well-worn French expressions, playing the exotic stereotype for all its worth.

We were discussing the riot when a distinguished Korean man in his mid-forties approached. He asked my French companion, "Monsieur Defferre, what brings you to Korea this time around?" The Korean wore glasses and had an engaging habit of smoothing his tie and conservative blue suit lapel while he spoke, as though every word were from the heart.

Defferre shook Dr. Kim's hand, then leaned forward in an A-frame hug and pressed his lips to the Korean's cheek, winking at me as he stepped back. We both knew such physical displays—

however exaggeratedly French—were against Korean custom. Defferre seemed to enjoy the other man's momentary discomfort.

"Monsieur Bannon, please allow me to introduce Dr. Kim Cholkyu, *directeur du centre medical.*"

Dr. Kim had known Defferre a long time. As I watched them, I realized that I was outside an old circle and was being slowly pulled in way over my head. Defferre wrapped his arm round mine. Then he led Dr. Kim and me to a table in a quiet corner of the room.

"You have heard, perhaps, of the Interpol?" asked Defferre. He sipped a glass of merlot—the same glass he had been nursing since we met.

"Inter-what?" I asked. Nineteen years old and the lessons learned in my international relations class had long since been forgotten.

Dr. Kim explained in English with a slight Boston accent, which fitted his American Ivy league education. "International Criminal Police Organization—ICPO—called Interpol for short. There are member countries across the globe that all cooperate to bring international crime to heel."

"In French, *Organisation internationale de police criminelle*— OIPC," added Defferre, knowing the affect of his appealing pronunciation. "Interpol." He leaned close, intimating that he was sharing rare secrets that only Dr. Kim and I would ever fully understand. "Crime is universal. We help keep it in check by fostering cooperation between law enforcement agencies across the globe."

Defferre and Dr. Kim laid out the Interpol party line well into the evening. I heard about databases and international goodwill, member countries, red notices on notorious smugglers and other legitimate roles played by Interpol. Every word was true; the same way that saying "Mozart was a musician" is also true. It just didn't tell the whole story.

From our conversation that evening I didn't realize the deeper, darker nature of Interpol's true role in hunting and punishing those who believed themselves above the law. Had I known, I might have been attracted to the venture—or run screaming into the night.

"So, Monsieur Bannon, perhaps you might consider our organization," said Defferre. This was the punch line. "We seek only the best recruits."

"My mission president might not like me just up and leaving the mission," I said.

Defferre smiled. "Mission President Pak, *n'est-ce pas?*" More exaggerated Frenchness. He looked at Dr. Kim, who nodded.

"We spoke with Pak earlier," said Dr. Kim. "And to other church officials, including Elder John Rane. We've worked with him before." I was stunned. John Rane was highly placed in the church. I met him once while on high school spring break and had a minor case of hero worship. It was only years later that I learned Rane had a few dark secrets and Interpol used that knowledge to encourage his cooperation on more than one occasion. When the secrets came out—surprisingly not as dark as Rane's fear had made them—Interpol washed hands and moved on. That night Dr. Kim noted my reaction. "Your church leaders are aware of the work we do and are willing to release you from service if you're so inclined."

I gasped as only a young man with a newly healed scar on his back can gasp. First, my small missionary world was turned

upside-down in a vicious riot; now I learned that the mission calling that I had held so sacred could be casually tossed aside by my
own church leaders. Dr. Kim continued. "Interpol has assisted your
church in other countries on occasions. They are willing to let their
best go to new 'good works.'" I felt Dr. Kim was being completely
candid.

"Thank you, Dr. Kim, Monsieur Defferre," I said, standing. "I'm feeling a little out of it. Must be my back injury and the
medication."

"Will you consider what we've said?" asked Defferre,
charm replaced with a piercing gaze I came to admire over the
years.

"I really don't think so. Thanks anyway."

"Dr. Kim and I will be around," he said, reminding me that
I still held their business cards. "We'd like to check in once in a
while."

I shrugged, smiled and left. Soon I would be grateful they
kept that promise.

three

PEANUT BUTTER CRIME

 Three months after the riots, a fellow missionary named Todd approached me. "Want some peanut butter?" he asked in a low voice.

It sounded like he was offering me drugs. But peanut butter? An American luxury I had missed! "Sure, you get a package from home?" I was still Mr. Naive.

Todd shook his head. "Nah, they sell it in Nampo-*dong*," he said, pronouncing even the Korean name in his deep Georgia drawl. He was referring to Nampo District, the shopping area in Korea's second largest city, Pusan. Anything could be bought there—most of it things to which a young missionary shouldn't be exposed.

"Peanut butter it is!" I agreed and we hopped on a bus to Nampo-dong.

Public transportation in Asia is always an experience in people, sights and sounds. Since violent crime on buses and subways is almost unheard of throughout South Korea, and since so many middle-class workers use public access vehicles rather than cram a car into the throng of too-many-autos-in-too-little-space, it's actually a pleasant way to experience the country. Invariably a pop radio station is playing in the conveyance and this was no exception. I remember clearly the tinny speaker blaring out one of my favorites, Jo Yongpil's *Ajik-un Salang-ul Molla,* "So Far In Love I've Got No Clue:"

> *So far in love I've got no clue, no clue*
> *Even so, I like you, like you*
> *Your "unknown confession" makes my heart pitter-patter*
> *And speaking about it is even harder*
> *It sucks!*
> *It sucks!*

Nampo and Gwangbok districts housed the largest shopping area in Pusan. Stretching between Kukje Market and City Hall were over 1,000 shops selling name brand goods. Because many street vendors with handbags and fashion accessories also lined the streets, the area was popular with the younger generation, especially due to nearby PIFF Square.

PIFF Square hosted the Pusan International Film Festival each year and held a plethora of theaters for every taste. Area officials attempted to create a Hollywood-like atmosphere by having handprints of famous movie stars and directors in the sidewalk. The movie theaters created a lot of foot traffic so local chic shops paid premium rents. At night, street vendors of all sorts came out and made the area even more crowded.

As we stumbled along the square, we enjoyed the occasional stare from the teen set. Americans were still rare sights in fashionable districts outside of Seoul, the nation's largest city. Two giggling teenage girls in matching school uniforms approached us, hands over mouths, pointing at me.

"Are you Mr. Bannon, please?" asked one, the stilted English completely charming.

"Me? Um…" I noticed one of the girls was terribly pretty, although both wore the same standard short haircut that made them seem like bobbing pigeons as they walked in unison down the road. The prettiness did me in. "Ummm… sure."

They had seen me on television and wanted an autograph. After the riots there was a small article about me in a Korean newspaper, so a popular game show trotted me out as a special guest one evening. Sort of a Hollywood Squares with food, in which correct answers were rewarded with yummies and the losers had to endure nasty bits of barely-edible (or recognizable) items. Still lost in the pretty girl's eyes, I stood there. My Atlanta friend saved the day. "TV? Yeah, he's the one!" Giggles from the girls. "Remember when he ate the fish head?" More giggles. "Tell me, Teacher Bannon, what year did WWII end?"

Okay, so I got it wrong. Okay, so it was fish heads. Gimme a break. Mr. South Atlanta smiled warmly and asked the girls to have tea with us at a local coffee shop or *tabang*. They agreed, although missionaries and girls were supposed to be far estranged. I confess that after recent events, a little flirting and female giggles did my heart good.

Pretty Eyes pulled up close as we walked. "Monsieur Defferre sends his regards," she said in perfect English. My head jerked and she smiled demurely in her schoolgirl imitation.

"That's nice," I said. "But I'm really not interested in talking about him."

"So what?" she said and her eyes suddenly betrayed more years than the school uniform indicated. Dark and glittering, secret eyes beneath a short hair cut that suddenly seemed daring. She was laughing at me. "He's interested in you."

PIFF Square had an underground shopping mall filled with the latest European fashions and international music. She guided me through the mall into a secluded tabang just as her partner was expertly charming my Atlanta friend into a booth on the other side of the room. The schoolgirl façade dropped and she got to business.

"We know what happened in Kwangju. Defferre only wants to see if you're suited for our line of work." She paused, ordered tea and a pineapple-orange juice for me. This popular drink, called *kool-piss*, was christened by an American soldier right after the Korean War and never lost favor despite the insulting brand name. "The boy's body is long since gone. There's no need to discuss him. But we can definitely discuss you. Give it some thought."

I was speechless. Still, I was just a little enchanted with her eyes and more than a little aware of how nicely she filled her uniform. Her lips were persuasive and not just because of the words they spoke. That effect, of course, was the point of sending her. I nodded and said I'd think about it. My reward was a bright smile filled with passionate promise.

After sipping our drinks and meaningless chat, she and her partner left the two gasping young Americans. Atlanta was all giddy. "Think we'll see them again? Did you get her number? I kept meaning to get her number, but it just slipped out of my head."

We headed to Kukje Market, only one of us aware of exactly why he never got around to asking her number. He wasn't allowed.

Kukje Market was originally formed by Korean War refugees and grew to become Pusan's largest. Wholesale clothing, silk, linen, curtains, bags, glasses and many imported items were offered by legitimate businesses in storefronts and carts. The stores were small and the vendor-filled alleys narrow. Kukje Market spilled out into the streets and continued into Kwangbok and Nampo districts. Along its southern boundary was the Jagalchi Fish Market.

We walked along the Pusan Harbor to the market. It had two main sections: one for fresh seafood, another for dried seafood. The name of the area came from *Jagal* (small rocks) and *ch'i* (a pure Korean word describing villages next to the seashore). Originally, the area had many small rocks, but where we strolled the wharf was concrete and lined with buildings.

The pungent, briny aroma of fresh fish filled our nostrils. Fish and shellfish were caught daily and sold fresh to consumers, almost right off the boat. We stopped for a bite at an open stall. The area was lined with tanks containing all sorts of fish, eels, squid, shellfish and mollusks. We watched as the fish were scaled, beheaded, chopped up, and dumped in a box of ice for long-term storage.

We continued walking after our snack. Down the alley I spied a familiar face.

"Hyung-Jin-*a*!" I cried and my friend from Hapkido class turned and beamed. He walked over to me, waving goodbye to the older man with whom he had been speaking.

"Hey, you!" he smiled, shaking my hand and bowing. "How's my younger brother today?" I laughed at the familiar appellation. Although he was only about a year older, in Korea our relationship was firmly set. We spoke awhile, passing the time and enjoying each other's company. I noticed the older man had disappeared.

"What brings you here today, Hyung-Jin?" I asked. He shrugged, his small lips forming the quiet smile that made him so appealing. At about 5' 7", he was short by Korean standards, but his balance and fluid gestures made this unnoticeable. He responded to my question with his usual directness. "Probably the same thing that brings you here."

Thanks, Hyung-Jin. Good answer; real clear. Atlanta spoke up. "We're after some peanut butter," he confided. It dawned on me—at last—that maybe there wasn't going to be a peanut butter shop in the alleys around the fish market.

Hyung-Jin took my hand, squeezing it as friends do in Korea. "Young brother, is this what you really want?"

"It's illegal, huh?" I asked. Good thing they hadn't asked about buying peanut butter on Hollywood Food Squares. I probably would have had to eat rooster testicles. Hyung-Jin nodded, eyes searching. I took it in stride. "Yeah, I could use some American food." It was that easy to cross the line.

Hyung-Jin led us to the eastern, dried food section of the market. Walking through I noticed dried squid, octopus, seaweed, anchovies, pollack, and codfish hanging in the booths. We stopped in front of a simple store that sold soda and snacks. Hyung-Jin's older friend—who had disappeared before—was behind the counter. He waved us through a door to the back.

Behind a glass door painted black was a world of black market goods. There were still heavy taxes on many imports. But any item with a heavy tariff is going to be smuggled in, even peanut butter. American and European candy, Swiss chocolate, jellies, liquor, magazines such as *Playboy* and Superman comics, nylons and many other items lined the shelves in tidy rows.

"If it's illegal," I whispered to Hyung-Jin, "how come it's all in a store like this?"

"It's only semi-illegal." Hyung-Jin smiled. He didn't know the score, either.

In the back room sat a tough, short, square-bodied *ajima*. The term literally meant "married woman," but in Korea had come to represent a type of older, single-minded shop woman. Although some may be kind inside, it rarely showed in their brusque exteriors. She spoke to Hyung-Jin, assuming that the Americans knew no Korean. "You want something today, sir?"

Hyung-Jin spoke with her at length while I shopped. With a basket full—yes, a basket like any other store!—I went to pay for the precious, long-missed American items.

"It's free today," said Hyung-Jin.

This was too much. Pretty schoolgirls who worked for Interpol and one of my best friends buying me food. "Nah, I got it older brother." I reached for my wallet.

He stopped me and the *ajima* looked up, intrigued. "Really, it's free," he said. "She's not charging us."

The older woman winked at me, smiling through some nasty teeth. I spoke to her in Korean. "*Ajima*, how can it be free?" She just laughed and pointed to the man in the front of the shop, indicating we should talk to him. Hyung-Jin smiled.

"God, I hate this mystery shit," I said.

His name was Chong Hongshik and he was a smuggler. Atlanta, Hyung-Jin and I went to his back room, sipped herbal tea and listened. Quickly he told us: "American missionaries are the best mules. No one suspects them and the merch could be tagged for Customs as part of the missionary's *sojipoom*, your personal items. What does a business traveler need with two year's supply of American stuff?" Chong asked. "Nothing. But a missionary, he brings enough stuff to last him cause he's poor. And his family and church send him stuff all the time. So supposing the box has five jars of peanut butter instead of one? So he likes peanut butter."

We nodded, trying to act sophisticated instead of like the novices we really were. We understood why they wanted us. We were both fluent in English and Korean and our Japanese wasn't half-bad either. It seemed innocuous enough. Over the line, but not by that much, I told myself. We asked questions about the transport, the buyers in the States and the cops. Chong was a noticeably skinny man, with smoker's breath and a twitching right eye. Maybe mid-fifties, his skin reflected a life on the commercial fishing boats before discovering the smuggling cash cow. "Cops and customs are paid off," he answered. "Don't worry about them."

Somehow, poor and needy, I bought it. I would be a peanut butter criminal.

Later, our smuggling careers were summed up neatly by Lee Hyung-Jin: "*Cham*! We were really bad at it!"

Pathetically true. I had a lot of free time. When I flipped the switch—went from the mission life to rationalizing I would cash in on smuggling "harmless" American goods—the transition was complete. We worked with Chong a few times. Laughably, the deals paid little on our end. We were a couple of kids pretending we were smart asses.

One day he sent us to the docks of Gamcheon Bay, where most of the smuggling traffic flowed. The bay was run by the Pusan Gamcheon Fisheries industry and while seeming clean on the outside was actually a perfectly sequestered arena for smuggling innocuous items. The merchandise came into the docks and made it's way slightly north to Nampo or up farther to Seoul.

Playboy and comic books were huge sellers. Hardcore porn held little interest in the Korean black market. Japan was right across the water and their hard stuff was perfectly legal. The airbrushed, buxom beauties of American *Playboy* held a Hugh Hefner glamour all their own. Because this magazine was banned at the time, men clamored for it.

To us, comic books, candy bars and nylons seemed harmless. We were unaware that the business of smuggling is dangerous. Like any crime, it attracts the most vicious characters. Hyung-Jin and I were babes in the wood, but we didn't like the vicious looks of those we were meeting. We began carrying with us telescoping batons and fighting knives, which were part of our Hapkido training. Chong saw them and smiled. A few weekends later, Chong sent us to a small basement shop in Nampo. There Chong's "old, good friend" supplied us with brass knuckles and lead coshes— both illegal in South Korea.

When Chong had said the cops were paid, it was no lie. The buy-in by customs and the police was a heavy cost of doing business. Chong let us know that the biggest offense would be to carry firearms, which were strictly forbidden in Korea. Although some smugglers carried them, if nabbed with a gun, the police would show no mercy. On the other hand, cops often would look the other way on smaller offenses.

We used a public bathhouse each morning after Hapkido class. Hyung-Jin may have been a criminal trainee, but he took great exception to posters of naked women. He thought they were exploitive. Our bathhouse, a quiet neighborhood affair, featured a framed portrait of a naked blonde in the men's changing area. Hyung-Jin complained about it every day—but only to me. One Saturday I swung by Nampo District and picked up a framed Monet print, which I presented to the bathhouse owner. "As a gift," I explained.

The older man invited me into his office and we sipped *Kin* Cider, a citrus drink similar to Sprite. We talked about the riots. He had served during the Korean War and spoke highly of America's assistance in that conflict. I shared with him tales of my father's experiences in the Korean War. He took both my hands in his. "For your father's sacrifice," he said, openly weeping as Korean's will in times of great emotion. "For coming to our land in a time of trial, thank him. For sending his son to us to share good works, thank him."

I felt like shit.

The next day, when Hyung-Jin saw the new picture, he knocked on the office door to thank the proprietor. The old man nodded, smiling warmly. "Your friend explained about the old picture," he said, pointing at the lovely floral art reproduction. "We respect that you are missionaries."

Hyung-Jin looked at me for a guilty moment then back to the proprietor. "Yes, honored sir," he said, using the honorific.

We showered in silence that day. I knew that our petty smuggling had to stop, but I also knew it wasn't going to be easy getting out. I had to handle it carefully.

I was still thinking about how to do just that a few nights later when Hyung-Jin and I planned to meet two Korean seamen at Gamcheon Bay. Since it was early, we spent the evening playing at PIFF Square. The area that had many small restaurants was called *mokja golmok*, meaning "let's eat alley." Street vendors sold all sorts of tasty (and not so tasty) treats, including my favorite sugar/rice cake, *dduk*, and the stomach-churning *bundiggi*, deep-fried, chocolate-covered crickets. Other stalls offered liquor. More standard fare was served in the sit-down restaurants. The area had many bars, karaoke rooms and clubs that stayed open well into the early morning hours.

After midnight we found ourselves in a popular karaoke club, where the bouncers eyed me menacingly. They had trouble with American soldiers before and to them, better safe than sorry when it came to big-nosed, white skinned foreigners. Can't blame them, but prejudice based on ones appearance—no matter how well earned through bitter experience—was still impossibly frustrating.

Our turn came to toss out a few notes and we took the stage, dismembering popular crooner Song Jangsik's *Salangia*, "This is Love:"

"I dreamed of a face for me alone
Always in my soul…"

I could list singing as one of my few talents and the well-liquored, pleasant crowd enjoyed the song enough to demand an encore. The owner graciously allowed a second song, free-of-charge, this time an American standard, "Moon River."

As we wrapped up the last chorus, I noticed Pretty Eyes of the form-fitting school uniforms waving at me. Was she following me? I hoped so. Generous applause followed us as we made our way back to the table, this time with Pretty Eyes sitting there. A pale pink silk dress replaced the uniform.

"I don't know your name," I confessed.

She laughed. No school-girl giggle this time. A woman's laugh, full and rich. "Eunmi, for tonight," she said and then requested that we speak only in Korean. "For tonight."

We danced and flirted and laughed and managed to share a little romance without a single mention of what I was doing to earn money—or what she did for Interpol. We even snuck away to a nice secluded part of the market. It's so seldom that an evening resembles the romantic interludes in movies, but that night I realized what films were desperately struggling to capture—a combination of attraction, loneliness and hope, joy, pain and need. And something more that we all feel but—not being poets—can only share emotionally.

Too soon Hyung-Jin and I had to keep our appointment. This time, Eunmi gave me a telephone number. "But tomorrow I'll be working again," she warned. "When you call, my first question will be about—"

My lips brushed hers, interrupting. "*Inseng-un kulun gosida,*" I whispered, the Korean equivalent of c'est la vie. She smiled and waved, not knowing I wouldn't be seeing her for quite awhile.

The dock was dark, the moon a sliver in the sky, the tide powerful and noisy. Dawn was still a few hours away. Deserted. Perfect for dark business.

The two stocky seamen met us behind a warehouse. Both were smoking and looked as if they knew how to handle themselves. One wore a jacket too heavy for the soft night, standing behind the crate of merch. The other was in shirt sleeves, like Hyung-Jin and myself. All four of us wore dark clothing. We exchanged their merch—a crate of Jack Daniels—for a case of cash. Suddenly, their faces tightened.

Dropping the case, shirt sleeves reached behind the guy in the jacket and drew a long, glittering blade. Seems they wanted both the merch and the money. I automatically set my right foot back, left forward, balancing. He poised and launched an underhand stab to the center of my body. As his strike came up, I leaned forward, sucking in my stomach, and struck downward hard onto his wrist with my forearms crossed, right over left. I kept my hands open to slide around the back of his hand and twist it up and around, but my timing was off. He was a powerful man who easily broke my grip and stepped back. Both of us were breathing heavy.

Behind the crate, the second seaman dropped his jacket, which had hidden a baseball bat with nails sticking out. From the way he swung it, lead was probably in the tip. Hyung-Jin kept the crate between them, drawing his sturdy seven inch blade similar to a Polish Paratrooper knife. Although a proficient thrower, Hyung-Jin was wise enough to know that tossing a knife meant throwing away his only weapon. Against that leaded bat he was grotesquely under-armed.

During our brief—only seconds, really—breather I extended my telescoping baton. I stepped to the side with my left foot as my opponent lunged at my throat with his knife. I slammed my left hand into his extended elbow, sliding my hand to his wrist and pushing down. His body followed the downward motion. I swung the baton on the back of his neck. He fell and I swung again. And again.

Hyung-Jin grunted. Turning, I saw the nail-studded bat arcing down onto Hyung-Jin's leg. I ran behind the seaman, swinging my baton onto the side of his knee. It caved. I swung it in an awkward blow to his head. He lifted his arm, blocking, and we both felt the baton shatter his wrist. Then Hyung-Jin and I knocked the two seamen out.

Hyung-Jin was bleeding from a nasty gash. I inspected the wound; luckily, it didn't seem too deep. Acting quickly, we got the hell out of there, snagging a bottle of Jack Daniels with the cash. Chong would forgive us returning without the merch, but never the cash. A few blocks south we stopped and I doused Hyung-Jin's leg with the JD. He screamed, of course. We bandaged him with my shirt. That's when I first noticed a deep cut on my chin, apparently from my attacker's last knife thrust. I tilted my head back and poured some liquor on the open wound.

We were both out of breath and near exhaustion.

"That didn't work out so good," I said, puffing.

He coughed up a laugh. "Yeah, next time let's bring more guys." We got solemn for a moment and he added, "Better yet, let's skip the next time."

"That's just what I've been thinking," I nodded. Then we saw the policemen running toward us.

four

DOING TIME

Caught with a bottle of Jack Daniels and the cash, it wasn't too hard for the authorities to connect the dots to the crate of JD on the dock. And the two seamen. On his only visit to us when we were in custody, Chong laid it out. "Most of the cash has disappeared," he explained, "and whatever money you boys put away has to find a new home. Give it to the policemen's fund."

The police knew who we were at the time of the arrest. Chong's previous graft paid for a less painful interrogation. The new contribution made for a sloppy investigation. Chong shook his head. "Those two seamen, who knows what they were up to? My mistake to send you, so I'm setting it right. They both have done time; they were wanted men." He stood up, done with the conversation. "I'm told that the police found evidence that they were North Korean agents, too." That North Korean spy card was played by the police often when there was something to hide. A couple of skells turned on each other. Two other suspects were apprehended and went down for smuggling. Hyung-Jin got sixty days. I got ninety. Case closed.

Except that we had to spend a few months in Korean prison.

I did my time in Taejon Prison, home of Korea's most notorious political prisoners. It was also the site of the infamous Taejon Prison massacre, in which eighteen hundred inmates were killed by the military and police during the Korean War. We were reminded of this often. Hyung-Jin was shipped to Taegu Prison.

In Taejon Prison, inmates weren't allowed to speak except for about an hour each day during exercise. Inmates walked a white line. Inmates did not vary from the rules in any way. The prison averaged one guard for every six inmates. Enough to keep things in line. Prisoners who forgot the rules earned severe baton beatings.

Christians in Korean prisons got the worst from guards and other inmates. They were considered insane; unreliable; they had no guts. They did not know about my missionary work and I never told.

However, my puppy looks did me no favors. Within a week I had to fight off a rape. When a huge Korean told me I was his, I knew that I was in for a beating one way or another. There was no backing down, no avoiding it, not unless I wanted to be everyone's playmate whenever they got the urge. A white face isn't popular in a Korean prison and anyone who thought he might find me useful was waiting to see how I stood up.

The huge man interested in my puppy looks seemed more Mongolian than South Korean—taller than me, muscled and scarred. Every prison cliché came to bitter life. He approached me on the yard the day after he made claim to me. I didn't wait for him to make a move.

Stepping in close, I rammed my left fingers into his eyes. Staying relaxed and balanced, I followed with a vicious right palm heel to the face. He staggered back. I stepped forward with my left leg, shifted my hips and swung up with my left elbow. I aimed for the chin, but hit his jaw instead. Dimly I heard other prisoners cheering or jeering.

Time was precious. Either I finished him or paid later. He was breathless, weaving, eyes bloody and shut, jaw painfully crooked. I grabbed his shoulders, rammed my knee into his groin and laid him down. I lifted my heel and stomped his face until the guards beat me away.

Later I took the guard's ruthless baton beating, but hoped I wouldn't be taking anything else on the yard. I spent the afternoon in the infirmary and—when I was able to walk on my own—I was shoved into solitary.

It was a twelve-by-twelve cell. Once a day I was allowed thirty minutes walking in the yard, alone. No talking. I spent hours reliving my last night in Pusan with Eunmi. I didn't love her or even want to see her again. It was just a pleasant memory that kept me sane during endless hours. Thank God I had spent at least one night of happiness before entering that pit.

My neighbor was Woo Yonggak, who had been a political prisoner since 1958. I only knew this because, after hearing a low moan in the night, I asked my guard, "Who is that?"

He backhanded me, told me never to speak and then

explained about Woo. "He's been in solitary confinement since the day he arrived," the guard went on. "He only hopes someday to send a letter to his wife and son in North Korea." I nodded and looked as eager as possible for more news. My lips were sealed.

I often heard the guard talking with Woo, who after all those years had earned the right to hold a conversation. He was allowed out of his cell once a day for thirty minutes. He never saw any other prisoners. Once, purely by accident, I was returning from my thirty-minute exercise as he was being let out. He was old, pale, gray, shuffling and beaten. I wondered what political crime had been so vicious to earn him a life in solitary.

"North Korean spy," my guard told me. His mood was lighter after the two weeks I'd been in the cell. I kept my head down as I'd been instructed. My mind's eye only saw a cap shoved low over his eyes and a baton. Mostly the baton. That day, he let me ask a question. It was like freedom.

"Pardon me, sir, but a true spy?" I asked, thinking that might be an old label used for crimes the police wanted to cover.

The guard caught my meaning. "Yep, a true bona fide spy. He had the chance to walk if he signed an oath of allegiance to South Korea, but he turned it down." The guard lifted his baton. I stepped back from the door, but he only twirled it. He liked the reminder of who was in charge and I let him like it all he wanted. "Woo's family would be executed if he signed."

After thirty days I was back with the others, but this time I had friends. An inmate of dubious age and even more dubious background slid next to me, voice barely audible. It wasn't time to talk and he was risking it. "Chong says you might want to know me."

I gave the sign that I heard, a twist of my left fingers on my ear and shuffled on, staring at his shaved head as he went in another direction on a white line perpendicular to mine.

On the yard, I saw Mr. Dubious surrounded by a dozen Korean inmates. He was holding forth and they all nodded respectfully. I put him at late thirties with a slight paunch that he carried well. Other prisoners kept their distance. I sauntered over and barely made it halfway before three of the dozen moved around me. If I was trouble, they had me tagged.

Dubious gave the sign and I passed through. This was safe ground—for those welcome inside the circle. Whoever this guy was, I was thanking God he knew Chong.

"Saw you in the yard a few weeks ago," he said, miming the finger jab. "Not bad. What did it earn you?"

"I got thirty in solitary and another three months in here," I said. Three more months in Taejon Prison. I needed friends.

"He got out of the infirmary after a few weeks," Dubious said, sizing me up. I assumed he meant the big guy I'd laid out. I waited, eyes dead center between his. Taejon had taught me how to shut up, wait and stare.

"I'm a friend of Chong." He sighed, rubbed his paunch. "My name is Kon. Someone tells your big friend that you stand with Kon, maybe he's not a problem anymore."

Kon took his time, but he obviously had the juice to handle anything that went down. "Chong, he tells me you didn't roll on him. You and your pal in Taegu."

"*Nun-do kkamchak anhamnida.*" I quoted an old proverb. "Not an eye blinks," a saying used by Korean criminals to indicate that they don't flinch and tell on their partners.

This seemed to confirm Kon's decision. "Chong's my friend, but I waited to see how you stood up." He waved his hand around him. "You want in this circle?"

"I'm with you, father," I said.

Kon laughed softly and turned to his man standing nearby. Kon's compact, balanced, dangerous-looking bodyguard had been waiting to see which way it went. "He's almost Korean, isn't he?" Kon asked. Kon's man didn't laugh, but he sat down. Better for me.

Kon got word from Taegu Prison that Chong's friend, Hyung-Jin, was all right. For me, life got a whole lot easier. Each day during exercise I took a place in Kon's circle. After solitary I was assigned cleanup crew, which included toilets and another hour outside each day working on the yard. This was the best work in the prison. Kon had arranged it.

"Chong sent over something for you," Kon said one day. "Guess he wants you to have some buying power inside. Like you need to go shopping?" He laughed, but we both knew that you got nothing without jack. No privileges, no extras.

"What did he send?" I asked politely.

"Three boxes U.S. Marlboro cigarettes," he said.

I gasped. So much for my tough exterior. Marlboro brand smokes were available in Korea, but cigarettes with tobacco grown in the United States were the premium goods. Chong was paying me back. With those, I could finish my time in style. But I knew the score.

"Father, please hold them for me as a gracious favor," I said, using the highest honorific form of Korean. Smart move.

Kon grunted approval, patting my back. "Maybe you don't mind spending two boxes for yard crew?"

"According to your wisdom, Father," I said, again in formal Korean.

"Good!" Kon laughed and gave the sign to his bookkeeper. "Done!"

Two hours of sky a day. Even when it rained I was outside. It was a slice of heaven every time.

But nothing inside is free.

Taejon Prison, I knew by then, had a life all it's own. Old grudges from outside remained and new ones were born. If I didn't stand up when the time came, I'd never see the outside again.

About a month after I emerged from solitary, Kon called in a favor. Seems two inmates had been planning a fistfight for a while. Guards were in on the betting—although they also got paid off for looking the other way. Time came, one man won and someone owed Kon some chocolate. Yes…chocolate. You read it right.

Kon sent me and another guy to collect. The guy who owed Kon belonged to his own group. They all stood up like they should. There were four guys plus our man, who announced to us that he wouldn't pay off the chocolate debt even if he was shitting the stuff.

We walked and came back later with two more guys. Things got nasty.

I got three more months tagged onto my sentence for being in the vicinity. A week later I helped with another favor: one of Kon's men had been raped and payback was due. Add another three months, because someone said they saw a white face in the crowd.

On the yard crew one morning, I looked up at the clouds thinking I'd never get out.

About three months in, I woke at the bell and stumbled on the line to the showers. I spotted some of my circle and we grouped, just like always. But a guard motioned me over.

I walked over and waited. A simple "Yes, sir?" would have earned me a backhand. I said nothing. The guard pointed down the blue line.

My head swam. The blue line was freedom. The blue line was for people who had done their time. I didn't mention to the guard the extra months I'd earned. I said not one single, tiny word as I walked the blue line to the gate that led to signing papers, getting my old clothes and walking just a little farther to—I still couldn't even imagine liberty.

I shot a sign at two of the guys from my circle to keep quiet (flick the lips) and let Kon know what's happening (hand rubbing over hair, indicating Kon's shaved head). Then I was at the gate.

Miraculously, it opened.

My personal items had been packed in a box, waiting for me. Inside I saw two packs of U.S. Marlboros. Kon had gotten my message and done the right thing. Signed papers, clothes. Suddenly I was at the final gate to the outside. The talkative guard from solitary was there with the regular guard. He pulled me to the side.

"Woo asks that you might give this to his son," he said, shaking my hand and passing a slim letter written on thin rice paper. I didn't speak. No need to blow it when I was this close.

"You may speak now," the guard said behind his low hat brim.

"Sir, Woo's son is in North Korea. I would never go to such a place."

The guard offered a thin smile. "Why does anyone do anything?" he asked nonsensically.

I coughed, acted as though I had to re-arrange my box and slid the two packs of smokes to the guard. "For your kindness, sir," I said, holding up a finger, indicating one pack. Then I held up two fingers for the second pack. "Perhaps the old gentleman might enjoy a taste on rainy days."

The guard nodded and motioned me on.

I walked out the gate and was free.

Outside stood a champagne-colored sedan. Four doors. Beside the back door stood the young woman Eunmi, whose image had brought me sanity on many days and nights of imprisonment.

"Um..." My mouth was dry.

Eunmi laughed. "You said that the first day we met! Get in. He wants to talk."

Jacques Defferre, French, Interpol, was emitting a slight smell of musk from his cologne. I crawled in the back seat beside him and Eunmi sat in front next to the driver. The car pulled away. I didn't look back.

"Have you ever heard of Eugène François Vidocq, Monsieur Bannon?"

By now I'd learned to keep my mouth shut and Defferre looked like he held most of the cards. He wore a dark blue suit that looked like it cost as much as the car. All part of his continental, celluloid image, I thought.

"No, sir."

"A great Frenchman, perhaps the world's greatest detective. Your own Sherlock Holmes was patterned after this man."

I didn't mention that Sherlock was a British creation. Clearly Defferre had a story to tell.

"Vidocq, oh, he was a terrible criminal. In eighteen hundred and something, he was released from prison to assist the French police. What a mind! The father of modern criminal investigation. In two years he rose from police informer to the most successful detective in all France. He was the first chief of the Sûreté." Defferre paused, patting the driver on the shoulder. "*Suivez cette route*," he said.

The driver was Korean and looked as though he didn't understand a word. All I could see was a thick neck and white-gloved hands. Eunmi smiled, pointed and translated into Korean, "He says follow this road." She was used to Defferre's insistence that French was still the global language.

Defferre sat back and sipped a slim can of Coke, the label written in Korean. He didn't offer me one. He continued, ticking off each point with a finger. "Monsieur Vidocq was a master of disguise. He founded criminology and ballistics. He invented plaster-of-Paris shoe impressions, indelible ink and unalterable bond. He helped the Paris homeless and publicly denounced the states of prisons. He freed innocents."

Defferre leaned forward again, pointing down a side road. "*Allez par ici.*" The driver didn't need a translator to figure out he should turn down that way.

Defferre turned to me. "Monsieur Bannon, why are you not in prison today?"

"I did my time," I said, gambling.

He laughed, head back, enjoying the moment. "Oh, no, no, no! Your time was much more than this. Tell me please." He lifted a hand, reassuring himself that his Bogey-style hair was still in place and stared hard. "Why are you free?"

"You need some work done," I said and, because he was expecting it, "Like Vidocq."

"Exactly. Interpol and I have a job for you. You will be my informer. Your friend Monsieur Chong has friends in Marseilles. You will help me watch them." He spread his fingers and laced them together. "Every action and reaction nicely arranged. Do you see how life always fits together?"

I sighed, seeing how my life fitted Defferre's world. We pulled up to Taejon Prison again, per Defferre's directions. We had traveled in a circle. "I say no and I go back?" Defferre nodded. Obvious question. Eunmi smiled encouragingly.

"Then how may I assist you, Monsieur Defferre?"

At the airport Defferre let me call Hyung-Jin, who according to Korean custom lived with his widowed mother. Hyung-Jin was an only child. His father had died in a train accident when Hyung-Jin was three. He'd been out of Taegu Prison for a month.

"*Yoboseyo?*" he answered the phone. The familiar voice of my stand-up friend.

"Guess who's going to France?" I asked.

"I know," he answered in Korean, adding in French, "*mon ami.*"

"Dammit, did everyone know but me?"

Hyung-Jin laughed. "They've got a little job for me, too."

We both knew enough not to ask the other's business. A pause, then I changed the subject to U.S. Marlboros. "Chong did all right by us inside."

"Yeah, he paid up." Hyung-Jin made a long, slow puffing sound. He hasn't quit smoking them since. "I got the word from Taejon about you. Thought your white skin might spell some trouble."

"I did all right."

I could almost hear Hyung-Jin's grin through the line. "Appreciate that you mentioned me to Kon. It helped."

With that we'd cleared the air and there was nothing left to say. Hyung-Jin wished me a safe trip and added, "We can settle up what I owe you sometime."

I smiled. "Will do."

five

HIDDEN TALENTS

M y first day in France, Defferre drove me to Lyon. When we arrived at our destination, he pointed out the window of his car at Interpol headquarters. "You see her? *Elle est belle!* Some day I will be a commissaire for her, although—" he shrugged, slipping the car into a parking space, "she does not reward some of us openly. There is dirty work in this business and you and I are some of those the queen never notices, but always needs."

Defferre often spoke of Interpol in this way, as the queen, a powerful feminine figure he served behind the public façade.

Defferre had laid out the public line on the flight over. We had flown first class. He encouraged me to enjoy the luxury. "After this, you'll be living economy-class all the way," he had said, chuckling at his private joke.

Sipping the port wine the air steward had offered, Defferre explained my new world to me. "What is Interpol? She is to be feared and respected and forever misunderstood. The criminals live in terror at the name, but it is all so unkind. She is nothing to them, really. Every member country follows its own guidelines and laws. Interpol is never an ultra police force, a powerful espionage group, nor does it have powers to tango into any country and pursue the guilty." He spread his hands innocently. "*En effet*, we are merely a database, a clearinghouse of information serving up red notices on active criminals and monitoring and handling world problems, like trafficking in human beings, smuggling and art theft."

He tilted his seat back and began chuckling. It rolled up inside him and spilled out over into the other seats. Passengers nearby noticed and smiled at his contagious laughter. Finally, it subsided. His face was red from the wine and his good humor, but his eyes betrayed no other effects. "If you believe such nonsense, then surely you believe that your CIA never assassinated anyone, Carlos the Jackal is a myth and President Reagan took no revenge for KAL007."

Defferre was referring to Korean Airlines Flight KAL007, a Boeing 747 that—en route from Anchorage, Alaska to Seoul—flew over Kamchatka Peninsula in the Soviet Union and was shot down. All 269 people aboard were killed. Tracking the event, all explanations pointed to a case of mistaken identity, misunderstood transmissions and a paranoid atmosphere created by the Soviet's new intercontinental ballistic missile, the SS-X-24. Defferre shrugged at this. "Yes, of course. That is exactly what happened. Please believe everything you're told."

"Even from you, Monsieur Deffere?" I said.

"*Bien sur.*" He laughed. "Of course!"

After we landed and were driving to Lyon from Paris, Defferre's mood darkened. He laid out the details of my new life.

"You are simply a number in her database," he said, referring to Interpol. "For now, you are known to only a few. I offered you the recruitment in Interpol and you walked away. Now you are back. And I expect you to do anything we ask to save your own skin." I cringed. Perhaps he was right but I didn't like hearing it put so baldly. Then, oddly, he smiled. "Do not feel so demeaned. I know of the riots and your bravery; I know all about how you handled yourself in Taejon Prison. Your guard, he spoke to me of you."

It dawned on me why the solitary confinement guard had said "Why does anyone do anything?" He had been Defferre's pipeline.

"Your old *connaissance*, Lee Hyung-Jin, has his own little job with the Korean NIS. He will watch Chong in Pusan while you watch things here. Eunmi will watch you both for me."

Eunmi was something of an enigma to me. I wondered how she fit into the agency but no information was forthcoming.

Defferre continued, "I know what sort of man you will be. Together, we will serve Interpol and do great things." I was shocked at his sincerity and fervor. It was contagious. And the spirit which had stirred me as a missionary began to take hold again.

"Your name is stored here." He tapped his forehead. "But you must be legitimate. When the time comes, we must present the precise account of your undercover work. So we will create your identity. Until then, we have temporary papers."

He handed me a passport, identity card, even ticket stubs and receipts from my travels in Europe from my home in Wisconsin. He laid out the entire legend of my cover: a young American student named Damien Williams who decided to take a walking tour in Europe. Only Chong would know that it was an alias. "Believe me, he will find it most satisfactory. His own secret man in Marseilles."

Damien Williams had fallen on hard times. Unemployed. "Like everyone else in Marseilles," Defferre added. The wallet had a little cash.

"Not much here," I said. That and the change of clothes in my bag represented all I had in the world.

"You are an agent, but you will play the criminal. Earn it."

I laughed, shaking my head. "My God, I'm a spy!"

Defferre *tsk-tsk*ed me. "You will play the traitor. Worthless scum." He paused. His eyes glittered playfully as they looked into mine. "But the truth will be pretty cool, huh?"

My room was in a cheap hotel on rue Bernard-du-Bois in Marseilles, just a block away from the best free jazz club in the world, La Cave a Jazz. It was adjacent to the city's rail station (La Gare St-Charles), a part of town respectable people took taxis to in daylight and skells ruled at night.

It was the thriving center of Marseilles' infamous smuggling and drug industries. In a city where high-level corruption was commonplace, Mafia rule was absolute and racial tension between the North Africans and the French was palpable, this area was the finger on its wanton pulse. Marseilles was France's ugly stepchild and those who tasted her wouldn't have it any other way.

Day one I hit a public phone and called South Korea as Defferre had instructed me.

"It's me. I'm out."

Chong wasn't surprised. "I heard you got out early. How much it cost you?"

I played it cool. "Enough to make me leave Korea for a while. I'm in Marseilles now under a different name. Maybe I'll catch an opera in Milano."

Chong said Hyung-Jin was in Pusan, looking for work. Marseilles was a bustling, thriving city that may have been imposing, but to someone who had run goods in the densely populated Pusan, it was just another cesspool. Marseilles was the third largest city in France at the time, with just under a million people. Pusan had nine million. I shrugged it off. "Got any work for *me?*"

I tossed him the phony name and he told me about his guys in Marseilles. "They're moving some high dollar merch for me, *Damien.*" He stressed the name, wrapping his Korean accent round it, trying it on for size. "You and Hyung-Jin stood up for me and I don't forget. Your end will be good on this one, okay?"

"Okay."

He said to give him a couple days to let his Marseilles guys know I was around. "Call me and I'll lay it all out."

We rang off. I stopped in La Cave a Jazz and took in a few sets. A trio was turning out some sweet fusion. After their break, a singer joined them, a short, dark-skinned beauty with soulful eyes and a resonant voice. She looked young, about my age, but wrapped her soul around the blues like she'd lived forever. Taejon Prison came back to me, cold like truth, but her voice took the edge off.

Back in my dive of a hotel room, the phone rang. I picked it up and listened without speaking.

"*Chanyoung-si?*" It was Eunmi.

"Did you just call me Chanyoung?" I laughed, speaking in Korean. "Hell, Eunmi, no one's called me that since, well, since I was a missionary." I paused, still soaking in those blues, I suppose.

My old Korean name brought back a time that seemed forever ago. I shook my head. Damn blues.

"To me you're Chanyoung," she said. "Safer to speak Korean and use the names."

I agreed. We skipped the obligatory small talk and got to it. "You talk with Hyung-Jin yet?" I asked.

"It's all done. After you're plugged in over there, watch and wait. And Chanyoung—" her voice dropped, perhaps she was even sincere, "this merch is dangerous. I don't know what it is, but there's a lot of jack being spread around to keep it safe when it arrives. Watch yourself."

"Thanks, Eunmi. Really." As I hung up, I heard her whispering, "*Inseng-un kulun gosida.*"

Yeah. C'est la vie.

Marseilles was big and sprawling, nasty and slumlike, but I confess I was enchanted with her dirty elegance and charm. Like a lover that's no good for you but drives you wild.

I spent days two and three watching *Columbo* on French television. He was on so much, I could catch the show dubbed in French or in English pretty much all day. That guy was brilliant, I swear. Smart, polite and an act of simplicity that fooled everybody. A man one could learn from.

Day four I called Chong. He dropped the names and a place. I tossed on some jeans, a loose shirt and caught the Metro to the Vieux Port.

Trade had always been Marseilles' *raison d'etre*. Geographically, Marseilles was nearly twice the size of Paris. Twice the crime, too. The Vieux Port, the old harbor, was colorful, somehow compensating for the dreary industrial dockland nearby. It was filled with fishing craft and yachts and ringed with seafood restaurants.

A few blocks west of the harbor, on the Cours St-Louis, was a sprawling building that overshadowed everything nearby. Toinou, the best shellfish restaurant in Marseilles, had dining rooms on three separate floors. I climbed to the third and took a table with my back to the wall, facing the stairs.

A thin waiter with a thick *marsaillais* accent and no English took my order. Easy enough. I tossed him 10F and opened the menu, shrugging. He laughed, winked and pointed to the photo of a dozen bi-valved creatures, artfully arranged on a platter. I laid out 100F and made a cutting gesture across my neck. He took the menu, nodding at the cash. Dinner and tip wouldn't cost more than 100F.

Waiting for Chong's guys, it occurred to me why Defferre was using Hyung-Jin and myself. His Vidocq theory held water. We had no training in undercover work or spying or whatever we were doing—but we could handle ourselves and knew the score. And we didn't flinch at taking care of business our own way. We came ready out of the box, no training required.

Chong's guys were heading up the stairs. I stood, balanced and relaxed. They weren't what I'd expected. These guys represented some high-dollar buy-in and it showed in their supple suits and polished shoes. I knew I was underdressed, but reminded myself that a twit like Damien Williams wouldn't know the score anyway. I was here ostensibly to run around for Chong, but my real mission was to keep my eyes open for Interpol.

"You Williams?"

I nodded and they sat, backs to the stairs. So much for experience. One of them was American, New Jersey from his accent. He had flowing sandy hair that seemed to be a source of sexual pride. He wore it like a badge of virility. "I'm Skip," he said, offering to shake. It was a name which always amused me and I could hardly believe I'd met a real Skip. The other, who's name was James, said he hailed from London. His brown hair was less assertive, although he constantly fidgeted in his chair and patted Skip's knee to emphasize his jokes. And why did this interest Interpol?

What was Chong doing with these jokers? They weren't serious. It was Amateur Night and I was the bouncer. What could these guys offer Chong that would pull down so much cash?

They talked all the way through dinner. Skip smoked non-stop. We left the restaurant and walked down Marseilles' notorious main street, Canebiere, toward the Vieux Port.

"You know that World War II GI's called this 'can of beers?'" Skip asked the air, waving his hands. He and James seemed oblivious to their surroundings. Canebiere was the seediest street in France. Lined with cheap hotels—and some not so cheap—shops and restaurants, it was filled with sailors from every nation. I was staring down every fourth or fifth skell on the street, who tagged Skip and James right away as easy marks. Something in me wanted to leave them to the street.

"Look, Skip," I said. "Let's talk about the merch."

Skip stopped on the street. Dumb ass. "Merch?" he asked.

"Yeah, the stuff we're moving. What Chong's paying for."

James stepped up. "The pictures," he said. He seemed serious now. About time. Skip nodded his head, patting James on the back. "Right, the pictures. We can take more tonight, if he wants. He's waiting in the room."

I stared between Skip's eyes, waiting. He looked desperate. "You could come if you like, maybe take the pictures yourself?" He looked at James for support. James got aggressive.

"Chong'll get his 'merch' just like we said." He stepped closer. "How about you back off?"

I felt stupid, but I played it smart. "Sure, James," I said, hands raised in surrender, stepping back. "Whatever you say. I'm just trying to hold up my end. You guys say jump and I say how high, okay?" Mr. Supportive.

"He's still in the room," Skip muttered. "We can go there."

Something sick dropped in my stomach. He's in the room. Pictures that cost big bucks. "How old is he?" I asked.

"Six," said James confidently. "Worth every penny."

"No, James, he's seven. He told me it was his birthday last month." Skip smiled at James, a secret between them.

"I think I'll pass on the room tonight, guys. You just keep walking on main street here, where it's safe. I'll get the word from Chong and we'll get the stuff moving." I walked off quickly.

Back in my hotel, I stared out the window at the train station. Skells were wandering the streets, girls looking for work, suckers willing to pay them. The moon was bright that night, staring over the dregs of Marseilles. Every one of them was a saint compared to Skip and James. I felt sick.

What had Defferre dumped me into?

Next morning I found a dive shop and picked up a sturdy knife, heavy fish line and two four-inch metal tubes, about a half-inch diameter each, with holes drilled in the sides. When I got back to my hotel, I heard a slight shuffle in my room as I opened the door. Dropping my bag, I drew the knife and stayed in the hall.

Defferre yelled from where he lay with his feet on the bed. "Stop that, Damien. Come in and shut the door."

I obeyed, tossing my bag in the corner. I sat in the room's one chair and waited. Defferre tossed a file to me.

"You've met them. Read it."

The file was thin. Brief descriptions of Skip and James, addresses and photocopies of identification. And a fuzzy picture.

"That was Skip's nephew, a few years ago," Defferre explained. "Skip disappeared from New Jersey shortly after the child was found strangled."

I stared harder at the photo. It was clearly a small child, naked, and what seemed to be the nude lower torso of a grown male. The child's face was turned to the torso.

"The child was eight years old at the time."

"How can you tell this is Skip? I'm out of my depth here, Jacques."

"That file is the only real evidence anyone has on Skip and James. They have been selling pictures of Skip with *les enfants* all over the globe. Beneath the smuggling world there is a darker trade. It pays well and no one talks. There is no evidence, no trace. But everyone knows what these skells sell. Custom pictures per customer request. Rape to order."

"They said they have a seven-year-old in the room with them. A boy."

Defferre sat up. "We know. They entered the country with him. His passport says he's James' son."

"I guess that's not likely."

"No, *mon ami*, not likely. But you see the tricks they play? He is a British citizen traveling with his son. There is no missing child report on Interpol records of this boy—we checked—and the documents are in order. The child even said he is the son to the airport officer. To enter their room, what is the cause? To arrest him, what is the charge?"

"The pictures," I said. "They've got pictures. That's what they're selling."

"*Oui*," agreed Defferre. "And so I am here. To help you get the pictures and arrest *ces betes*. These beasts."

Things didn't work out the way we hoped. That morning, James took the child for a week-long stay in Paris. When I called Skip, he pouted about it.

"We can't take any more pictures. The ones we've got will have to do." He whined some more and I let him. We set a time to look over the merch. If it looked good, we'd set up the trade. I asked about the package.

"Pocket size," Skip said.

We met around sunset in the waterfront district south of town center, Escale Borely on avenue Mendes-France. I tasted salt in the air mixed with Skip's pungent cigarette smoke. He plopped on a bench, all arms and legs, and began extolling the virtues of his product.

"Let's see it," I said.

He produced a floppy disk. One of those big 5¼" suckers. "Is the sample on that?"

Skip giggled. "Let's go back to my place. See what it does for you."

It was a long walk. It was dark by the time we passed under the famous and forbidding Basilique Notre-Dame de-la-Garde. I would say it was a better part of town, but Marseilles didn't have one. We turned up an alley and Skip caught Defferre out of the corner of his eye.

"Is someone following us?" he screeched, suddenly spooked like a scared rabbit. I stared him down. Defferre heard and stepped from the shadows. No wonder he needed to use guys like me. Little Bogey show off.

Skip took out his lighter and torched the floppy disk. It crackled and disappeared. "No samples today," he said.

Now we knew without doubt that Skip was guilty but had to find a way to catch him, just like Columbo. Where's the clever guy when you need him?

I stepped in close, eyes hard. "Duck," I said.

"What? Why shou…" Skip fell, with a bullet in his head. A few moments later, Defferre walked up to Skip's body.

"Told you."

Defferre lifted Skip's wallet and watch, then motioned me to follow him. We headed for Skip and James' apartment. There was a dead man in an alley and we were strolling to his apartment. I let it sink in a moment.

"You know, Jacques, I felt pretty bad about that guy in Kwangju." Defferre cocked an eyebrow sideways toward me. I scratched my head. "But this guy—" I paused, thinking it through. "This is the first time I'm glad to see someone dead."

Defferre looked forward, motioning the apartment ahead. "I knew you were right for this work," he said.

At the apartment door, Defferre produced a mechanical lock pick and we were in. I asked to see it.

"Later, Grasshopper," he said, and the Kungfu joke nearly doubled me over with laughter. It wasn't that funny, but emotional release is sweet when it comes.

Defferre used the phone to call a gendarme who would find Skip in the alley right away, a poor victim of street violence. This was all happening fast, but something dawned on me: Skip was meant to be killed all along. I had to mull that over.

Skip's computer stood in the corner. Defferre told me to check it while he checked the room. He got on the phone again.

I flipped it on. Flicker. Buzz.

"Some people are on the way," Defferre said, hanging up the phone. He had called the DST, whose counter-intelligence role often overlapped with smuggling investigations. "I'd like to find something before they get here."

The hard drive was clean. The floppies were clean. How did he get the photos onto the computer? Then it hit me.

Floppy my ass. My entire ass. It was all a smokescreen for Damien. Wave a floppy around, act all high tech, and if things go bad, it probably just had his mom's birthday list on it. He even burned it, so I'd think the merch was gone. How could he know Defferre didn't care?

I was beginning to worry that an innocent man had been killed—but he'd said "He's in the room," hadn't he?—when Jacques whooped and waved a floppy Smurf stuffed toy.

"Squeeze him, Damien."

I did. Sneaky bastards. Inside Smurfy's stomach it felt like a key. I sliced the doll open. Where did the key fit? A train station in Pusan.

"They had delivered the pictures all along," I said, shaking my head. "The whole amateur hour routine was designed to throw us off. They knew you were sending me."

Defferre agreed. "I think so, yes. When they said the child is in the room, it was a test. *C'est vrai.* You could not hide your emotions and the next day," he snapped his fingers, "James is gone. Skip stays to sell the toy, which you deliver to Pusan and they never touch the photos."

Defferre was on the phone to Pusan. Eunmi busted open the locker within an hour and found the stash. She called us in my hotel room.

"There's only pictures of the sandy-haired guy," she said. "No brown hair anywhere."

"Is the kid in them? You see his face?"

Eunmi's voice was filled with rage and disgust. "Yes, I see the face."

Hearing that, Defferre left. He had work to do in Paris. I spoke with Eunmi a moment longer. "You know what happened to Skip?" I asked.

"Yes, I do, Chanyoung."

In my mind I saw the frightened face of a seven-year-old boy. I sighed. "I guess I'm in this for the full ride. One way or another."

six

SPY GUY

I arrived at Kimhae International Airport in Pusan from Paris. Defferre had sent me off to Korea within a week of the Marseilles assignment to work on a new one. Eunmi met me. We talked over going to see Chong first and agreed that it might be a good idea.

Eunmi was laughing as we walked into Chong's shop. I looked over at her. Her snug black leather jacket was so completely modern and spy-like. She seemed to love the self-image, so I told her, "I saw the same outfit on *chic* French women last week—but of course it didn't look as good." It was a sincere compliment that earned a cheek kiss and those beautiful eyes lingering on mine.

Hyung-Jin opened the black glass door in the back and waved us in. We strolled through the shopping mart and went to Chong's back room, where he sat nervously fiddling with his cigarette, skinnier than ever. His hair seemed to be thinning, too.

"Bannon," he said. His eyes were angry and scared.

"Teacher Chong," I replied respectfully and sat down. Hyung-Jin positioned himself behind Chong. He wore a loose long-sleeved shirt and held his right hand in the back pocket of his slacks, where I knew he would either have brass knuckles or a folder knife. Eunmi stayed by the door.

"You know what happened to your man in Marseilles," I said, more of a statement than a question.

Chong slowly took a drag on his cigarette, held in the smoke, then blew it out. He peered behind him at Hyung-Jin, then back at me, eyes hard. "I've played it straight with you," he said in cold, even tones. "I did the right thing."

I was about to speak when I caught Hyung-Jin's eyes. He was telling me to go easy on Chong, but not too easy. The man was scared of us. Chong looked over at Eunmi, a question.

"She's with me," I said.

"She broke into the locker," he said, referring to the Pusan train station. "I figured maybe she's with you. I figured maybe you got out of Taejon 'cause you rolled on me."

"You know what was in the locker, right?" I ignored his accusation.

Chong nodded.

"And you know those guys, what they did, right?"

Another nod.

"Then don't ask me to do that again. We work together, maybe make some cash, but I don't do that shit. I cleaned up the mess and no one knows your name, so we're even on this." I didn't mention Defferre or that Interpol had Chong tagged. "The gendarmes nabbed James in Paris with the kid; cops were on the way to the locker when Eunmi took the merch."

"I did you a favor," said Eunmi, using that smile in a way even cynical Chong couldn't resist for long.

I continued, "The minute they showed me that kid, I stopped caring what happened to them—or the deal. I didn't roll; I just didn't let them know that I spotted the gendarme on our tail. I got the hell out and they took the weight." I was laying it out pretty thick, just like Defferre had coached me. "I got Eunmi to dump the merch—it's gone so don't even think about it—and now we're even."

Chong looked from Eunmi to me and back again. He puffed and drank his tea and puffed again. I tossed a roll of Korean won on the small table between us. "That's your end of what I took off Skip."

"He won't miss it," said Hyung-Jin. Chong agreed.

I tossed another roll of currency, smaller. "And this is for a carton of U.S. Marlboros to send to Kon in Taejon. I don't forget what I owe." If Chong caught the double entendre, he didn't let on. He pocketed the jack and puffed again.

"Maybe we won't do business for a while," he said, testing the waters.

"Good idea. I'm tagged in France, anyway." I stood slowly, no quick movements. "Besides, I've got business here that won't wait."

Chong stood and I noticed for the first time that his hand was shaking slightly. He was a tough man, bitter, but this deal had been his first foray into kiddie porn. He may have expected he'd get a piece of Skip's pie. I laid on the honey.

"Teacher, there's no future in some merch. Let's stay friends with peanut butter and JD."

Back on the street, Hyung-Jin shook his head, laughing. "I just can't take you seriously."

Eunmi agreed, laughing with him. "Oh, I know! He's so cute!"

"Wait a sec!" I said. "He was shaking in there! I'm all like—" I swaggered, almost tripping, "—a spy guy! Show some respect!"

"Cute," said Hyung-Jin, smooching the air.

"And cuddly," echoed Eunmi.

So much for my macho image.

The main reason Defferre had sent me to Korea was to see Dr. Kim Cholkyu, director of the South Korean National Medical Center in Seoul. Eunmi took me to his Pusan office the next day for a psychiatric examination.

"Why an exam in Korea?" I asked Defferre.

He smiled benignly. "Ah, the sweet innocent!" It seemed to me Kon in Taejon Prison was the only one who didn't comment on my looks. I thought I'd send him another carton of Marlboros just for that. "I told you before, we need you legitimate for the paper work," Defferre said. "We need to present the standard Interpol recruitment papers, the evaluations, the training. This way, I can use you for our little assignments and she will be satisfied." She was Interpol, of course. "So Dr. Kim will date your exam a few months before your bad luck with Taejon and Chong."

I got it. Dr. Kim was Interpol's man, but more important, he was Defferre's man—on a deeper level within Interpol and beneath the public servant exterior. Dr. Kim could evaluate me legitimately—it was a bona fide examination with serious results from a qualified professional—and when someone asked about the recruitment process all the paper work was in place. At the same time, Dr. Kim was not in easy reach of the nosey.

The exam was a standard psychological review: numerous tests that included multiple choice, fill-in-the-space and mental and physical acuity. Some sensory deprivation was tossed in to make the whole experience completely excruciating. Prior to my entering the deprivation chamber, Dr. Kim announced: "You have nothing to sense or feel except panic in a small place. Your body is feeling nothing, but your mind may revolt at the confined space. Concentrate on breathing, on your own pulse, but never on the time. You cannot count minutes in that situation. When you feel your mind slipping—and it will, it is natural and part of the test—try singing or reciting poetry or going over favorite movie scenes. This will keep your mind focused."

It worked.

After the standard examinations, Dr. Kim spent hours with me each day discussing my thoughts and experiences. I had to add him to the list with Kon as someone who didn't judge me strictly on looks—but then, that was Dr. Kim's job. We did the usual: my family, friends, sexual preferences, fighting, prison, first job with Defferre. Afterward, he shared some of his notes with me:

"Subject displays keen interest in mastering testing materials; however, after mastering the exercises, he pressed to know the purpose of the exercises and showed little patience for repeating the tests without this explanation. Possessing a keen intellect and predisposition toward thorough mastery of any challenge, he expressed a great respect for 'breadth and depth' of knowledge in any field. He offered… variations or entirely new approaches to the tests."

He also noted that despite displaying strong ethical convictions, I held the belief that the use of violence is a viable option in difficult situations. In this vein, Dr. Kim seemed particularly interested in my thoughts on Skip's death.

"Good riddance. When James dies, I'll buy the champagne," I said.

"You think Defferre wants to hear that?" Dr. Kim wasn't so dense.

"I'm sure he does."

He laughed. "You're probably right! But don't worry, I know you better than that." We had discussed the docks, the riots, even prison. "I'll report here—" he pointed to where he wrote in his notebook, "—that you do not prefer that type of assignment."

I accepted this, but he wanted to instruct me further. Dr. Kim explained "Two percent of the male population, when given a legitimate reason or are pushed unnaturally, can kill without regret. They are like the protector of the innocents or a lioness," he said, watching me all the time. "She would never harm her cubs, but will kill without remorse to defend or feed them." He added that such men do not have the resistance to killing that is common in the other 98 percent of the population. "These men may be called sociopaths, but in the medical sense, not the popular vernacular. In a combat situation or as policemen, this trait is desirable," he said, "and movies and novels glorify just this type of capacity to kill." Dr. Kim further explained that "Anti-social personality disorder," that is, the disorder of sociopaths, lends itself to rebellion against authority and highly assertive insistence on doing things in unconventional ways. In this sense, the sociopath is one who behaves in a way deemed inappropriate by society, but whose role is essential nonetheless. He added, "Just because a child molester is a sociopath does not mean that all sociopaths are child molesters. In a smaller way the school clown or the man who leaves a salaried job to be an artist might also be anti-social."

His arguments sounded valid and even reasonable. I do not doubt that he believed them himself.

He laid out two equations on his notepad:

Aggression − Empathy = Sociopath

Aggression + Empathy = Protector

The protector, he explained, does not have a classification in the medical community because such behavior is not considered a disorder. "But take away the empathy and you have a sociopath."

He made a note and showed it to me. It read: "Subject expressed pleasure at physical confrontation with those harming others, but felt empathy toward his opponents."

"You are in the two percent." He smoothed his tie, hand on heart. His deeply pocketed eyes were sincere behind his glasses. "And in times of danger, there are innocents who need you desperately."

He made me feel like I was a rare breed, part of something bigger than myself, but at the same time the only one who could do what was needed. The disgust I had always felt at vigilantism was momentarily forgotten. Dr. Kim's little talk had done its job.

My last night in Pusan, Hyung-Jin, Eunmi and I watched a KBS television *MacGyver* marathon in my hotel. MacGyver did something clever with some stuff lying around and managed to save the day—in Korean so expertly dubbed you'd swear that Richard Dean Anderson spoke fluently.

Eunmi hugged her pillow like a teenager. "Dreamy, I tell you. Dre-e-eamy."

Hyung-Jin smiled in that quiet way of his. We were all in jeans and floppy t-shirts, eating an obscenely expensive meal on his dollar. "It doesn't settle up for what you did for me in Taegu Prison," he said. The food was sprawled across the room.

I burped because I'm so charming. "It's a start!"

"Dre-e-eamy!"

Hyung-Jin and I rolled our eyes. After all this, we were having a slumber party. Unbelievable. He tossed a pillow my way and I deflected it with my foot onto Eunmi. She dodged, eyes never leaving the television. The phone rang.

"*Yoboseyo?*" answered Hyung-Jin, then in English, "No, I'm sorry, sir. He already left for Seoul. He's on the late train." Hyung-Jin hung up.

"*Cham!* Defferre's like my dad!" I said, reverting to Korean.

"Yeah, but he knows what you do," Hyung-Jin said, waving a finger. "Unlike your dad."

"And he has more money," tossed in Eunmi.

"And my dad doesn't think he can—" I slicked back my hair in bad imitation "play it again, Sam."

Eunmi squealed. "Bogart! I never realized it before. Defferre looks like Bogart!"

Hyung-Jin had never met Defferre and ate it all up. Before he could ask more, though, Eunmi said, "Now shut up. *MacGyver's* back on."

Dre-e-eamy.

Defferre met me at the airport terminal in Paris. "How was *MacGyver?*"

Bastard.

We spent some time in Paris, stayed at a nice little hotel. Even went to the Louvre. Each morning Defferre went over tactics and training. He taught me the secrets of lock picking. "Handy, but try knocking first," he advised. We went over the business of dead drops for exchanging information, concealment devices, miniature cameras, creating a "legend" or cover identity when caught unexpectedly in a strange locale. We discussed the concept of "assets"—people who are used then tossed away when the job is done. I didn't care for that one, but the rest of the spy stuff was a lot of fun. Good tradecraft can be the difference between life and death, but that doesn't make it any less cool.

Defferre took me to the gendarme shooting range and had me try out a SIG-Sauer. I sucked. We tried a Beretta. Still sucked. We tried everything in the range and had some good instructors try their best to teach me the basics. Hopeless. Imagine aiming a pistol at a wall and missing. That was me. I sucked in Paris and I've never improved.

Defferre strongly encouraged me to practice, but also advised me that most of the work I would do would be quiet, quick and close. "I do not need a marksman. I need someone who can pull the trigger when it's time."

I told him, "I can pull any trigger when I need to defend my life or those of others, when the threat is imminent." But not like Marseilles. Defferre said nothing. He just invited me to lunch.

One day while we walked along the Ile St-Louis, Defferre picked up a hand towel at a street booth. It was a warm day and, although he wore slacks and a light cotton shirt, he was sweating. He used the small towel to wipe the perspiration from his brow and hands. We sat outside the Café-Brasserie St-Regis on rue Jean-du-Bellay, across from pont St-Louis. Defferre ordered a *plat du jour* for me. He also ordered *bouillabaisse* and requested a beer in a plastic cup, "for a stroll around the island later." The food arrived.

"You recall James?" Defferre asked. "He walked."

I stopped mid-chew. "How could he walk?"

After Skip died in Marseilles, Defferre and a team picked up James in Paris with the child. Seems that James got himself a good lawyer. While I was in Korea taking tests, he was handed over for trial. The rest was just legal hoops. The kid said he was on a trip with his "new uncle" and nothing happened; the lawyer's doctors found no evidence of abuse; the lawyer pointed out the kid had run away from an orphanage in London, that James' only crime was taking in this poor child rather than following the British adoption process. The kid went back to the orphanage in London. James was deported for an initial hearing—charges pending—in the United Kingdom. He walked out of court the same day. Then ran.

"And now he's gone, to find more children," sighed Defferre, stirring his saffron-tinted bouillabaisse soup, absently poking the poached fish. "You see the tricks they play? That is why you are needed."

I tore off some bread and munched numbly, barely tasting it. I dipped it in Defferre's soup and gave it a try. Didn't improve any. "Games of death and deceit," I muttered.

"Pardon?" Defferre smiled at two women his age walking by. One returned his smile as she moved on. He self-consciously slicked his hair and returned his attention to me. The hand towel slid across the back of his neck.

"It's from a comic book I read as a kid," I said. "*Master of Kungfu*. He's this super martial artist, right? But his dad is Fu Manchu." Defferre nodded, recognizing the famous literary villain. "So this kid, he starts working with MI6 to stop his dad. But then he gets a taste of the whole international spy thing and hates it. The bad guys get away; the good guys are bad guys, its all a game. The guy who wrote the comic, he called them games of death and deceit."

In France and Belgium (as well as all over Asia), comic books don't have the stigma attached to them that they do in the States. Saying that comics aren't just for kids is like telling a Belgian that the sky is blue. Brussels is actually considered the world capitol of comic strips, where they are taken very seriously as an art form. So Defferre listened carefully and—culturally—his reply was not at all strange.

"So life imitates art yet again," he said after some consideration. "I would like to read this book."

"It's called 'Avengers' in Britain." A weekly anthology with other comics reprinted from the States.

"Avengers? *Incroyable*. How appropriate." He took out his tiny note pad—a slim metal case with pencil attached—and jotted the American and British names of the books. Very thorough, my Jacques Defferre. He took a bit of my bread and dipped it, eating thoughtfully. He looked up at the sky. "What are we to do with James? More games of death and deceit, you think?"

"I don't know."

"But I do know, *mon ami*. Someday—" he slid the hand

towel across the table to me. "Someday, you will take care of him. For the children."

I took the towel and felt it, damp and gritty in my hands. A cartoon smiled back at me. *Hello Kitty*.

We drove to Brussels. During the trip Defferre explained my new legitimate life. "You are now a major in the Belgian *Gendarmerie*. Your post is the *Formateur Maitrise de la Violence*." I was the Close Quarter Battle Instructor for rookie gendarme. Easy job for someone with my background and the cover let me disappear when needed. But a major?

Deffere grinned. "Major Bannon has such a nice ring to it," he said. It was enough rank to get things done and avoid questions. According to my file, he said, I had graduated at the top of my class in Lyon, was older than I looked and had an important relative. "And all the other instructors are majors," he added, winking.

Defferre told me he had a nice apartment for me in a lovely part of town. It would be my semi-permanent home, which was something I hadn't had for nearly two years. I was pretty excited when we drove along the eastern edge of the Bois de la Cambre on the Avenue Franklin D. Roosevelt. "Your only decent president," Defferre offered. The avenue was lined with elegant villas, embassies and old government offices. Best of all was the *Universite Libre de Bruxelles*, which had been standing since 1834. I was stunned.

We passed it all.

About two kilometers to the northeast was the active campus of the universite, on the site of the old *Champ de Manoeurves* Parade Ground at Ettterbeek. We passed that, too.

As with university districts the world over, there was dingy housing nearby. We pulled up to an apartment building that looked a lot like any other craphole in the world, only with cobbled streets and no air conditioning. But inside, I was surprised. It was pretty nice. Best of all, most of my neighbors were either young teachers or graduate students. Close enough to the college so no one would notice my odd hours, but with an older crowd that would mind their business.

I planned to teach close quarter combat class for two weeks, and then head to Lyon for an assignment. Defferre tossed me some cash along with a city map.

"Enjoy yourself while you're here," he said. "Teach the recruits something useful you learned from prison." We shook hands and I felt a taste of freedom. My own place, a little jack and an interesting job.

"But don't make too many friends. You may have to betray them in the end." He paused at the door. "Or lose them."

seven

CLOSE QUARTERS

As I got reacquainted with having my own apartment, a sense of place overwhelmed me. I hadn't realized how much I'd missed this basic comfort.

My neighbors were talkative—being teachers—but tended to keep within their own university group. One, Karl Couble-mann, a German physics instructor, had an unpleasant way of pushing himself on his neighbors when he was bored. A knock on my door one night around 9:00 P.M. reminded me of this trait. *Knock.* I didn't expect anyone, so I didn't answer. *Knock* again, more insistently. I slid beside the door. *Knock* with the physics voice: "Are you in there? Open up. I'm thirsty."

I opened the door a few inches. He was tall, sallow, in his late twenties with a gasping little attempt at a moustache. "How about a beer?" I noticed that he didn't bring any.

I shook my head and shut the door.

The rumors were that close combat instructors like me weren't friendly. I now know some teachers were weird.

On the other hand, I liked my new occupation even if it was a cover. Training the gendarmes was a lot of fun. Defferre's pitch had been that a martial arts background would be an important supplement to their overall training. The classes were held in English. I managed to toss in some of my Hapkido instructor's wisdom, since I had so little of my own to offer. The stereotype of a brash young student challenging the new teacher to prove himself had no place in the structured atmosphere of these sessions. My students were uniformly well behaved and eager.

We broke the class into unarmed and armed combat training. They studied firearms with experts in that area. Very wise. The only real focus in the armed training was the baton, a particular favorite of mine. Hapkido was rich in baton techniques and I had mastered many of them.

Thursday afternoon, after the last class of my first week, a student about my age pulled me over. He fidgeted and his eyes wandered everywhere but to mine. "My uncle owns a small shop," he told me, running his fingers through his thick brown curly hair cut so short that it looked like a brillo pad. "Sometimes he imports things from Asia and sometimes needs help."

"Lots of nice things in Asia," I said, looking at him appraisingly.

"Yeah, well," the student coughed slightly, digging his toe in the mat. "My uncle said you might like something from Korea."

He handed me a small package, wrapped in white paper. Then he took off.

I opened the package. A *Hello Kitty* key chain.

"Why not just call me?" I asked on the phone. "I like the spy stuff, too, but the key chain is a little silly."

"Ah, Americans! No panache!" Defferre treated me to an exaggerated sigh. He didn't worry too much about secure phone lines and other essentials of the trade. He just made sure we never talked about anything important on the phone. "I think you understand from my nephew that there is a little family business to attend to. Should I instead call at your home and say—" he adopted a flagrantly bad U.S. southern drawl "Ya'll need to come see meh, sawn."

Why do all Europeans think all Americans have southern accents? I wondered.

So it was that I was off to Lyon. The kid wasn't really his nephew.

Jacques met me at the train station and we drove immediately to the Interpol building. On arriving, I saw that Interpol's offices in Lyon were located in a building whose exterior was an exercise in non-descript, nestled in an area equally banal. Significantly, there was only one small sign to indicate that it was anything other than a business concern. Or maybe a utility company.

We walked in without incident. No metal detectors, but security cameras were everywhere and I noticed seven guys in the lobby who tagged us the minute we hit the door.

Defferre's office was cramped but tidy. "The Interpol building looks like a utility company," I said.

"Utilities?" he laughed. "Yes, we fix things, *mon ami*." The wall behind his desk was dominated by a poster of Humphrey Bogart, the famous scene from *Casablanca* where Rick is leaning back against the bar.

"I knew it," I muttered.

Defferre pretended to ignore me. He had prints from all over the art spectrum—French impressionists, Japanese *ukiyo-e*, rococo, even Warhol's depiction of Marilyn Monroe. His bulletin board was filled with notices on missing children. This was his legitimate role with Interpol—tracking missing children and policing the traffic in human beings.

His rich, darkly lacquered desk seemed out of place in such a tiny office, as did the two matching mahogany bookshelves. One was filled with law books from all over the world. I could only recognize the English, French and Korean titles. His chair was practical and simple—again a mismatch to the high-backed leather armchair facing his desk. He waved me into it.

Defferre told me there were many more then seven men watching me as I entered. "The madman, he cannot be stopped by the metal detector or the trained dog," he said, referring to lunatics who might rush into the building with a bomb or rifle—maybe even try to drive in the lobby with a van full of explosives. He tapped his temple. "Only the trained eye and the nose for such things will stop them."

I almost sat down before I noticed a flash of red color on the dark brown leather. Three issues of the magazine *Shang-Chi, Master of Kungfu*.

"My friend in the U.S., he sends to me the latest issues for you."

I laughed and picked them up, thumbing through. One issue even had a title cover, "Games of Death and Deceit." Nice touch.

"I am applying the butter," confessed Defferre. "You like my little surprise?"

I couldn't stop smiling. It was remarkably thoughtful of him. I found myself remembering the Marseilles alley and comparing it to this office, this chair, this kind little gesture. "I love it, Jacques. Thank you. But why are you buttering me up?"

"Because I need my master of the Hapkido," he said, winking, "for something that is not a game."

Defferre went on to explain "I called you in a week early, because a nasty little bit of business came up—and only you can help the innocent." This was Defferre's talent, to make me feel that I was the only one on the planet who had that something special to thwart evil. It was like Dr. Kim's pep talk, only much more French and *charmant*. Dr. Kim used logic and powerful propaganda to convince me that I was unique and part of something more important than myself—that my personality was well suited to righting wrongs the law couldn't. With Defferre, on the other hand, it was all emotion.

"You see this child, Damien?" He pointed to a girl's picture on his bulletin board. "And that one? And there?" He continued to point. Two children, three; a girl, two boys. Seven years old, four and a half, two. "They all have been taken from their homes by one man. Finding him has been the ultimate nightmare for me. But he is in Osaka this week."

Defferre went onto explain that Shoaib Akram was a Pakistani citizen who sold kiddie porn across the globe to fund his particular brand of terrorism against neighboring Middle Eastern countries. "The problems in that part of the world are so ancient that the children he snatched could never begin to understand the complex factors that led to their rapes and deaths."

"Neither can I."

Defferre gave a slight smile. "I knew you were right for this assignment." He looked out the window for a moment, then sought my eyes. "He is meeting *yakuza* to sell a tape and photos for a special request," Defferre said, referring to the Japanese mafia. "They will then go on a Sex Tour to Korea, the Philippines and Thailand."

"And what is my job?"

"Your job is to keep an eye on him and his pals while they are in Korea. Some Japanese men like to travel to poorer countries across Asia on tours, buying whores and generally acting like big spenders. The salary guys aren't so bad, but the skells sometimes get rough, so they go to brothels suited to their tastes. In Pusan, they will be visiting an expensive house in Nampo. It is run by Han Namhun," Deffere said. "He works for a man that works for Kon."

I knew Kon was connected and kept his hand in things from inside. He wouldn't be out of jail for a couple years, but his name carried weight. "You want me to watch the house. Let you know what Shoaib's doing, if his plans change, that sort of thing. Maybe get inside the house on security?"

Defferre nodded.

"I can't guarantee Kon will vouch for me on that one."

Defferre shrugged it off. "Kon's sister is married."

In prison Kon had mentioned her husband, some taxpayer with a sweet salary job in Chunju. Kon seemed to like the fact that his sister was legit. He bought their house for them as a wedding present.

"Her husband beats her," Defferre said. "Kon doesn't know."

The line would be that I was in Chunju for a checkup on my back from the riots. Defferre would have Eunmi check Kon's men in Chunju. When I pay my respects to Kon's sister, maybe with some fruit or something, I'll notice trouble at home. "So I visit the husband at work, straighten him out. Be sure he knows the score."

"Then you tell Kon's friends what you had to do, they tell Kon and *voila*! He owes you a favor."

I nodded grimly. "Kon pays what he owes." I liked the idea of dancing with a wife beater. I hated Shoaib preying on those who couldn't defend themselves. Dr. Kim was right about that.

Defferre laid out the Shoaib deal. The Japanese government had a working relationship with the yakuza with which Interpol was not going to interfere on this one; the Korean NIS didn't want any trouble if our guy was paying for legal sex (part of the "tour"); so the best place to nab him was the Philippines. "On his last trip, he killed a prostitute—which in itself does not bring attention—but then he took two young girls from the brothel. They have disappeared. We have pictures with *les enfants* and Shoaib in disgusting acts."

He showed me the photos. What I saw is illegal in most countries, but not in Thailand or Pakistan. So this guy was untouchable in his home country. He was also careful when he traveled abroad; thus it was hard to nab him with photos in countries where his acts were a crime. He'd been snagging kids from all over the world for years and selling the photos and negatives to skells for thousands. His crime in the Philippines? He failed to pay for the girls.

"The brothel owner will work with us," Defferre said. He stood, motioning me to remain. "Enjoy the kungfu books, Damien. I liked them very much." He walked around the desk and opened the door. "I'll be back shortly."

Two hours later, Defferre returned with the prettiest man I've ever seen. Tall, willowy, full lush lips—I swear if he grew his dark hair long and wore a dress every man in town would have made a try. As it was, his hair was short and he made a conscious effort to seem older than his early-thirties, maybe to compensate for his good looks. He stood with hands crossed behind him, legs apart. Military at-ease.

"May I present Major Damien Bannon," said Defferre. He chose that name for me and refused to let it go. "This is Captain Henri Wolper, DST. He will assist us in the matter of Shoaib Akram."

The French *Direction de Surveillance du Territoire* (DST) served its nation as a counter-espionage organization. Their teams were on par with top-flight counter-terrorist groups all over the world, ranked with the efficient British SAS and the brutal Israeli Mossad. At the time, Interpol was not officially battling terrorists, but the boundaries were often blurry.

"Many terrorist cells are funded with smuggled goods and with this—" Wolper waved at the pictures of children on the bulletin board, unwilling to explain further. Defferre's work was obviously distasteful to him.

"You will meet with the captain's team, *Major* Bannon." Defferre was enjoying the difference in rank. Internal politics were as palpably invidious in Lyon as anywhere else in the world. "After the Shoaib affair is concluded, we will share the report with them."

"We would like to be debriefed prior to the subject's arrival in France," said Wolper. Defferre gave me the sign and I played Mr. Cooperative.

"Sure, Captain Wolper." I saved "will do" for when I meant it.

It was all Wolper's team at that first meeting. They seemed competent professionals and pleasant enough, but I was distracted.

"Who's the *American*?" One DST agent asked, tossing her hair with disgust. She emphasized the nationality like it was a disease. "Seal? Delta Force?"

Her friend sneered, removing a dark beret as he sat down. "Some guy with Interpol."

"*Mon Dieu*, why us?"

Wolper introduced me to his team in the DST briefing room in Marseilles. I said a few non-sentences, rambled on about teaching with the Belgian gendarmerie and assured them I was eager to cooperate on the current assignment. Wolper went over a few logistical details, in particular the hand-off of Shoaib when he arrived in Paris and the meeting was over.

"So you're some sort of Korean expert?" A rich, hard, feminine voice demanded.

"That's the rumor." I looked up. Her tall, slender form was outlined against the bright lights of the room. I took in the vivid sense of slumbering fire that seemed to find expression only in those tawny eyes; the intense power of stillness she possessed, which conveyed the impression of a wild untamed spirit in an exquisitely trained body—all these things burned into my memory in an instant. In heavily accented English she said her name was Sidelle Rimbaud. She was twenty-four, had recently joined Wolper's team and could shoot my pupil out at a hundred paces.

"At a hundred paces I could hurt your feelings pretty good," I said. "With a megaphone."

She gave me a hint of a smirk. Those astonishing eyes seemed to smile just a little. But if I were looking for a date, I could tell I'd have better luck with a street lamp.

I left for Korea the next day. With a little spare time before the operation was to begin, I decided to keep the appointment I'd made at the Chunju Presbyterian Hospital. The doctor poked, prodded my back and asked about a few other scars I'd earned. He figured a missionary shouldn't be falling off of his bicycle so much. I agreed.

Dr. Kim had suggested I drop his name as my primary care physician. Worked wonders. The Chunju doctor perked up at the name. "Please send my best wishes to the honored doctor." He mentioned that he would see personally to Dr. Kim's request to send my records to him in Seoul. Positions in Seoul were hard to come by. Maybe he figured a little sucking up wouldn't hurt.

The nurse was pleasant and eager to try out a little English. She wasn't pretty in a way that would be noticed in a crowded room, but her smile was dazzling. She suggested that I might meet her and a friend later at a coffee shop. This was pretty standard in Korea—bring along a friend on a first date and if it looks all right, just the two of us for a movie or something later on. She was two or three years older than me and I thought she'd be fun to make friends with over dinner. But I knew I was heading out of Chunju soon and, worse, there was no way I could make any kind of friendship work with people outside my newfound career path. This spy stuff was cool, but what about dating a nice normal girl for a while? Picnics, first kisses, meeting the folks. All the stuff that people do when there's no thought of "for tomorrow we die" attached to it. My only date since I'd joined Interpol had been one night with Eunmi—we were both lonely, caught up in a dirty business. So we reached out. We hadn't talked about it since then, even to Hyung-Jin. We settled into a sort of brother/sister thing—a much more realistic and satisfying relationship given our work environment.

Having gently deflected the nurse's invitation, I left the hospital whining to myself. I pouted all through my meal, a delicious plate of Chunju's famous *pibimpap*—rice with veggies and egg. That and Chunju *kimchi* were worth the trip. I moped about eating it all alone. I called Hyung-Jin from my hotel room near the Chunju Rail Station.

"Yeah, you're right," he said. "Women are beating down your door and poor Race has to turn them all away. Whine, whine, whine."

"Hey, I just want a normal date!"

Hyung-Jin laughed. "There's no such thing in our business, dumb ass!" He said that we were both lucky, anyway. "Lucky to be alive, lucky to be out of prison. Just do our jobs one day at a time, right?"

He was right. Of course. We discussed our meeting in Pusan. Just before we hung up, he asked, "Hey, you think Eunmi might go out with me?"

Whine, whine, whine.

I called Kon's guys in Chunju. I told them to check me out; that I was looking for a little work while I was in town. Next day, they let me know it was square and to come on down.

Five of them were shooting pool. I showed up and made small talk. One of them had done time in Taejon before I got there. We swapped a few stories. He was short, a stocky, laughing crustacean with hands that hung down to his knees. Mr. Crab. His lower lip twitched when he shot pool.

"How can I pay my respects to Kon's sister?" I asked, tossing a dart. Crab looked over at a slender guy who was reading a sports magazine. The guy wore slacks and a nice shirt. Prettier than the rest of us. He didn't look up from the magazine.

"Usually Yongdo takes things to the house," Crab said, nodding at the reader. The others snickered softly.

"Fair enough." I tossed some cash on the table. "Send over a fruit basket or something from me." I leaned on the table, stopping Crab's shot. "Make sure it's from me." They knew I had history with Kon. The magazine reader got up and pocketed the money.

"No problem," he said in English. I stared at him hard between the eyes until he backed down. Time to go.

I found the sister's house on my own. No—I didn't trust them. Korean houses were often surrounded by twelve-foot fences, usually of cement. The cement was covered with broken glass on top. The outside door was solid steel with an intercom attached. I pressed the button.

"*Yoboseyo?*" A woman's voice.

"I've come to pay my respects to Kon's sister," I said in formal Korean.

The door buzzed and I walked the short path to the front door. Kon's sister. She was surprised that it was an American, but recovered immediately. She had long dark hair and looked like she was after the film-noir siren look with dark circles under her almond-shaped eyes.

"For the honored sister of my dear friend Kon," I said, bowing and with both hands presenting the fruit basket I had just purchased.

"How sweet!" she said softly. Her long neck turned as her eyes wandered to the door. There were red bruises on her neck. "Will you take tea?" This was half-hearted, a courtesy at best. I declined.

"I must leave. Please accept my gift graciously and send my regards to Kon." I got out in a hurry, closing the gate behind me.

I caught a cab to her husband's office.

I tagged the husband as he left and followed him to a bar. They knew him; so I figured it was his usual. He knew a little English so didn't mind making friends when I started buying. Now he was on beer six—or so—and it was all Korean. About one thing.

"She's a flirt. She drives me…" the husband took a long drag on his beer. "She drives me…" Another drag. "Oh, hell, she just drives me!"

"She puts out to everyone, huh?" I asked. Mr. Subtle. "How dare she?"

"My feeling exactly. She's lucky to have me. I ought to leave her, but I'm stuck. Her brother, he's the tough guy, right? And if I divorce her, he'll kill me!" Divorce was uncommon in Korea and the woman took the weight of the stigma afterwards. Kon wouldn't like that. "And the brother has friends, they're always at the house." Another drag and the glass was empty. Bartender dropped a fresh one right way.

Husband had on a blue suit, conservative gray tie, clean cut. There was nothing distinguishable about him. He clenched his fists. "Sometimes I get home and I swear I can smell a man's cologne, you know?"

"So you slap her around or what?"

He said he did. All the time. His hands hurt from it. It didn't stop her. I nodded. "What else can you do?" The words almost stuck in my throat.

When he was toasted enough, I led him outside. Behind the bar, I smacked him across the throat. He caved. I hailed a cab and told the driver to take my unconscious friend and me to a cheap hotel. Husband reeked of booze. Not the first pair of drunks the cabbie had ever seen. I paid the fair, paid the dive hotel, carried husband upstairs.

And waited.

He came around just before dawn. I slapped him. Hard. He jerked up and I slapped him down again. He mumbled and whined, but the only coherent thing I heard was, "Why?"

"You don't like how your wife acts, you sleep in another room. Get out or get a little honey in town." I slid on my brass knuckles. "But you don't lay a finger on Kon's sister."

He took a beating.

I left husband in the dive and headed to the pool hall. I figured I'd let them know I settled the score and maybe it would get to Kon. As I walked in, Crab slapped a pool cue across my neck. I spun, dizzy, and felt my knees caving. Reader kicked my legs out. I hit the cement floor hard and tried to cover up. They worked me over with the pool cue and heavy boots, but stopped short of killing me. Crab lifted me up.

"No one visits sister's house but me," Reader said. I should have known not to go there. Dumb ass. "And Chong," he laughed, slamming a fist into my ribs, "says hello."

Chunju was complicated.

eight

WALKING THE PATH THAT'S GIVEN

Kon's guys tossed me onto a deserted street corner near Jeonbuk University. I dusted off and hailed a cab. The cabbie shot by me like I was a leper. Another cab; same luck. Finally, I waved some jack in the air. Mr. Samaritan threw on the brakes. Nice big cab, too.

"Hospital." Like I needed to say it.

In the emergency room, I laid out the missionary line. My passport and bona fides all held up. Told the cops that some *kkang-p'ae*—gangbangers—had done the damage and snagged my briefcase. "It was full of bibles," I said. The cop loved the irony and told the story to everyone he saw the rest of the night.

When they finally wheeled me to a room alone and before the painkillers kicked in, I phoned Defferre. "Bit of trouble here in Chunju," I said.

Defferre told me they would take care of the hospital. "But it will take about a week for me to send someone. We'll miss our man in Pusan. You got a place?"

"I might. I'll let you know."

And I drifted off into nothing.

My doctor showed up the next morning. "Dr. Kim called me and asked that I look in on you," he said. "There is no internal bleeding; just bad bruises and a nasty cut on your forehead." The doctor threw his considerable weight around, made sure that the nurses were nice to me. I figured he was hoping that Dr. Kim owed him one.

The coffee house nurse came later that day, all concern and big smiles. It wasn't her shift—not even her area—but she came by to put in the word with the other nurses and keep me company. She even brought a little stuffed E.T. doll. I'd been inside Taejon when the movie came out, but I'd seen the ugly/cute little spud's face all over since I got out.

I called a number I had written down during the riots in Kwangju. Moon Jongjin. His mother picked up and I remembered he would only be seventeen now. Just out of high school. Well, I wasn't so old, either.

She said he'd be back and I left my name, room and number. An hour later he was standing beside my bed. "How's the back?"

"Nice greeting, little brother," I said, trying not to laugh. "I took a beating."

"That's why tae kwon do is better. Less beatings."

"You weren't such a smart ass in Kwangju," I said and this time I did laugh. It hurt, but it felt good. We passed some time. He was fuller, grown up, but still a foot shorter than me. He had a stomach like iron and his jaw looked like he'd taken a few hits with it. And not just in tae kwon do class. He caught me up. Yoon Myungju had kept in touch with him. She was in Kwangju, working a bookstore job.

Moon said he'd finished high school and was getting ready for the mandatory draft. "Three years military service. Can't wait," he grimaced.

"Maybe I got a friend with the NIS that can hook you up with a good post."

Moon cocked his head. "You got a place to stay?"

I shrugged. "Maybe a hotel."

"Ri-i-ight! A hotel!" He rolled his eyes like I'd said something funny and called his mom. Looks like I had a place.

I walked out of the hospital that day. Moon's house was in a run-down part of town. His father was working construction in Inchon—"Good pay these days"—and Moon's mother thought having a missionary stay there for a week was a good idea for the afterlife. "Please pray for us," she said, preparing my sleeping mat. Moon and I were bunking together. I assured her that her good heart was all the prayer she needed, but that I'd do my part just the same.

Korean homes are heated by an *ondul* flue system that runs hot water under the floors. Uniformly covered with linoleum throughout the home, floors are toasty and perfect for sitting or sleeping. My mat was plush and inviting. I lay on it, trying to momentarily forget the nasty business behind me. And in front.

Moon wanted some answers. "NIS friend, huh? Maybe it's time you caught me up."

So I spilled my guts about prison, about my friend with the NIS, even about that nurse at the hospital. Didn't mention Interpol.

He listened to every word. Moon was good at that. I could see he didn't like most of what I said, but I never felt that he judged me.

I dozed off. When I woke I flipped through the television channels. *Columbo* wasn't on.

Later that night Moon brought in a beat-up slipcase volume of *Korea's Best Loved Poems*. He opened it to his favorite poet, Yun Dongju, and read to me. I watched the moon from his bedroom window, heard crickets outside.

Prelude
Let me have no shame
Under heaven 'til I die.
Even winds in the brush
Pained my heart.

With a heart that sings of stars
I will love all dying things.
And I must walk the path
That's been given me.

Tonight also, the winds sweep over the stars.

"This is *han*," he said. "You know han?" I did. Unrequited sorrow. With a little revenge tossed in. It was a uniquely Korean word that represented a bitter acceptance that life is misery but also beauty. The poet wrote *Prelude* during the Japanese occupation of Korea, from 1910 to the end of World War II. Koreans were forced to speak and write only Japanese—their native tongue was forbidden. Their great works of art were taken to Japan, where they are still housed in the Osaka Museum of Oriental Art. The poem was not only about the feeling of *han* that the occupation inspired—it also described a rare glimmer of hope.

I memorized the poem. "*I must walk the path that's been given to me.*" Moon and I talked about it many times during the week. If life is filled with *han*, the poet seemed to say, then the only important thing is how we live.

Among the stars.

Hyung-Jin hit town and we took a bus to Cheongju, a quiet little town south of Chunju at the foot of Mt. Naejang. It was October. The mountain was beautiful, alive with all the rich reds and golds and oranges that make autumn so impossibly heart wrenching. In Korean there is a term for a live leaf on a tree— *ipseh*—and a dying leaf that is about to fall or has fallen—*nakyop*. Mt. Naejang was filled with nakyop when Hyung-Jin and I hiked its paths.

Hyung-Jin told me that Shoaib Akram had never gotten to Pusan. Seemed his tour had changed. "Eunmi says he's probably postponed for a few weeks."

"Either way, I'm no good over there. Something stinks with Chong."

"Chong put the word out about you and that business in Marseilles," said Hyung-Jin, stepping off the path and plucking a red leaf from a tree. "He says you can't be trusted."

"And what do you think?

"He says you rolled on him."

"True enough."

Hyung-Jin smiled quietly, crumpling the leaf in his hands. "Kon's losing ground. Chong wants to cut into kiddie porn and move up a few notches. NIS tells me to side with Chong, get deep in his trade."

Defferre and NIS played ball sometimes, but on this we were way out in the cold. I had no idea about the recent shifts among the skells in Korea and Defferre hadn't been told. Or didn't tell me.

"Those guys in Chunju, they're Kon's men," I said. "But they sent me a message from Chong. Maybe they're playing both sides."

Hyung-Jin agreed. We laid it out between us. We would settle things with the Chunju pool hall. Hyung-Jin would tell Chong he had cleaned up Kon's men in Chunju—setting him up good on that side—and I would tell Kon that I settled the score with the traitors who were boffing his sister. Pipeline to both sides.

"And Defferre?" Hyung-Jin asked.

I hunkered down, drawing in the dirt. "NIS and Interpol have a few agendas that we don't know about and we get stuck in the middle with too little intelligence and too late help."

"They weren't there at Gamcheon Bay," said Hyung-Jin.

"Or the pool hall."

Hyung-Jin looked up at the trees, their brilliant colors dancing in the afternoon sun. "We're just leaves to them. We grow a little while, do our jobs, then when we're not useful, they'll let us fall off." He kicked a pile of leaves. "Nakyop are beautiful, but people walk all over them."

I stood, handing a fallen leaf to Hyung-Jin. "Then we need to keep ourselves useful."

We didn't care about the whole crew in the pool hall, only Reader and Crab. Reader was Chong's new man in Chunju and as a bonus he was doing Kon's sister. Crab seemed to be his only ally. We watched them for a few days, got the feel of their habits.

Reader and Crab liked to watch the strippers in Kunsan, next to the U.S. military base. Unlike purely Korean clubs, Kunsan clubs allowed a wilder crowd, suiting their GI audience. Korean clubs were almost temple-like: quiet, with the strippers in complete control. Payment was made to the proprietor and the customers gratefully sat enraptured. The Kunsan clubs, though, were riotous affairs, with money dipped in g-strings and constant vigilance by an army of bouncers. Our guys liked that.

We tagged them coming out of a club, stumbling back to their crap hotel. It was around 3 A.M. as they walked on a nice quiet street. They were a little drunk and didn't have pool cues this time. Payment came due.

We sent some flowers to my friendly nurse and called the hospital a few days later. She agreed to meet us with her pal at a local coffee shop.

We were so nervous Hyung-Jin couldn't button his shirt. "She's really nice, huh?" he asked again and again. "You don't think I look like a punk ex-con?"

"Hell, Hyung-Jin, you're a responsible taxpayer, an NIS guy!" I showed him his fresh new ID. He had become legitimately NIS about the same time Defferre made me a major in the Belgian gendarmerie.

The girls were a lot of fun. Neither of them really took

much interest in me, but the nurse got one look at Hyung-Jin and set her cap.

Hyung-Jin decided to stay in Chunju for a few weeks.

Defferre told me that he hadn't been looped into the information on Chong's bid for trade. But it didn't surprise him. We got word to Kon inside that I had cleaned things up in Chunju. By the time I was in Pusan, I already had a case of JD waiting for me, courtesy of Kon.

Eunmi set me up in a nice condo in Namchon district—not too far from where my old missionary companions still plied their good works. It was better than the dive in Belgium. She took me shopping so I would "look less like a bum and more civilized." I picked up Itzhak Perlman and Pincas Zukerman's *Mozart Duos* on cassette and we listened to it on the beach, letting the music wash over us.

"Shoaib's coming in over the weekend," she said. "Probably be here for three days."

I looked at the waves, at how the wind teased her glossy hair. Like normal kids; friends whiling away the afternoon. I shook my head. I really had to stop whining. "I'll get into the whore house— oh, um, excuse me—the brothel right away. Kon owes me one now."

Eunmi laughed. "Excuse you? No one's said that to me in forever." She put her head on my shoulder and we laughed. I thought I was lucky to have a sister like her.

The house was unbelievable by Korean standards. The rooms were huge and ornate with every opulent decoration they could stuff in. The colors were garish—green, red, yellow—insulting to the eye, but it all blended in the atmosphere of flowing money. I wore a black suit, black turtleneck, and acted respectful. Security and service with an international flair. The girls were between the ages of eighteen and maybe forty or more.

Kon's man, Han Namhun, ran the house. He told me that they had a girl for every flavor. "But no kids," he added. He'd heard about Marseilles. "Just adult entertainment." He handed me the case of JD personally, sending Kon's formalized thanks for "that small business in Chunju." He tossed in that there was going to be trouble with Chong. "But Kon's always come out on top," he said, a little too hopefully. Wishful thinker.

Shoaib turned up Saturday with two Japanese yakuza. Defferre made it clear that the yakuza weren't to be touched. I was to watch Shoaib and keep the intel pipeline open. The Japanese played it rough with the Korean girls, but we knew that going in and used the girls that do that sort of work. I didn't like it, but the girls said the yakuza didn't cross the line. Rough but not dangerous, they said. That line was too blurry for me.

Shoaib liked the schoolgirl routine. The whole bit—ponytails and plaid skirts—but there were girls who specialized in that, too. The first night went without a hitch.

Night two, Shoaib wanted the youngest girl they had. Turned out she was seventeen—legal in Korea—and he spent a few hours with her before it got boring. Skells like Shoaib want really young ones and aren't satisfied with play acting substitutes. Remembering the bulletin board in Defferre's office, I knew this guy was going to ask for a pre-teen.

Han told me to take Night Three off. Guess who had asked for a kid. Han had to walk the line between my working for him and Kon saying to treat me right. He didn't want trouble with Mr. Wildcard Marseilles guy. Funny how Defferre's reputation was following me.

Defferre and I talked it over on the phone in my condo. "DST needs this guy," he said. "He can be turned and used as an asset to locate terrorist cells."

"DST knows what he sells?"

Defferre laughed across the globe. "You saw Captain Wolper. He can barely stand to talk about this business, but doesn't mind that we get our hands dirty with it." I knew the type. I asked what we were going to do about Shoaib. "Nothing until the Philippines," Defferre said.

I told him that there was a kid involved and Defferre just sighed, truly unhappy but resigned. "The child they bring to him will be a professional. A child prostitute who has done such things many times before—and will do them many more times even if we stop Shoaib tonight."

That was hard to hear. I understood what was going down—stopping Shoaib in the Philippines would be the right move for Interpol and DST, because he could be shipped to Paris without a hitch. Moving now would irritate the Koreans, who would probably deport Shoaib to Pakistan. And the kid would be spared only one night of misery in a young life filled with it.

I felt bile rising in my throat. "Okay, Shoaib is hands-off," I said. "But before I leave Korea, I want to know who's pimping out these kids."

Defferre chuckled, a deep dangerous sound. "*C'est ca*. Now you are catching on and becoming one of us."

Was I? I was caught in a melee of conscience between my desire to stop real evil and the methods that had to be used.

Nabbing Shoaib went down as planned. We picked him up in the Philippines and exported him to Lyon.

I told whorehouse Han that I wanted to try something on my own, but maybe I'd be back later. If he still had work for me. He said I could come back anytime, which I took to mean as long as my credit with Kon was good.

Eunmi was still working on tracking down the kiddie pimp when I flew out of Pusan. Whorehouse Han's contact had been a middleman who had disappeared after the yakuza left town. We filed it away for the future.

I joined Defferre in Lyon and watched as he spent a few days helping Shoaib roll on every contact he had in the kiddie porn world. We didn't ask about terrorists—that was for DST. On day three we dumped him on DST, a little worse for wear. He rolled for DST, too.

Before I knew it, I was back in Brussels teaching again. I realized after the first class that my whole body ached from the beating I took in Chunju. It would be a while healing. And the scars I was collecting were starting to itch. I went to the gendarme doctor. He'd seen plenty of scars over the years.

"I could prescribe for you the addictive narcotic," he advised. I guessed he was late sixties and more than a little tired of young gendarme. "But my best advice is to be more careful. You know there are policemen who spend twenty years without ever drawing a weapon? Learn from them!" He shook his gray head, burping his next pearl of wisdom. "Forget the medication. In the evening, when it itches so, take a glass of wine. Don't overdo it or you will lose the benefit. Just one glass when you need it. You will sleep well."

It worked. I had never had a sip of alcohol in my life, outside of half a beer at a party when I was fifteen. After all the jokes I'd heard from drinkers, I was truly sipping wine "for medicinal purposes."

Defferre left me alone for a while after that. I actually got to know some of my neighbors, wandered into some nice shops and bookstores in Brussels, even read those comic books Jacques gave me. Most of the best cafes in Brussels have comic strip collections for customers to peruse while eating. I felt on vacation, even though I was teaching every day.

After a Saturday of strolling, I relaxed with the prescribed glass of merlot and searched the channels for an episode of *Columbo*. Found one. Some skell committed a murder and Columbo was going to catch him. Just the sort of plot I liked.

The phone rang.

"I got your number from Jacques Defferre," she said, voice rich, slightly nervous. "You may not remember me." I did. Sidelle Rimbaud. Ms. 100 Paces. "I'll be in Brussels this week. Would you like to join me at a café for lunch?"

I would indeed.

nine

TRICK OR TREAT

"A thirteen-year-old was enjoying the first Halloween Party at a friend's basement/recreation room. Friend's parents were upstairs and the seventeen-year-old sibling was watching the group of giggling seventh graders. Evening wore on, Seventeen pulled Thirteen aside and started dancing. Nice and slow. Thirteen had never danced like this—a bit of the bump and grind. Then some serious kissing—something else Thirteen had never experienced. Seventeen's bedroom was downstairs, too." As I spoke, I looked lingeringly at Sidelle. We had been seeing each other seriously for a few month and were relaxing at her villa.

"'How about we go in there for a while?' suggested Seventeen, opening the door and pulling the younger child inside." I went on. "On the bed, serious kissing and a little more."

Engrossed in my role, my voice broke a little.

"'I'm not so sure I'm ready for all this,' said Thirteen. Seventeen didn't listen. And didn't stop."

Sidelle's eyes met mine. "What happened to the seven-teen-year-old? Did the girl's father find out and punish him?"

"I purposefully left the genders vague, Sid," I said. "If Seventeen is a guy and Thirteen is a girl, then he's a no-good son of a bitch, right? But if Thirteen is a guy, then it's like 'oh, lucky little guy got some from a hot older chick.'" Sid shrugged, pulling her long auburn hair from its ponytail holder that matched her light blue cotton jumper. I continued. "But when you take the gen-der out, you realize that anyone that young doesn't have the jungle skills or the sense to say no—or to even know what to say."

Sid's eyes were dark amber swirls in mother-of-pearl, large and expressive. She took my hand. I felt the callous on her trigger finger and a scar across the back of her wrist, "from some bad men in Paris." The bad men had been part of a terrorist cell of North Koreans intent on leaving a car bomb in front of the South Korean consulate. Sid's DST team had stopped them, but not without leaving some scars. She caressed my hand gingerly, looking first at my own wrist scar from a Taejon cafeteria seating arrangement debate, then in my eyes. "So what did you do?"

"I was only thirteen, right? So I'm all in love with this gal 'cause I don't know what she is. And my brother was all, 'Hey, I heard you hooked up with Dee at the party. Way to go, man!' cause he had no sense that maybe a little kid didn't want sex so soon." I paused, kissing Sid's hand, a laughing sigh. "This is the first time I ever told this story."

"Nice girl," said Sid. Sarcasm after my own heart.

"So two months later I'm knocking on her door. 'Is Dee home?' I asked and she looks right at me and doesn't remember me."

"Maybe she had her own problems."

I nodded. "Yeah, I figured something like that. I mean, I was only a young kid but I figured maybe there's no difference between boys and girls—that they all are pretty messed up and don't know what they want at that stage. There are a few manipulative punks but most others are just stumbling along like me. That's how I learned to live with the fact that I said no and she didn't stop."

"That's rape, *mon cher*," said Sid, leaning closer.

"Yeah, I figured something like that. So I got to thinking and decided that my first kiss—hell, my first everything—was pretty confusing and pretty bad and if I was dating a gal, and I knew it was her first kiss, then I'd do whatever I could to make it special. I mean, even if we weren't in love or whatever, at least she could always look back on her first kiss and say, 'That was nice.'"

Sid kissed me then, lush parted lips brushing mine. "Sort of like that." I gasped slightly, a teasing smile. "Only not quite as good. I figure I need more practice."

Later, we got back to the Halloween story. "What about love making, Damien?" Sid had adopted the name Defferre gave me, because it was the first name she ever heard in reference to me. "I already have a crush on Damien," she explained with her crooked half-smile, eyes glittering. "I couldn't betray him with Race."

"I never had sex again in those years," I said. "I got all religious, even though I suppose I lost all those naïve thoughts that women are more virtuous and pure than men." Sid snorted at this. She had often mentioned that she felt women were no better or worse than men, just their methods were different. While I held that all people wanted the same things—to be loved, adored respected, trusted and have great sex—Sid held the same ideals, but felt that women were more likely to stab each other in the back and lie to their men to get these things. I insisted that even though cultural training may alter behavior in men and women, they are essentially the same. Mr. Egalitarian. Funny that I was espousing that and Sid was the socialist.

I laughed at her snort and picked up the story. "So, I dated a lot in high school and you'd be surprised at how many gals broke up with me 'cause I wouldn't put out." I laughed at this, but Sid wasn't surprised one little bit. "And then I did the mission thing and here I am in France with you."

"All those years without *l'amour?*"

"I guess so. Weird, huh?"

Sid smiled softly, sliding her fingers through her hair, then through mine. "We should make up for the lost time."

The *Direction de la Surveillance du Territoire* (DST – Directorate of Territorial Security) had offices at 1 *rue Nelaton* in Paris and was organized in five departments: counter-espionage, internal security, international terrorism, technical administration and general administration. The DST also had a special office of national and international relations that included countering illegal drug trade, organized crime, money laundering, and arms proliferation. Sid worked with this special office on assignments that often crossed paths with Interpol.

Sid had rigorous DST training before her induction into the rarified ranks and it was still a daily effort. Every day that she wasn't on assignment she honed her skills in combat, jungle training, endurance, interrogation resistance and the specialty of Sid's team, Close Quarter Battle. This was practiced in the *hôtel de la mort*, the Death Hotel; a training simulation like the SAS Killing House. It housed five rooms, dressed up in complicated scenarios, such as embassies, aircraft or power stations. Dummies were in place and occasionally there were experiments with "live" hostages. The walls of the rooms were lined to prevent ricochets and the team often formed smaller combat groups armed with a variety of weapons. There, the team practiced their ability to fire accurately and quickly. Some scenarios required the use of knives.

Sid tried to get me admittance to the training as a participant—no chance—then as an advisor—not likely—and finally just as an observer. No go on all counts. After all, those Interpol guys couldn't be trusted. On official levels, intelligence agencies simply refused to share. Covert organizations across the world often wasted more time watching each other than watching the enemies.

Who were the enemies? For Sid's team, they were the skells who funded terrorists. She wanted even more training than the DST provided—and that's saying a lot. She and I practiced sharp shooting. She was an expert on all counts. Had a few badges to prove it. I tried my best, but still just plain stunk.

"*Mon Dieu*, my grandmother shoots better than you!" cried Sid after I failed—again—to hit the chest of a target.

"But I wounded his fingers pretty good. Too bad I was aiming for the head." I tossed out a lame excuse.

Sid rolled her eyes, "You must practice. I want you alive," she tilted her head and pursed her lips in a way she knew I couldn't resist, "for later." Her Mademoiselle Coquette routine was something she rarely got to explore at work and she enjoyed the exaggerated affect it had on me. I did, too.

She and I also practiced unarmed combat, along with baton and knife training. Sid was DST trained and in superb physical and mental condition, but my techniques had come from a whole different world. First, Hapkido, which is an art designed to maim and kill; then the docks, alleys and prisons of Korea; finally, the assignments for Defferre. Sid's training was practical and dangerous, but she had only used her excellent marksmanship to date. She had never known the dull, thick horror of feeling another human being die by her own hands. It showed in her sparring.

So at first I went a little easy. She waited until I was sipping some water and laid her baton on the back of my legs. I collapsed and she crawled on top of me. "No more easy stuff, *mon cher.*" She covered me with kisses; then rolled me over in a choke. "I mean it! My life depends on this stuff, too, you know."

Good point.

Talk about the best way to relieve domestic stress. No wonder we never fought.

Saying "*l'amour*" or "*mon cher*" was Sid's way. Unlike Defferre, whose clichéd demeanor was calculated to impress with an exaggerated Frenchness, Sid simply had French words that she preferred. We used to play a little game, comparing the best words around the globe for a given meaning.

"For love, definitely *l'amour*," she stated emphatically.

"The Italian *amore* is pretty good though," I tossed in. "Has a great Dino song." We launched into verse: "*When the moon hits your eye like a big pizza pie, that's amore!*" then realized that was the only part of the chorus we knew.

"Americans have the best way of saying *democracy*," Sid said, a little serious. "It's not completely their word, but they've used it well." It was rare for Sid to say anything positive about America—a culture she thought was crass, over-bearing and morally hypocritical. "A country where ballet dancers—male bodies in perfection— are called effeminate," she sometimes complained, "where violence is shown to children on television everyday but *l'amour* gets an R-rating at the movies; where religion is used as a weapon to beat down individuality." There was more, much of which I'd heard from other Europeans. Sid acknowledged this. "I suppose I'm just frustrated at America, because they're so damned rich and know it!"

I laughed, allowing that I wasn't so rich. "But Americans do have endless hope, resolute hope—it's what I love best about my culture," I said. Sid had never seen America that way, but when I said it, a light went on. She said that sense of grueling hope was what made me so appealing, despite being so American. Then why was she with me? She didn't know either.

"Who has the best word for *yes*?" she said.

"Japanese all the way," I said, and grunted a low gutteral, "*Hai!*"

She tried it on; then laughed, a full-throated lyrical sound, fresh and inviting. "So you ask a little Japanese chick for a date, and she grunts, '*Hai!*'"

"Nah, the girls say it different!"

"And how is that?" she asked, stretching like a cat. So I showed her. Lucky us.

Although I could be released for special assignments with the Lyon headquarters of Interpol, Defferre had not used this privilege for months. Over the summer, Defferre stressed my legitimate role with the Belgian gendarmerie. He had me teach as many classes as possible, sometimes ten sessions a day. I attempted to ingratiate myself and fit in with my neighbors and colleagues.

I worked this rewarding job and saw Sid whenever time allowed. By September we were spending weekends together in her villa just outside Marseilles or at my apartment in Brussels. Her father, a bank vice-president in Paris, seemed to really like me. He said that Americans were trustworthy husbands and my job was stable. The instructor cover was coming in handy.

He commented once that he liked the way I treated Sid, "Candid, like an equal—not like the pretty boys before. They always asked for the money and stared at her figure too much." Sid hated that sort of talk, insisting that her previous beaus had all been interested in her, not her father's jack. I just listened and kept my mouth shut. Sid's brother, the French equivalent of a CPA, thought I was the worst thing that ever happened to his sister.

Their mother had passed away when Sid was fourteen. "She watches over me always," Sid confided late one night. The moon glistened in her eyes the way poets have been trying to tell us about for centuries. That night I finally appreciated the sentiment. Sid continued, "She is an angel now. When I need guidance, God sends her to speak to me."

"Do you see her, like a spirit?" My tone was sincere, curious.

She shook her head. "*Non, non,* but I feel her here," she pressed her hand to her chest and then my hands to that dear spot that housed her heart. "Before mama went to heaven I didn't listen to God. So He sends her to speak to me when I need help."

Sid was a devout Catholic and wore a small gold cross every minute. Since my missionary work and introduction to Interpol, I had fallen away from organized religion. This was another area about which we disagreed.

"You know what I've seen and been through, Sid," I said. "Prison and my own life aren't too big a deal, but what I've seen done to kids. Why does God allow evil to flourish? Is He good or a mean son-of-a-bitch?"

She slapped me. Hard. "He took my mama, *non?*" She hugged me tight, head on my chest, tight so I couldn't breathe. "Are you the only one to suffer? We are nothing!" Tighter hug, loving and punishing me at the same time. "He does not explain to us about the torture of *les enfants*, but He is there. My mama tells me so."

Sid convinced me to give prayer another try. We attended a few masses. Whatever faith I had lost when I stopped being a Latter-Day Saint missionary was reborn that summer. Not because of Sid. She agreed with me that the romantic idea of a "good woman" saving a man's soul was not only a lame excuse for not owning one's personal actions, but also too heavy a burden on the woman in question. "*Beauty and the Beast* is a horrible story," Sid explained. "Where the beauty is always trying to change this miserable beast. Better that he changes himself and comes calling when he knows how to behave."

My new and deeper belief in God came from within, just as my decisions and actions to that date were from within. I came to see faith as a companion to make life endurable and God as a Being in whom one could place the misery of life and find comfort.

Sid thought maybe I wasn't such a bad bet. "Mama tells me that you are a good man," she said that night. She kissed me, long, in a way that only love and passion combined in true commitment can kiss. She pressed her lips to my ear, whispering. "Let's grow fat together."

"Fat?" I laughed softly, enjoying the thought.

"*Oui*. Fat, *mon cher*." She laid an arm on my chest, propping her head on her wrist. "I will quit DST and you will quit Interpol. We will find an oasis from the evil in the world." She kissed me again, deep amber eyes wet with pleading, hair falling across us. "We will attend university and you will become a professor of history. Then I'll take your classes and flirt with you. I'll never stop taking classes."

It was a beautiful dream.

"I hate what I have seen!" Her voice filled with venom. Emotion took her for a moment as she searched for the right words. "I wish I were still ignorant and innocent."

It all sounded strange coming from two people so young. "*Mon cher* Sidelle," I said, equally serious. "We can. We will escape."

"Soon?" She kissed me. I nodded. She lay her head on my chest, drifting back to sleep, murmuring. "Grow fat together."

Defferre loved Sid. He made a lunch date with us one September day in Lyon. At the time, Lyon was the second-largest city in France, filled with the noise and stench of urban sprawl and smog. September in Lyon is the hottest and most humid in the country. I wore a beige double-breasted suit with a light brown band-collar shirt. Sid wore a beige summer dress with a cream scarf wrapped round her waist. It made you notice her beautiful hair and eyes even more.

Before we went to lunch, Sid and I meandered in *Vieux Lyon*, taking in the late blooms, the sidewalk cafes and debating whether the distant skyscrapers were eyesores or wonders of modern architecture. Neither of us cared much.

Lyon is all industry on the outer fringes, but where we were, in the heart of the city, the history is rich and elegant. Even though Vieux Lyon was a slum in many ways, on a clear day the old medieval and Renaissance buildings were thrilling. The bizarre shops on *rue du Boeuf* offered so many obscure and fanciful items that we endured having to stare down skells every block. Sid bought a silk cream scarf, which she wrapped round her neck with a flourish. "*Est-ce que je charme?*" she asked, posing for me.

"Yeah, the most charming secret agent in the world, Sid." I meant it, but she slugged me anyway. Being with Sid was a bruising experience.

We wandered across *pont Bonaparte* to the *place Bellecour*, one of France's largest squares, to admire the statue of Louis XIV looming over the historic buildings. Many of the old buildings, dating as far back as the eighteenth century, are covered with graffiti, referred to as *trompe l'oeil* murals and hailed as modern art. We guessed that elegance was in the eye of the beholder after all.

A humid drizzle started as we grabbed a cab to the Alain Chapel restaurant, where Defferre had made reservations a month before. Not only one of Lyon's most expensive restaurants, this stylishly renovated nineteenth century postal station offered food that was just plain sinful. Sid the Catholic swore she had to confess the meal later that week. Defferre caught the twelve-hundred dollar tab courtesy of Interpol. If the meal were on my budget, it would have been bread and cheese in the park.

We sat in a relaxing window table, watching the rain outside. Lyon is known throughout France for her food, particularly *quenelles* (poached fish balls), tripe Lyonnais and the famous Lyon sausage. Defferre made a point to wear his sharpest double-breasted suit, stylish and conservative blue with a diamond tiepin. His hair was so slicked that it seemed a little closer to Bela Lugosi than Bogart. Sometime during the meal, Defferre presented an envelope.

"Let me guess, Jacques," I said. "Holiday is over." Sid cringed.

"Not at all, Damien! This is a present. Opera for two."

We opened the envelope. Train tickets going the long way to Milan, and two La Scala tickets for Verdi's *Otello*. I'd never been to the opera, but Sid was a great fan. The tickets were for an October performance.

"I can personally guarantee that you will have the week off," Defferre said, enjoying our surprise and his little present. "As for you, Mademoiselle Rimbaud, is this enough time for you to request a holiday?"

It was and we couldn't wait.

ten

TERROR IN
MARSEILLES

Sid planned to take a month leave from mid-September
through our opera date in October. I requested that all my classes
be cancelled from the schedule for the same time period. We spent
the month in her Marseilles villa.

Before I was free, however, Defferre had one small job for
me. "Kon will be released from Taejon Prison in three days. I want
you to pay your respects and give him this." Defferre slid an
account book across his desk. Bank of America. Ten thousand dollars, U.S. "He will expect a token of your esteem. Withdraw the
complete amount in Korean won and present it with all appropriate formality. I want you to continue in his good graces."

It was expected that I would personally call on Kon at his
Chunju office to present the non-traceable gift—if I wanted to do
business with him in the future. That's just what Defferre wanted
him to think.

Eunmi and Hyung-Jin met me at Kimhae Airport outside of Pusan. I was pleased to see them and to be speaking in Korean again. All the pop songs on the loudspeakers were new, though. I had to catch up.

In the taxi to my little condo in Namchon dong I noticed they were holding hands. Very cosmopolitan and a rare sight outside of Seoul. I ribbed them about it and Eunmi blushed. "We hear you have someone too, Chanyoung?" she asked, using my Korean name.

"*Kulotji-ye,*" I confirmed in Pusan slang, using the familiar form reserved for close friends. "Best thing to ever happen to me."

They smiled in the way of happy couples who want everyone else to have someone, too. Go figure: Hyung-Jin and Eunmi. At least they didn't have to keep secrets. That was a bonus with Sid, too. No secrets. She even knew the real story behind my work with Defferre.

The three of us whiled away the afternoon in Pusan. Eunmi giggled a lot and whispered to me more than once. Hyung-Jin didn't care for that one little bit. He and I took a stroll on the beach after dinner. Eunmi said she wanted a nap before we all gossiped away the night.

"I got it," Hyung-Jin said, passing me a small dime-sized package. "All the way from Brazil."

I slid it into my pocket and squeezed his hand in Korean fashion. "Thanks, Hyung-Jin. You're the best friend I ever had." A moment passed, then I added, "After Sid, of course."

"Same here," he said. "After Eunmi, of course."

"I guess this squares us."

Hyung-Jin shook his head. "This squares us for Taegu Prison. I still owe for Gamcheon Bay."

I told him that he didn't owe me for saving his life. We were square. He insisted that in our line of work, it was a good bet he'd return the favor someday.

Next morning, they saw me off at the bus stop. "Be careful over there," said Hyung-Jin. "Chunju wasn't so good for you before."

Eunmi handed me a fruit basket wrapped in an oversized silk scarf. "For the trip." They were both leaving town on separate assignments, but assured me that Hyung-Jin might see me in France soon. "There's a little job Defferre is lining up for late October," Eunmi said. "Something to do with smugglers funding a terrorist cell."

Hyung-Jin had heard the same. "A pipeline from Pusan to Marseilles, with the jack going to a North Korean group. I don't have the details, but ANSP is playing ball with DST, if I hear right." ANSP (South Korea's Agency for National Security Planning), was the current alphabet soup for what would become the NIS years down the road. It had been established in 1981 under direct authority of President Chun Doowhan. Warrants were optional; recruiting guys like Hyung-Jin was standard procedure.

On the bus, I opened my fruit surprise. The scarf was a silk screen of a Picasso—my favorite artist at the time. Eunmi had included an origami swan and a note in Korean:

"My dearest Chanyoung. I am honored that you remember me as your friend and hope that you will always think of me as your older sister. I will always cherish the memories of the many nights we spent on the phone when you first went to France. Please think well of me. Your Truest Friend, Eunmi."

I smiled at how life had turned around. Maybe Sid was right. God did watch over us.

I wore a conservative blue suit and gray tie to Kon's office. He didn't keep me waiting on line with all the other well wishers. I was ushered in immediately. I didn't recognize any of Kon's men, but noted that none of the crowd I'd dealt with at the pool hall were around. Kon was free and it was time for some house cleaning.

I knelt. "Greetings to Honored Kon." I pushed toward him a large cube-shaped bundle, wrapped in plain paper and tied carefully with silk thread. It was the $10,000 Defferre fronted for the assignment. "May you enjoy good fortune and a life of sound health."

Kon's nose told him what was in the package, but according to Korean custom, he waved to his bodyguard to pick it up and place the package with the other presents. Safer than any bank. They would open it later.

Formalities concluded, Kon walked over and stood me up. Some of his men were wide-eyed at this singular honor. He waved them over. "Greet my good and true friend from Taejon. He protected my interests inside and watched over my sister while I was unable to protect her."

The light dawned on who I was. Kon's men realized I was the one who tipped Kon to the pool hall boy's move with Chong. And I was the one who had paid back the two guys who worked me over. Their greetings were sincere. Loyalty to Kon was paramount in all their minds. Tipping him to what was going down wasn't snitching—it was what was expected within Kon's family. I was an American—very bad thing—but had been loyal to Kon against a group of traitors. That fact, plus my Korean language skills, the respectful jack and Kon's complete acceptance of me were my ticket into their circle.

Defferre was right. This trip was necessary if Interpol wanted to continue using Kon's connections.

I waited the correct amount of time, chatting with Kon's men and enjoying the expensive Korean delicacies that had been ordered for Kon's return. His sister and her husband arrived later in the afternoon. He wore a dark suit and she was in a conservative dark dress, almost matronly. She averted her eyes and kept to the corner. Her husband slunk there with her, flinching every time I walked near. This was a source of great amusement to Kon's men, who knew the story. Kon loved his sister deeply, but he demanded she always behave in a way that kept his honor—and her own.

After making excuses, I slid out the door and headed to the bus depot. A trip to Pusan, a plane to France, and I was home in Sid's arms again.

Our month of heaven passed quickly. The day we were to leave for Milan, Sid and I shared breakfast on her balcony in Marseilles. We were enjoying an early-October warm spell before the real cold set in. I had walked to the local bakery for croissants and milk. Sid didn't share her countrymen's penchant for wine with every meal.

"This meal will put some pounds on us," I said, laughing at the butter dripping from our fingers. I wore slacks and a dress shirt; she was in tight jeans and a loose-fitting blue sweater. My tone was deeply felt. "Maybe we will grow fat together after all."

She dropped her croissant on the plate. "*Ce qui?*" What?

"I mean that growing fat with you at some university is all I could ever hope for."

"*Que voulez-vous dire?*"

"In English, please Sid." I smiled warmly.

"What are you saying to me, *mon cher?*"

I cupped her hand in mine, placing a small black ring box on her palm. A tear trickled from her deep amber eyes, down her cheek. "If you will have me, there could be no greater joy than sharing all the love and pain and hope of life with you."

She opened the box. Solitaire cut blue diamond, one carat, all the way from Brazil. I had it set after I got back from Korea. We slid it on her finger together. She kissed me, tears mingling with our parted lips. "I'll love you till death, *mon amour!*"

The rest of the morning was ours alone.

On October 19, Defferre assigned me to work with the Korean NIS representatives and Sid's DST team in an Interpol sponsored kiddie porn bust. The team leaders set up a command post in Marseilles and began surveillance.

A North Korean had been caught by the NIS a few months previously. Under drugs and torture, he rolled on a smuggling ring that funded a cell of North Korean terrorists operating out of Marseilles. Sid's team had stopped the terrorists' previous attempt at bombing the South Korean consulate in Paris. Now they had larger plans: a Korean Airlines passenger plane.

Terror isn't cheap. This smuggling ring, according to the skell who rolled, specialized in fetishist pornography—anything illegal for which customers would pay high dollar. Child abduction, rape, porn and selling of the victims to high bidders were part of the package.

Using this information, a DST team had watched a number of suspected North Korean terrorists throughout France. Two were tentatively identified in Marseilles. It became clear that they were not planning any terrorist activity; instead, they were aggressively raising funds with drug traffic and kiddie porn. Because this fell under the special DST office that countered organized crime, Sid's team was assigned to watch and apprehend. The North Korean's drug traffic was primarily focused around Marseilles, but they moved a huge volume of fetishist porn into South Korea.

Interpol coordinated the joint efforts between the Korean NIS in Pusan with the DST in Marseilles. Both organizations sent team members to the opposite country to observe and assist in deporting prisoners. Hyung-Jin arrived on October 20.

Hyung-Jin and I worked the afternoon shift on surveillance. The rest of the time we bunked together in the same crap dive hotel on rue Bernard-du-Bois near the La Gare St-Charles train station that I had stayed in on my first trip to Marseilles. He talked about Eunmi a lot. He really loved her.

Sid was deployed with her team. We spoke on the phone and stole moments at the command post when possible. Her teammates knew all about our engagement and ribbed us frequently. I had told Hyung-Jin, of course, all about it before Sid said yes. He insisted that we all pose for a group photo. One of the Interpol officers assigned to the surveillance obliged and snapped a shot of the DST team (with Sid) with Hyung-Jin and myself.

On October 21, our surveillance conclusively identified the two North Korean agents. There was reason to suspect the small warehouse they stayed in housed a significant amount of drugs and child pornography. That morning, a South Korean arrived with two Iraqis. DST believed they were exchanging goods and cash.

Captain Henri Wolper of the DST got the final go ahead. He didn't seem quite so pretty now that he was leading his excellent team into action. Hyung-Jin and I, along with other Interpol officers, were assigned positions surrounding the building. The DST team prepared to enter the structure. Sid found me.

"*Mon cher*, tell me again," she said, hugging me. Her heart was pumping through her Kevlar vest, hand on my chest.

"*Je t'aime*," I whispered. I love you.

She smiled and sprinted to position. Wolper gave the signal and the team stormed the warehouse. DST knows its business and within minutes the building was taken. We heard shots fired but there were no reported DST casualties. One Iraqi was dead, a North Korean wounded. The South Korean and other Iraqi were in custody. The DST team began a thorough search of the building for the second North Korean. Interpol officers entered the building to effect arrests.

Sid and another DST took positions at the entrance of the building. Others were deployed throughout the structure.

The North Korean was across the street. Sid's partner saw him first. He was casually walking along the sidewalk in front of a brick wall like nothing had happened. Cool as ice. Hyung-Jin and I ran across the street as Sid and her partner approached the North Korean from behind. Hyung-Jin drew his weapon.

"Stop!" he ordered.

The skell flinched, turning to run. He saw the DST, weapons trained, and turned again toward us. He dodged into a dead end alley. Superior position and difficult to capture. DST radioed the skell's position. The North Korean fired from the alley at Hyung-Jin. We hit the ground, returning fire. The skell was buried behind trash cans, opening fire on anything that moved. Hyung-Jin clipped his leg. I fired and missed. Missed again.

Because DST is better at this, Hyung-Jin and I stopped and let them do their jobs. Sid and her partner were running to position themselves at the mouth of the alley, other DST on the way from the warehouse. The North Korean must have realized he was getting boxed in. He ran from the alley, screaming in crazed panic.

Before the DST team could train their weapons he was within a few feet of me. I fired. Missed. Pathetic. Hyung-Jin was angled behind me and couldn't get a shot. The North Korean raised his weapon and I stared at the dark barrel of my death.

Sid fired. A hole tore open in his side, twisting his pistol enough to miss me. He kept firing as he fell. Firing and firing until we heard the dull click of empty chambers. He was prone, surrounded by DST weapons.

I turned. Sid lay on the street, dragging herself toward me.

I rushed beside her. A bullet had torn away part of her shoulder and neck. Blood was gushing out of her Kevlar, just above her heart. Teflon-coated bullets. I lay next to her, trying to cover the impossibly large wounds, holding her as she twitched and gasped. Vaguely I heard Wolper call for medical assistance. No one approached us. Then her breath slowed.

"*Je t'aime, mon amour,*" she whispered. She felt cold beside me, then flushed hot. Her eyes lingered in mine and I moaned her name. She coughed blood, heart punctured, perfect neck ripped apart. Her life was pouring through my hands onto the street. *It's hot,* I thought. *Her blood is hot.*

"*Je t'aime,* my darling," I said, throat tight.

She lifted her hand weakly. I pressed it to my cheek. Her voice was low, only a hint of sound, "*Je t'aime, je t'aime, je t'aime.*" She fell silent, mouthing the words until her lips stopped moving.

After that, it's all a blur of agony. The slow cleanup; the ambulance taking Sid to the morgue; the debriefing. Hyung-Jin told me that a DST fired a round into the North Korean's head. I don't think anyone even bothered to make up an excuse for it. I returned to our villa alone.

Hyung-Jin flew to Pusan. He and Eunmi tried to call me, they said, but I did not answer the phone.

Sid's father came down and cursed the day I came into her life. "You could have quit—she said she wanted to! You waited and now what?" Tears poured down his cheeks, standing in Sid's villa. He hit me again and again. "She died to save you! You! You!" He hit me until he could hit no more. Then he left.

I used every penny I owned to pay for Sid's funeral, a plot and statue of an angel looking over her in a graveyard just outside Marseilles. I bought orchids to strew over her casket. She loved orchids.

At the funeral a soprano sang Sid's favorite aria, *Vissi d'Arte* from Giacomo Puccini's opera, *Tosca*. In the song, Tosca wonders why God has rewarded her tender heart and absolute devotion with such misery.

Vissi d'arte, vissi d'amore,	I lived for art, I lived for love
non feci mai male ad	...Never did I harm a living
anima viva!	creature!
Con man furtive	Whatever misfortunes I
	encountered

quante miserie conobbi,	I sought with secret hand to
aiutai...	succor…
Sempre con fe sincera,	Ever pure in faith,
la mia preghiera	my prayers rose
ai santi tabernacoli sali.	in the holy chapels.
Sempre con fe sincera	Ever pure in faith,
diedi fiori agli altar.	I brought flowers to the altars
Nell'ora del doloer perche	in this hour of pain. Why,
perche, Signore, perche,	why, oh Lord, why,
me ne rimuneri cosi?	…dost Thou repay me thus?
Diedi gioirlli	Jewels I brought
della Madonna al manto,	for the Madonna's mantle,
e diedi il canto agli astri,	and songs for the stars in heaven
al ciel, che ne ridean piu belli.	that they shone forth with
	greater radiance.
Nell'ora del dolre Perche,	In this hour of distress. Why
perche, Signore,	why, oh Lord,
perche me ne rimuneri cosi?	why dost Thou repay me thus?

Sid's father screamed at me before the funeral and barely spoke to me after. But while the soprano performed, we wept together and he grasped my hand.

The day after the funeral I went home and torched the villa. Everything went up. I walked away.

Eight months with Sid was too short. A lifetime would have been too short. I slept with the silk ivory scarf she bought in Lyon wrapped round my hand. Sometimes I woke in the morning and—for a few blissful seconds—didn't remember she was gone. I lived for those moments.

One night, unable to sleep, I put my feelings down on paper.

L'Envoi
It's not the blood, so, or
how she limped heavy in my arms;
cold then hot then empty
("*Je t'aime, je t'aime*," was all she said.)
or the casket-smooth wood
over eyes and curved innocent;
that was benediction:
"*Vissi d'arte, vissi d'amore*." She did, you know.

Before that, before then,
in waking hours and breath sour sweet;
hair fell across my chest:
"*Let's grow fat together*," was all she said.
It's not that I regret
her sacrifice, holes in dear flesh;
only life without her:
"*I'll love you till death*." She did, you know.

eleven

HOW TO "CLEAN" PRACTICALLY EVERYTHING

After Sid's death, Defferre moved quickly. He invited me to a café on the *Cours Julien* in Marseilles for brunch.

When I arrived, Defferre was sitting with two men I had never seen before. Defferre embraced me and as I sat down, the two men rose and Defferre introduced them. "Smith" was mid-fifties, with a crew cut and a burly demeanor that defined stout, like those pictures of people who look like they're bulldogs. "Jones" was perhaps ten years younger, taller than me, with less severe close-cropped hair. He wore sunglasses.

"Good morning, Damien," said Defferre. I cringed.

"Not that name, Jacques. Never that name again."

He nodded at the other two, as though my reaction confirmed something. "Now it is time to go with these men," he said. Then he stood up and walked away.

"Go where?" I asked his back. He shrugged as the men approached me.

"Let's have no trouble," said Smith in a clipped Scottish brogue, grabbing my right arm above the elbow. I resisted and he rammed a thumb into my kidney. Pain blinded me. I almost fell.

Jones spoke calmly in my ear with a thick French accent: "The *commissaire* has a special job for you. Our job is to get you to that job." The pain was down to a dull throb as I translated that peculiar sentence.

"What's the job?" I asked as they led me to a nearby car. Smith planted me firmly beside him in the back; Jones got into the driver's seat and pulled into traffic.

"It's in Lyon," Jones said. "You'll love it."

That was the last word either spoke for the rest of the drive.

We didn't go to Defferre's office in Lyon. Instead, Jones took the Grenoble highway to La Verpillere, which was about twenty minutes from the center of Lyon. We drove to the quiet industrial district on *Chemin de Malatrait* and stopped at a large tan warehouse with offices alongside. This was the home of Archangel.

Smith showed me to a small studio apartment on the third floor of the warehouse. "Just relax a bit. Commissaire Defferre will be along shortly."

Commissaire? Since when was Defferre a commissioner? Shortly turned into an hour, then two. When I wandered into the hall, three of four hard looks from other crewcut leather jackets convinced me that I was going to play the waiting game. Heading back to the apartment, I looked around. The room had a television, a small kitchenette, a huge bathroom, full-size bed and a small round table with chairs. By this time I knew I wasn't leaving until Defferre gave the sign.

Defferre came in around 9 P.M. He wore black boots, durable dark work pants and a heavily starched, tan long-sleeved shirt. He sat down at the small table and motioned for me to join him.

"What's this all about, Defferre?" I spat out.

"*Cher ami*, I know about the villa." He sat back, one hand on the table and the other oddly hovering over his hip. I noticed he had a pistol on his belt, stuck behind his back. His hand casually covered the weapon. "Let's talk about it, Race."

I shrugged and glowered. Defferre reached across the table to slap me. I blocked and twisted his wrist just as his free hand brought the pistol across my temple. I fell from the chair, blood already in my eyes.

"See how upset you are?" he demanded, firearm still drawn. "When has anyone so easily pistol-whipped you?" Defferre overestimated my inabilities. I'd taken plenty of beatings.

I got back in the chair, using a napkin to press against the wound. My head throbbed and the blood was already slowing. Defferre ignored it. "Race, there is no time for the brooding young man today. I will not beg for your attention and there is no clichéd Hollywood actress eager to calm the troubled hero while you" he waved off into an imagined horizon "stare off into the distance of your troubles."

I got his point and, searching for something to say, asked nonsensically, "You're now a *commissaire*?"

Defferre seemed pleased. "Exactly. My role here, in this building. A part of Interpol that you weren't told about."

"Why not?"

"And why would we tell you? Until we are sure of your loyalty?"

"I thought I had already proved it," I said quietly.

He laughed, deep and long. "It takes more than superficial skirmishes. You must persevere." He stood and walked to the kitchenette, wetting a towel, his back to me. A gamble, but he knew I was listening. "If you are unwilling or unable to meet the test, you can leave." He waited a few moments and when I didn't, he handed me the towel.

"So a mysterious trip to a warehouse? Sort of cloak and dagger, if you ask me, Jacques. Don't you know real life isn't like the movies?"

He fell back on the bed, bouncing slightly as he looked at me with a crooked smile, head tilted. "*Incroyable*! Listen to yourself! You lived in Korea, Brussels and Marseilles; a beautiful Asian girl adores you and our dear Sidelle was to be your bride; you have a job with the Belgian Gendarmerie that has a second, deeper more important mission beneath it. Today I will tell you about a third, even deeper level. Now you tell me, Mr. Hollywood," he leaned up on one elbow. "What exactly is NOT like the movies?"

He had me there and we both chuckled. It was the first time I had laughed since Sid died.

"Okay, what's the third deeper level, then?"

Defferre repeated that I could leave. "Go now, if you choose. I will see that you have a ticket home."

"I have no home, Jacques. My parents and family seem so distant; the only home I had was with Sid and she is gone. Pretty pathetic, huh?"

"No, you are not pathetic and you have the opportunity to be noble."

Defferre joined me again at the small table and laid the plan out. Archangel had a type of international cooperation that the United Nations never imagined. In a cold, desperate voice he described the nature of global child pornography rings: kidnapping young children, taping and photographing their rape and torture. If the child lived, selling him or her to another collector. And selling the porn across the world.

"They are above the law, Major Bannon." Defferre always used the rank he created for me when getting to the point. "You remember James in Marseilles? He is in Romania now. The laws do not touch him there. He can travel to Thailand, Pakistan, even Japan if he greases the *yakuza*."

Skells like James snatched kids and headed to their favorite basements or out of the country. They had a network of other collectors, some highly placed, that facilitated their travel plans in exchange for time with the child or photos. There were as many reasons for these heinous acts as there were people. "Some act out of greed or fanaticism," said Defferre. "Like the terrorists who sell kiddie porn to fund their cells."

"Like the guy that killed Sid."

He nodded. "They never stop, because they enjoy it. That is the common denominator, Race. They enjoy abusing the children. The man who shot Sidelle was a small part of a much larger *evil*." He enunciated his last word carefully. His eyes blazed. "They are only ever caught for other crimes, like drugs or terrorism. Never for the worst crime of all."

"But a lot of countries have laws against kiddie porn. These skells can be punished."

Defferre shook his head, leaning on the table so it almost toppled. "Imagine you are in Brussels, *mon ami*. You know your neighbor is this type of man. You know all about him. But he has no pictures or tapes at his home; he has no children. Even if you and other gendarmes watch him for days and weeks, there will never be evidence. The photos are in a country where it is not illegal. The children are taken while on holiday trips." Defferre reminded me how James had snatched a kid from a London orphanage, falsified papers and got the little boy to say James was his father. "It is a problem that crosses all borders."

"Archangel is the answer. With cooperative law officers and organizations—and just as often without—Archangel deals grim justice to those who can not be convicted."

"Like Skip in Marseilles," I ventured, knowing the answer.

Defferre barely shrugged, eyes locked on mine. Not staring between the eyes like prison. Directly *in* my eyes. "Sid died stopping these beasts. You can make them pay." He spoke slowly. "I want you to be a cleaner."

Archangel had "a certain number" of cleaners, Defferre told me. There were many other operatives or officers or agents. Defferre was never really clear on what they were called. "They work for Archangel, like you," was all the explanation I got. They also all worked for Interpol. Eunmi wasn't part of Archangel, but helped often enough as an Interpol officer to be considered a reliable part of assignments in South Korea.

Silence filled the air. Finally, I broke it.

"Will do," I said. Quiet and sure.

Defferre smiled. "You will start training in the morning."

All that night I lay awake in the small dark room, two words twisting inside me and I did not know which ruled: *Justice. Revenge.*

Before eight the next morning I went to the offices beside the warehouse. This held the organizational headquarters of Archangel. The warehouse itself was primarily for training. There were two other students. One, a small, grotesquely bitter Irish woman of about thirty, had dark red hair and an overwhelming hatred of child pornographers. Her four-year-old son had been kidnapped while she was on duty as a police dispatcher in Dublin. Three weeks later he was found, strangled to death; his body showed signs of rape and mutilation so vile she could not repeat them. Even worse, about a month after finding the body, some pictures and a tape showed up in a skell's house during a drug bust. The images recorded the little boy's agony all the way to his death. The kidnapper and mutilators were never caught.

Her name was Margaret. She came up to my chest and was very solid, but not overweight. More like a wrecking ball. She heard of Archangel through the grapevine in her department and contacted Defferre herself. She had arrived three days before me.

The other student was an American from Torrence, California. He was a little older than me and said his name was William. He had been recruited by Defferre after washing out of the SEAL program. Seems he handled the training okay but didn't respond well to authority. He was tall with muscles like an Oregon logger, close-cropped hair and a continual sneer. He loved milkshakes. When his time was up with the United States

Navy, he flew to France. He'd been training for about a month with Archangel.

Our instructors rotated every week or so. The most frequent face was Smith, the Scottish-brogue bulldog himself who had rammed a thumb in my kidneys. I finally learned his real name. "Call me Mr. Bennet," he said the first day. He occasionally wore glasses when we watched films. Otherwise, he squinted. He was fluent in French and had a perfect American accent—when he used it you'd swear he grew up in New Jersey.

"The idea is to teach you the essence of cleaning," he said. "You will learn the nuts and bolts of behavior and intelligence gathering and how it's used to identify and eliminate a target."

This was the beginning of a whole new language for killing that was a denial of the act itself. We did not "kill"—we cleaned or eliminated. The people we were to kill were not humans—they were targets or skells. Even the weapons we used had nicknames, all the way down to bullets being called rounds.

We received intense and repeated affirmation that we were morally superior to our targets, child abductors and pornographers. The most frequent term applied to the child rapists and murderers was "*evil*." The name of our organization itself, Archangel, imbued us with a vision of a vengeful vigilante wielding the sword of justice.

The old "cultural differences" chestnut was also trotted out to lesser effect. We were told that some cultures do not have the same compass for good and evil as Christians—and therefore legalize child prostitution and porn. William bought it completely. Margaret and I rolled our eyes at such blatant propaganda. Like a Pakistani father doesn't love his daughter as much as an

Englishman. Ri-i-ight. She and I wanted to get back to the nuts and bolts.

Killing was so abhorrent on a gut level that these exercises in denial and rationalization seemed natural. By giving different names to the act itself and cloaking ourselves under the guise of moral authority, we were able to deny the true nature of our actions—to ourselves and to others. Even so, it was very difficult to overcome the moral inhibitions of a lifetime.

Killing in self-defense may have seemed an acceptable act, but aggressive pursuit and murder of other human beings was a completely different matter. Our natural resistance to killing was mixed in with an overwhelming need for vengeance, on the part of Margaret and myself. Our trainers subjected us to a continuous list of justifications: instinct to protect children, coercive obligation to our leaders and peers and, when on an actual assignment, self-preservation. Our training included numerous scenarios in which we distanced ourselves emotionally and morally from our targets in order to treat them as alien or evil beings that needed to be eliminated.

All of this was designed to expunge blood guilt.

We were lectured on behavior, security and reliability in action and information. We were trained in the basics of international purchasing and business transactions to match our future covers, which would frequently include posing as professionals. Shipping, inventory, TQM, JIT, Kaizen, all the then-popular concepts and lingo of global business were included in detailed essay and oral exams.

We practiced our covers, learning how to use identification from various countries, different passports, entire legends built around each new identity. We drilled on being detained by police, enduring interrogation, then being released and acquiring a new legend. As soon as the new identity was in place, we were arrested again—usually within hours—and had to support the new cover as plausibly as the old.

The training also included lessons on how to kill leaving no clues. William had some training in this with the SEALS before he washed out. Margaret may have been a dispatcher, but she knew how to handle herself. Bennet asked if I had any experience in this area. Margaret and William both looked at me, waiting. Not wanting to reveal too much of my past and experience in this area, I shrugged and said, "I knew a guy in high school that ws a pretty good boxer. Does that count?"

We learned how to develop "assets" and "agents." The definition of the terms changed depending on which instructor was talking. Even worse, the terms would change across the globe and even between organizations within the same country. An asset was any human resource, technical or otherwise, available for an assignment or operation. An agent was a person controlled by an intelligence service to obtain information—a nice term for a snitch.

Bennet referred to any legitimate law officers as "angels"— a term in intelligence communities that usually denoted a member of an opposing service. I wasn't sure that I liked the fact that Archangel saw legitimate police officers as the opposition. "About the time they catch you," Bennet said, "you'll know what I'm talking about."

It was clear that, just as the child pornographers had their own nefarious network, Archangel used its association with Interpol to develop a system of contacts across the globe that was not condoned by standard procedure. This was the "third, deeper level" to which Defferre had referred.

Inside me revulsion and commitment churned, yet I couldn't seem to leave. I began to wonder what the hell I was doing there.

We practiced killing scenarios. We were each given a practice "target" on whom to gather information and prepare an elimination plan.

I took three days to gather the information on my target in Lyon. The only consistent trait he displayed was his likelihood to stop at a favorite café near his apartment sometime between 8:00 and 8:30 each morning. Other than that, his schedule was erratic. I decided to work the café.

On day four, he stopped to have a croissant at about the right time. I tagged him and followed him to the bus stop. He stood with his back to me, reading a paper. No one else was around. I rolled up and mimed sliding a stiletto through his lower back and into the kidney. The stiletto is a sharp dagger with a narrow blade that widened near the end, then narrowed again at the point. Although I had grown accustomed to the traditional US military KA-BAR, an exceptional utility and fighting blade that held it's edge and was hard to break, it wasn't the right tool for this job. The stiletto was ideal for a quick silent kill, because it could be slid in, twisted around for maximum damage and then pulled out without much external bleeding. The flesh closed back over the wound. The kidney strike was so painful that it paralyzed him, killing silently and quickly. The instructor acted out his death and swore he never saw me coming.

Margaret made her cleaning look like an accident. Her target showed a taste for hookers; so she conned her way into his car by promising a three-way with her nine-year-old daughter. Then she mimed knocking him out with an ether mask and drove near the Rhone. She poured vodka down his throat with a paper funnel, let the alcohol soak into his bloodstream, then put him behind the wheel. She poured the vodka over the seats and planted a lighter and cigarette butts. After she torched it, she'd roll it into the river. Her target/instructor said there were only two flaws. First, the target didn't smoke. Second, our skells probably wouldn't want Margaret watching while they entertained the little girl; so she'd have to devise another way to get in the car. Hard on the vanity, but Margaret didn't seem to care.

William tagged his target at the same club every night. Using blanks, he walked up to the target outside the club, pumped one in the head and two in the body and drove away in a car he'd boosted for the occasion. Full marks for William.

William had used the Parabellum, a type of German Luger. Bennet vouched for a Beretta high-powered .22 caliber. "It goes in but doesn't always come out. Nice and tidy and no need for a silencer," he said.

Bennet went over edged weapons. "Race was the only one who used a knife. Nothing wrong with your other approaches. Always use the tools at hand—the right tool for the right job." This was one of Bennet's favorite expressions. "Since bladed weapons are perfect for our work, we're going to learn them."

As we trained, I noticed that everyone—including the instructor—preferred a slashing or hacking blow to the piercing strike. This was an obstacle Kim Changsik had discussed in

Hapkido class during weapons' training. "To pierce is to penetrate," Kim had said in Korean as we drilled on lunging techniques. "But slashing seems less repulsive because we resist piercing our enemy's essence. To reach your hand and pierce another human being's life— his vital essence or *qi* force—is repugnant." Kim explained that the ancient Korean *Hwarang*, or flower warriors, were the fiercest knights of the Silla Dynasty (57 B.C. - 935 A.D.). They forced their warriors to pierce with the blade. Death to the soldier who slashed. "Do not cut; thrust," Kim said. "A stab is usually fatal."

Having the benefit of Kim's training, I was prepared in ways the others were not for blade drills. Bennet and William preferred the commando-style kill—an effective and horrible method. We practiced sliding up behind our target, holding a hand over his mouth and thrusting the blade into the side of his neck, ripping outward. This method, when performed correctly, was almost as silent as the kidney strike and far less repulsive to the students. However, holding one's hand over a victim's mouth can be tricky and easily lead to bites and screams. We practiced on each other, acting out as best possible the bucking and shuddering of the body, even using warm liquid in balloons to simulate blood. We faked the final breath hissing out of the wound.

The purpose of the repeated exercises was to prepare us to act instinctively, without thought, when faced with real danger.

Margaret had the most to learn in hand-to-hand combat. It quickly became clear that William knew a lot of moves but lacked the stone cold delivery it took to do the job. We covered crushing throat blows. I shared a Hapkido move that reportedly had its roots with Korea's *Amhaeng osa*, Horsemen, the dreaded secret service of the Yi Dynasty between 1392 and 1910. The move countered an opponent's right-hand strike by stepping into the punch with the right foot, blocking the inner arm with both forearms, then delivering a smashing blow with the side of the right hand to the opponent's throat.

"You didn't learn that from your boxer friend in high school," Bennet said one day. Defferre was looking on, as he often did when his duties permitted. "Where'd you pick up that trick?"

"Here and there," I shrugged.

"Maybe there," Bennet said, practicing the move as he smiled at Defferre. "But definitely not here."

We also drilled punching a thumb or finger in the eye of our opponent. After puncturing, the thumb was stirred in the eye cavity, then cocked to the side and yanked out, bringing the eye and whatever else with it. We practiced with lemons strapped to our targets' eyes. We also practiced on the lemon eye patches with short, dull blades.

It was so horrendous to Margaret that she had to stop and retry it later. William puked. I took their turns, thinking maybe I had been too easy on that wannabe-rapist in Taejon Prison.

twelve

DRACULA BY DAYLIGHT

It would have been our first Christmas together. I had nothing left. She was gone. The pictures were all burned. I had only memories. Cold comfort before dawn. Lying in bed, I tried prayer, begging God to explain this miserable world to me: the tortured children and horrific images we had seen as part of our training; Sid's death; the need for an organization to conquer evil that laws should but could not touch. I needed a sign. If I believed in the existence of Evil—as Archangel's propaganda so fervently insisted—then perhaps there was Good? I spent a few hours pleading.

"I'm lousy with subtle hints and hidden meanings. Like some guy shows up and says something all wise or whatever. Or I get my answer by reading some mystical Bible passage. I don't need secret codes today. I am weighted down by darkness and despair. I know my life so far has been no use to You and I'm not sure that what I'm doing here isn't worse. I read the sixth commandment and it is pretty clear: *Thou shalt not kill.* It doesn't say,

Thou shalt not kill except for child molesting scum." I was wrestling between a last hope for redemption or the only Christmas gift I knew to give Sid: Revenge. "I need a straight answer that even someone as broken as I am can understand. How about it? You say and I'll do."

My prayers were never eloquent. And that day I seemed to get no answer. The children in the tapes, calling on Jesus to save them as they were tortured, weren't answered in any way I could see. Unless Defferre and Archangel *were* God's answer—but how could a good, gentle, just God use such horrific means to achieve justice? Or was it only my own lust for vengeance? Around and around I went.

Mid-morning Defferre strutted in the room, double-breasted blue suit, hair in perfect order, two presents and a small, decorated tree in hand. "Today I spend Christmas with you, *cher ami!*" He set the tree on the table and arranged the two presents under it.

"I've got nothing for you, Jacques."

"Just as well, for my gifts are not special!"

Defferre didn't have any family with whom he wanted to share a holiday. Sid had told me the rumors. My mood wasn't too festive; so I brought it up. "You don't want to see your family this Christmas?"

He shook his head.

"Cause of your uncle, huh?" Defferre recoiled like he'd been slapped. I continued. "Sid told me there was a rumor about you and an uncle. That's why you're so harsh about the kiddie porn. She said maybe your folks knew about it."

Defferre unbuttoned his jacket and sat with a sigh, pushing

the small tree to the round table's edge. "The rumors, they are just rumors, *non*?" He choked for a moment, struggling with rage and pain. Pain won. "Christmas day there are no walls between friends. You are my only friend, Race. So I speak. Yes, my uncle abused me. I believe my parents knew and did nothing. It is all as our beloved Sidelle spoke."

I sat with him at the table. "I'm crazy after what happened to Sid and pissed at you for dragging me into Archangel. Mostly I'm mad, because I am beginning to feel like an avenger and I like it. So I struck at you. Sorry."

Defferre smiled wanly, the only completely genuine smile I'd ever seen on his lips. "*Mon oncle* is dead. My father is very old and misses my mother. She passed to heaven a few years ago. He will not speak to me. He blames me for the death of his brother."

"Even though he knew what his brother did to you?"

"Even so."

Archangel was on our minds; so I had to ask, "Did your uncle take any pictures?"

"I search for them every day," he said. "I was only five when he started. He died when I was fourteen."

We sat a moment in silence, both aware how deeply we shared scars.

"Do you believe in God, Jacques?"

"With all my heart."

"So did Sid." I choked back a sob and Defferre stood, shaking off the melancholy.

"Enough! Today we are together and alive. Let's honor that fact by going out and dining well. But first," he presented his gift, a long tube. I opened it.

A poster of Shang Chi, Master of Kungfu. I laughed and taped it on the wall beside my bed. "My God, Jacques! It's so cool!" Shang Chi was in an exaggerated—and poorly balanced—kung fu pose that was miles away from any type of reality I'd endured. But I loved it all the same.

"I have read some of these books, Race," Defferre said. "Shang Chi is a most thoughtful man." Every moment was a surprise with Jacques.

The second present was a small handkerchief with a *Hello Kitty* motif embroidered in the corner. The tag was Japanese. I arched an eyebrow.

"It will be something between only you and myself," Defferre explained. "There are many internal politics within Interpol and many more dangerous enemies in this world. Evil of many kinds like child pornographers are everywhere, in every level of society. When I give you some small token with Hello Kitty on it, like that day in Paris, then you will know the assignment is real." I held the handkerchief carefully in my hands, feeling the light cotton grow heavier with each word. Defferre pulled on his jacket. "James is in Romania. Before the new year, he must be cleaned."

I pocketed the kitty. "Will do."

"And you'll feel justified and thus good," he said quietly.

Romania under Nicolae Ceausescu was a nightmare for children. Although genuinely popular when he took power, as his reign went on his economic gymnastics and obsession with foreign affairs had created dismal poverty for his people. Ceausescu believed that the key to industrial growth was a larger workforce; so in 1966 he banned abortions.

Women bore the double burden of work and childcare. The pseudo-women's movement was headed by Elena Ceausescu and was nothing more than a cover for greater oppression. Soon the Ceausescus created the "Baby Police" and compulsory gynecological exams to ensure that women were performing their procreative patriotic duties. Contraception was illegal for any woman under forty-five with less than five children. Unmarried people and married couples without children were taxed exhaustively.

So many children and such dismal economic development led to overpopulation and rampant disease. To those who traffic in small children, Romania was a field ripe for plucking. They offered money and food to buy a child for a night, a week or even to take out of the country. Pimps peddled children as young as two years old on the streets of Bucharest.

All of this was overseen by Ceausescu's powerful secret police, the *Departamentul Securitatii Statului* (Department of State Security), known as the *Securitate*. The Securitate guarded internal security and the Ceausescu regime by suppressing all challengers. Their tools included illegal imprisonment, horrific torture methods and multiple rapes of prisoners and celebrities, including their children, as well as several well-known female Romanian Gymnastic team members. Murder and assassination were common currency. Interpol and Archangel had no friends in the Securitate.

Romania was perfect for a guy like James. Greasing local officials was easy in the corrupt environment. Ceausescu's maverick foreign policy, independent of the Eastern bloc party line, allowed foreign visitors and even some industrial "advisors"— translated as investors who would enjoy monumental kickbacks from the regime. James was posing as an import/export broker in Bucharest, but he actually traded in children and pictures of children.

My cover was simple. I was the front man for a global company with offices in New York, Paris and Tokyo. They had plenty of money to toss around and didn't care too much about working conditions. I aggressively worked to fit the stereotype of the young well-dressed hustlers. That was me: Mr. Fast Track-MBA-Yuppie-Punk. My suit was so expensive I was inwardly embarrassed to wear it amid all the squalor. It came with a nice tie, though.

I greased customs with *Playboy* magazines and nylons. I greased the Securitate with cash. I had appointments with three factory heads before the plane landed. If the young punk liked what he saw, his company would send the bigger dogs and the US dollars would follow. My cover was no problem as long as the cash flowed and Archangel had plenty.

I stayed at the Athenee Palace Hotel on the northern corner of *Piata Revolutiei*. Although it was Romania's most famous hotel, with a long history of intrigue and espionage, it was actually a crappy dive. It was cold outside—about 20 degrees F—and the hotel didn't bother adding much heat for its patrons. Romania's most bitter cold usually came later, January through March, with snowdrifts that held the city hostage. The snow was light this time round.

My television was black and white. On the second night, to my surprise when I clicked on the television, *Columbo* was on. I later learned the show was hugely popular in Romania. But as I sat and watched, I wondered if my being there at that moment watching an American television show was a sign.

This unexpected taste of normalcy brought home the fact that I was completely isolated. I couldn't call or contact Defferre with the Securitate watching every move. And a wrong move in Romania was suicide. Mr. Tough Guy spent the night cowering in his hotel room.

Next day I headed to a hiking shop to pick up some goodies for a short day trip in the country. Walking down the street was like walking in a prison without guards. A Securitate guy had picked me up as I left the hotel; I wasn't supposed to know he was there. I bought some good boots, a hat and a small pack. I boosted a utility knife so the owner couldn't tell my Securitate tag about it when he checked what I'd purchased.

Bucharest was an architectural nightmare of Empire-style, concrete and poorly disguised ghettos. Its lush greenery was hidden by the blistering cold winter winds. Fresh produce was the highest-priced legitimate item on the street corners, since it was not as readily available as it was in more rural Romanian towns. Bucharest was filled with Romanians, Gypsies, Turks, Arabs, Africans and Pakistanis—with the occasional yuppie American.

Every hustler and punk wanted to try his luck at copping my wallet or offering up some overpriced crap. I was offered women and children on every corner. My cover didn't include slapping punks around, so I endured most of the entreaties.

A Pakistani in his early forties tried the wallet lift at a crowded intersection. He was smooth. But his nimble fingers didn't find the wallet in my breast suit pocket—I wasn't even carrying one. I grabbed his wrist, twisting down and to the right, so his palm was facing the sky. I continued the thrust until his wrist gave. He cried out softly, gritting his teeth and accused me of attacking him. Other people at the intersection moved away. Another Pakistani rushed up, probably an accomplice. It might have turned nasty, but petty skell #2 had caught my Securitate tag out of the corner of his eye. They disappeared.

We knew James's office address. My excuse to the Securitate for looking it up was the same yuppie cover—with a kiddie twist. James was too much of a whore to have one specialty. He liked his work—needed it, actually—but I couldn't ask my hotel concierge for one particular fetish and expect James to pop up as the only supplier. He offered too large a variety of child prostitutes and porn; an equal opportunity scumbag.

I had to watch James without being seen. He would remember my face from Marseilles. And I would remember his. The job wasn't to make friends; it was to track him down and eliminate the monster of so many children's nightmares. That little poetic flourish was Defferre's contribution.

I tagged James two days before New Year's Eve. His office was on *Magheru*, a perfect location for his import/export business. He locked up early and headed to the *Gara de Nord* train station, a busy, squalid hive with queues for everything. He bought a ticket to Transylvania. Me, too. For the trip, I dumped the yuppie suit and switched to my boots and hiking hat with matching pack. I adopted a whole new demeanor. Mr. Tourist. James didn't tag me, but Securitate wasn't fooled.

James took a bus the next morning to tour Bran Castle, the infamous but misnamed Castle Dracula. Not the real Castle Dracula, which was a dilapidated shamble restricted from the public. This castle professed to be an occasional home of the infamous

Vlad Tsepes, described as the impaler and recognized as the historic Dracula. Ceausescu had tried to paint Vlad as a national hero. Fifteenth-century German pamphleteers had tried to settle old scores by depicting him as a sadistic dictator. He was neither. A ferocious warlord who soundly defeated 70,000 invading Turks with an army of 10,000, his methods were vicious and sometimes brilliant. His torture of captives was grotesque. To his own people, he provided security and—based on church and personal records—was admired for his punishment of the invaders. Like any leader in the history of the world, he was both hated and admired by his people—depending on whom you asked.

Watching James cast furtive glances at children taking the tour, I knew Bram Stoker's fictional vampire was alive and well in the here and now. But garlic and crosses didn't stop this monster. Dracula by daylight.

As I followed him, James' reason for taking the tour became obvious. A Romanian in his middle years approached him and they chatted in English, like two old friends. They left the castle. My Securitate tag was in the small gift shop, industriously plowing through the same brochure for a hundredth time. The tour wasn't due to finish for another hour or so. He didn't look up as I slid out the exit following James and his pal.

They walked to a particularly nasty network of alleys near the bus station. Following them was tricky. English and Canadian tourists filled the castle, but in the alleys James and I were the only two foreigners around. Just as I was about to turn off and wait at the train station, James and company turned into a dingy deserted alley.

An old woman wrapped in dark scarves and heavy coat walked by, pretending not to notice me. In Ceausescu's Romania, it was better not to get involved. I peered around the corner.

James was having a heated discussion with his companion. A decision was reached and James laid out some jack. The Romanian opened a side door and ushered out a small girl—no more than three years old, barely walking on her own. James slid his fingers between her legs. The Romanian laughed. James unzipped his fly.

I slipped down the alley. The Romanian was closest to me. He caught the butt of my utility knife in the throat and collapsed. James recognized me and stood like a deer caught in headlights, his organ dangling in the open. The girl ran behind a trashcan and cowered. My knife slid easily up under James' rib cage, twisted and punctured the heart. I turned to the Romanian. The throat blow had killed him.

"Hello, kitty-kitty."

I wheeled toward the voice. It was the old woman. She stood at the mouth of the alley, stripped of her scarves and heavy coat. She was in her mid-thirties with dark hair and brooding, angry eyes. She leveled a pistol at me. Securitate. Damn.

"Back up," she said. Her English was perfect British upper class. She looked at the bodies, then at the little girl. Her eyes softened. "Dump the knife."

I wiped it clean. "Did you say, 'Hello Kitty?'"

She stepped over the Romanian. "I have a child. We are not all monsters here." She was Securitate, an intelligence officer with an organization that did not usually cooperate with Interpol. She was an *angel*—but not in opposition. Archangel's reach was long. She lifted the little girl and carried her to the mouth of the alley.

"My colleague doesn't know what you did here, Mr. *Businessman*," she said, emphasizing my cover to show that she knew the truth. She was assigned to follow me if I left the castle. The guy reading the brochures let me think I lost him. Mr. Amateur. Sometimes I wasn't as smart as I thought I was. "I will finish this mess. You must hurry to the castle. My report will show that you took lunch. Go now." She shoved me, then added in the same efficient tone, "And thank you."

I hit the castle, finished the tour and headed back to Bucharest. My mental state ranged from an eerie dead calm to whirlwinds of adrenaline-driven anger and worry. All without remorse.

On the train back, I thought about how Archangel had prepared me for my mission. They had instilled a powerful sense of accountability to Interpol, motivating me by showing the horror-filled deeds of those criminals above the law. They did this so I would do the unthinkable—kill or be killed. They provided me with a sense of anonymity within a group that was depicted as larger and better than myself—making the cause the killer, not me. Before Interpol, I had learned how to momentarily withdraw my emotions. Then it had been for self-preservation, but now the same cold distance worked as a cleanser.

The arguments of moral and social distance from skells like James seemed plausible on the train. To me, he was evil and I was an avenger. Archangel's training had done its job.

Back at my hotel room, I had time to think.

I knew that revenge killing in a burst of rage was common throughout history. The recent loss of a loved one could stun or paralyze some people and in others cause that well-known response stage of grief: unrequited anger. Archangel had helped me nurture this anger, even inflame it, but there was no effort to work through it. I didn't want to anyway.

I hadn't been concerned about how I would perform when it came time to clean. My actions had been completely reflexive, based on years of training and a few curve balls from life. My sense of remorse at killing another human being was real and intense. But I'd gotten the hang of denial.

Some cleaners felt exhilaration in killing. I wasn't sorry that James and his friend were dead, but I wasn't thrilled at what had happened, either. It scared me, as potential death should scare anyone. I closed my eyes and remembered the Securitate woman holding the little girl. To anyone with children, what I did may have seemed necessary and right. Had I allowed myself to buy into all of Archangel's rationalizations and propaganda? One over-riding emotion swept over me. Grim satisfaction.

Next day I took the train out of Romania. The Pakistani pickpocket was at the station, but my Securitate bodyguard was all the motivation he needed to head in the other direction. By evening I was in my room at Archangel.

Defferre called and asked me to his office. I stumbled over to the offices attached to the warehouse, suddenly tired beyond reason. Defferre sat behind a steel desk, so unlike the lacquered wood in his Interpol office. This room was much larger, but just as crammed with books. His bulletin board held pictures of skells and missing kids alongside a world map dotted with multi-colored pins. A red pin was stuck in Romania. There was no Bogey picture, though. I began to wonder just how many of Defferre's eccentricities were real.

"You didn't mention there was a friend in Romania," I said casually, without accusation. Just a fact.

"How could we know what she would do?" He sniffed, waving his hand dismissively. "Communists!" Defferre told me that they had sent a message to "a few people we know in the Securitate" that I was on an assignment. "The government in Romania is so vicious, we never know if our friends can help us. Or even if they will be alive the next time we try to reach them."

Having just made it out of Romania alive, I knew exactly what he meant. But why couldn't the Securitate officer have arrested James? Or cleaned him herself?

"She has her own job and security to worry about. There are powerful people in the regime who make a lot of money from the child trade. She would be no good to her son if she were dead. Or her new daughter."

Orphanages in Romania were living hells. The Securitate woman had taken the three-year-old girl into her home as her own. I knew nothing of her husband or her life, but at that moment I realized my job wasn't about Archangel. It was about a little girl in Romania—and helpless children all over the world.

Exhaustion had caught up with me and my head swam. Defferre saw this and walked around his desk to help me stand. "*You* are the cleaner, Race. She has her job and you have yours." He put his arm round my shoulder, "But we all have the same mission."

thirteen

BUG HUNT

B yron Hotel, Bayswater, London. Our target, Jergens, kidnapped children and did dark, sweaty things to them. He sold the videotapes of what he filmed before, during and after.

Jergens was the head of a particularly disgusting circle of sleaze that Archangel had tagged months before. But no one could touch him. He kept himself just remote enough and his partners were too scared of him to talk. Until Margaret caught Narit Chaiyasut in Thailand.

"When Dublin police found the pictures of Margaret's son after the drug bust, they were poor copies," Defferre said. "The addict had picked the pictures up on a child sex tour in Thailand." The addict coughed up the name of a Bangkok brothel where he bought the photos. It specialized in kids—perfectly legal in Thailand. Defferre sent Margaret. "You know how someone always says, 'You can't work this assignment, because you are too close to it?'" Defferre asked me, then slammed his hand on the desk hard. "I sent Margaret exactly because she is so close. She understands what these beasts are." Margaret had left her husband after her son's death; she lived only for revenge.

The brothel walls to which she went were covered with glossy 8x10s of children in sexual acts with adults. One wall had only European kids. This was the brothel's special appeal. It's neon banner read in English, "Kiddie House," emphasizing its international cosmopolitan offerings.

The photograph of Margaret's son was on the wall. She ripped down the picture. Defferre told me that she only had a few words to say that night. "Picture's down. Brothel's still standing." Typical Margaret.

Next day she tracked the local photo supplier to the provincial capital of Phetchaburi. It straddled the River Phet about 120 kilometers south of Bangkok. Narit Chaiyasut was cutting a deal to buy the two-year-old son of a poor family from a village near Pak Chong, skirting the Khao Yai National Park in Southern Isaan. They had brought the child to Phetchaburi under the promise of big cash. Chaiyasut would use the child for his own fetish; then sell him to a brothel in Bangkok.

Margaret cut the deal short and the parents high-tailed it back to Pak Chong. Chaiyasut must have picked up some Muay Thai kickboxing in high school. He tried it on Margaret. Like kicking a wrecking ball. She lost her temper and broke him in a few places. That red hair was no lie.

"The skell in Thailand rolled and gave up some tapes," said Defferre. Chaiyasut only knew one name: Father Jergens in London. Defferre had strongly cautioned Margaret not to lose it in the Kiddie House brothel. We didn't want to tip Jergens.

Defferre showed me some tapes of Jergens *"with child."* Then passed me a pink Hello Kitty hand-towel. All those suffering kids and Jergens was in a ritzy London hotel. I went there.

Jergens put up a fight. It was messy and slow.

There was a video camera and lights set up by the bed. I used it. Before he died, he told everything he ever knew since childhood to that camera. Every time he got loud, I popped him in the throat. Near the end, he told me about a four-year-old red-haired boy he had taken "while on holiday in Dublin." Kid died and Jergens dumped the body and scooted back to London. Just one of his many "holidays."

Defferre hated the tape. *"C'est mal."* Margaret kept a copy by her bed.

Archangel's man with the Metropolitan Police caught the case. He found the tapes and pictures of torture/rape kiddie porn, some starring Jergens. When the facts came out about this guy, London didn't spend too much time searching for who killed him. No one signed for the expensive forensic work on the scene. A few weeks later, Scotland Yard submitted copies of all the kids' photos found at the scene to Interpol headquarters in Lyon. The arduous task of matching the photos with international missing child records might take years—and many of the children would never be identified.

Jergens' accomplices—the distributors of the tapes—were all over the globe. Germany, Israel, Thailand, Japan and South Korea.

Defferre fed the Isreali distributor's name to Archangel's contact with the Mossad. A few days later the Mossad's man in Lyon delivered a large package. It had the skell's diaries and a lot of pictures of kids: some porn and others just normal photos. Many of the pictures were of children the scumbag had abused— he was *with child*—and other pictures were just part of his collection from Jergens.

When the Mossad took down the guy, they knew something was wrong as they walked into his house. The skell was in his mid-fifties and the first things they saw were pictures of young boys on the walls: at the park, at the beach, all between the ages of about five and fifteen years old. They were normal photos, but the man had no children. His porn pictures were hidden.

Guys in Jergen's ring—like most child molesters—kept personal collections. These collections became the skell's whole life. Not just for the cash to be made selling them, but for personal satisfaction. Jergens had a huge collection in his London hotel room, hidden in a large trunk with a fake bottom. Child pornographers keep collections that go back for years. Pictures of kids in underwear ads pasted into scrapbooks, pictures taken on the sly at parks, kiddie porn pictures that had been taken by the skell or traded and bought from other porn rings.

They also kept souvenirs of the kids they molested: a lock of hair, a ribbon, a baseball. The skell's diaries were carefully accurate, detailing every nuance of their "encounter" with the child; even recording later events in the child's life, like a party or report card. The collections were a plethora of disgust, including records and photos of their own abuses as well as pictures purchased across the globe. They built their own secret world. The Mossad's guy even had a hidden room where he took kids or went alone to be with his private collection.

The Mossad package also had some new names and locations. Defferre added them to his billboard: Saudi Arabia and New York. The Mossad wouldn't say what they did with their scumbag.

Defferre called a meeting. Bennet, Margaret, William and I attended. The board was covered with the same colored pins, but there were two new red ones on London and Thailand.

"Individual assignments are highly effective," Defferre began. He smoothed his hair back frequently as he spoke—a speaker's nervous habit. "Margaret and Major Bannon have shown what an individual working for the greater good can do." He detailed the assignments in Thailand and London, along with other information that had been uncovered about Jergen's kiddie porn ring to date. When he got to the events in London, he walked round his desk to Margaret. He motioned for her to stand.

"May your son's soul rest in heaven now, *Madame*," he said. His tone was slightly formal and completely sincere. Defferre kissed each of her cheeks with great ceremony; then presented a small package. "Archangel offers you the only justice that can be found on earth."

Margaret opened the package with her typical cold, detached calculation. It was a small silver box. An avenging angel, wings spread wide and spear at the ready, was engraved on the lid. She lifted it. Inside was an exquisite white porcelain figurine of a small boy praying. The compartment beside it held a plain silver lighter and some negatives.

"Are these...?" Margaret's voice trembled.

"*Oui, Madame*," Defferre assured her. They were the negatives of Jergens and Margaret's son. "Major Bannon rescued them from the hotel. No policemen, no journalist and no beast shall ever see these pictures of your angel again."

Margaret sat. Her full chest heaved, hands shaking as she lifted the lighter. She couldn't make the flame catch. I leaned over, wrapping my hand around hers to steady it and thumbed the flint. Flame erupted.

"Thank you all," she whispered and torched the negatives. Defferre and I wept as Bennet and William watched respectfully. Margaret's eyes were dry. Her voice was filled with raw pain. "Rest in peace, my darling."

Afterward, Margaret sat straight in her chair, as determined as ever. Defferre laid out Archangel's plan to clean the rest of Jergen's ring. He passed out assignments.

"I've always been pleased with the name we chose for ourselves," Defferre said, carefully enunciating it. "*Archangel*. A good name, *non*?" The name had worked wonders in training—giving us all a sense of purpose and moral legitimacy. Defferre walked over to his billboard and took out a red pin, tossing it on the floor. "For this operation, we also should have a good name." He slammed his heal on the pin, cracking the red plastic. "This is a Bug Hunt."

My first assignment was in New York City. Bennet feigned pouting; he said he wanted to come along and practice his Jersey accent. After New York City, I would fly to Seoul. William took Saudi Arabia and Germany; Margaret was heading to Tokyo. The board had a more extensive collage of colored pins than just those cities. Defferre caught me lingering over it. "We have," he said, "many ways of catching and punishing."

We all looked at him. We were aware of the many other people coming and going in Archangel, but everyone kept their assignments and personal lives to themselves.

"We expected to work with some of the others after our training," ventured William. Defferre glanced at Bennet, who responded in his thick Scottish brogue. "We choose the groups of trainees very carefully. You three got to know each other, your strengths and weaknesses. It was natural that you shared some personal information during the hours and days together." He never looked more like a bulldog, leaning elbows on his knees, earnestly explaining his strategy in selecting us to work together. "You were trained to work alone, but sometimes you'll need a helping hand. We prefer to keep the same team together whenever possible."

"*Esprit de corps*," pronounced Defferre, smiling.

"Right," nodded Bennet. "Team spirit."

My plane to America arrived at JFK Airport. I disembarked and took a taxi to the Skyway Motel in Jersey City. My British passport had some goofy name and I had a stack of business cards that said I was a management consultant specializing in TQM. My legend even included an appointment in a few days with a trucking company. After unpacking, I flipped on the television. All in English, all 100 percent American TV. I surfed until after midnight; then switched it off in disgust. I was back in the States for the first time in years and Columbo wasn't on a single channel. "What a gyp," I muttered and headed over the bridge to Manhattan.

Archangel's profile had an address for my guy in Brooklyn. It was a craphole apartment building. He was on the fourth floor.

This neighborhood didn't have security guards on duty. I was in worn black jeans and a beat up brown jacket. Fit right in. I took the stairs and knocked. No answer. Yelled and knocked. Same result.

The hallway was deserted and not too well lit. I peered down the key way of the lock: basic pin tumbler. I slid my pick into the lock, keeping the hook up toward the internal tumblers. I slid it to the back tumbler; then slid in my long tension wrench. I raised the back tumbler with my pick until I felt it break. Tumbler lock pins divide where they break with the internal cylinder wall, called the shear point. The pins have to be lifted so their break points match the cylinder line, so the cylinder can rotate and open the lock. When a pin's break point is aligned correctly it is called "breaking." I worked frontward, breaking the other four tumblers; then rotated the lock.

Inside I saw a family photo on the wall. Hispanics and my guy was Caucasian. I slid down the hall, peering in the bathroom. The kitchen opened to the living room. A boy of about fourteen was sleeping on the sofa. I heard a sound in the bedroom and worked my way over. Mom and Dad with another kid sleeping on a mat on the floor. They had pictures and mementos from Puerto Rico all over the walls. Just a family trying to make do on too little cash. I shook my head. Archangel's file must have it wrong.

As I worked my way out, the kid on the sofa woke up. He stared at me hard, scared but tough, too. Brooklyn had probably already beaten all the surprise out of him. "I'm Santa Claus, kid," I said, dropping $200 on the floor where he could see it. "Merry Early Christmas." I got the hell out.

We knew that our guy liked to hit Times Square to swap photos, buy and sell kiddie porn. I headed there.

Times Square was still a squalid cesspool at the time. The hawkers lamely tossed some vulgar offers my way, but I looked like I had no cash and even less interest. I heard the wares being hawked as I wandered slowly down the streets, eyes sharp like I might be looking to take down a taxpayer. They offered drugs, girls, boys, kids, even animals. I wasn't part of the New York crowd, but Times Square wasn't any different from Bucharest or Pusan. I just understood the language better.

The guy's name was Kenneth Roades. He was a middle-school teacher in Brooklyn. On top of moving product for Jergens, he was also in a position to enjoy his own fetishes. He sold his personal pictures to Jergens and others across the world.

As a teacher, Roades had access to kids the age and disposition he liked. No one should ever be surprised that a skell is in a trusted job with children. They find out early that they like children and aggressively pursue careers that keep them close. They really are attracted to kids—and they also want to have sex with them. Roades routine was to pass out a questionnaire to the kids; find out who was having trouble at home. He'd spot the loners and talk with the other kids about them. "He having trouble? Oh, his parents are divorced? His mom is a drunk?" That sort of thing. Then he'd invite the kid to his place. He had it all there: workout area, cool posters, music. He offered emotional support and understanding—something the troubled kid needed. The place was great to hang out. He'd turn down the lights and read a pornographic magazine. He didn't want to scare the kid off. The kid would get all excited, maybe a little drunk or high, and Roades would help himself. From the file, it seemed that Roades didn't go in for the torture stuff, but he moved the pictures and videos that depicted it.

I wandered Times Square for an hour or so. Roades didn't show. Back at the motel, I lost the jacket and shirt and plopped on the bed in my jeans. I let the tension run out of me. "So strange to be in America again," I murmured. Then I dozed.

In my dream I was walking down a hallway. Expensive London hotel. I faced a door. I knew this hall. I entered the suite.

There was smoke floating on the ceiling. Water on the floor to my shoes. The water was rising. The smoke was thick, and I could smell burning flesh. The same smell of *his* blistering flesh before he died. The water was to my chest.

Something in the water touched my leg.

I couldn't move and slowly the water rose above my head. The water was dark, fetid. I couldn't breathe and the liquid was thick.

"It's blood," I murmured. *"I'm drowning in blood."*

The something touched my leg again. In the dark, faces floated in and out of view. Children. The children. So many.

They were smiling.

They lifted me up so my head was above the water. Their small hands were strong. I couldn't resist. I breathed deep. The air was sweet.

I raised my hands.

And I was no longer in the room. I was nowhere. It was perfectly dark and I could see myself reflected in the dark. My skin was bright.

"I was young," a voice said. Its owner stepped forward. He was perhaps twenty years old. Korean. "I was young and you killed me." He stared at me. He was accusing. "Whatever I might have been ended because of you."

His face bloodied. His head tilted at an unnatural angle, just like it did when I saw him the first time in that Kwangju alley.

"You tried to kill me," I said. My hands were dripping with his blood. "I'll have the scar on my back all my life." I twisted my body to show him, but the large scar was gone.

He laughed. "I should have killed you. Look at what you've become!" He pointed behind me, and there, faces in the dark as far as I could see—all the people who had died because of me.

"Murderer!" he said, and the faces nodded in unison. "Murderer! Murderer!" they chanted and I was surrounded by zombies. They bit. I couldn't move.

"I have a tape!" The man from the London hotel suite waved a tape above his head. "He killed me. He tortured me!" The tape played above us. A giant movie screen, filled with his grotesque death and my grim face.

I screamed and pushed the zombies away. I tried to speak. I could not. Futile, impossible, my voice wouldn't work. The zombies surged forward.

"Stop." A small voice. A child zombie. The child touched me and faced the others. "Wait."

No. Not a zombie. Who?

"My parents still miss me." The child—boy? girl? I couldn't tell—seemed to glow. "But I'm happy now." The child pointed at the man from London. "You hurt me."

The zombies disappeared and I was alone with the child.

"You saved me." The child took my hand and smiled. "I was trapped in that room until you killed the bad man. Now I'm free."

"Your soul is free?"

The child nodded. "I'm dead. But now I'm free."

"Can I be free?" I asked.

The child didn't answer. It was a girl. She kissed my cheek and I saw her pretty hair and dress. She left and I was alone in the London hotel hall again. I opened the door to the suite. It was empty.

"That dream haunts me," I moaned, rolling out of bed. My jeans felt like I'd worn them for a week. I'd been enduring dreams like it since Sid died. I figured more were on the way, so I tried not to let them bother me. Too much.

I phoned Defferre. "Bad intel, Jacques. Nobody's home."

"*C'est mal.* Can you make a new friend in Times Square?"

"I'll try. May be a few days. Will Seoul wait?"

"It's been there a long time," Defferre said.

That's the way we talked. I knew that experts in trade-craft—especially the KGB guys—had reserve code words for everything. We were just really vague all the time.

I tagged Roades in Times Square the second night. He was in his late thirties and looked like the most pleasant, non-aggressive, upstanding school teacher ever imagined. Blue jeans with a matching blue shirt under a tan blazer. He sauntered into a strip club and sat close to the stage, sliding singles into the g-strings of dancers who all looked underage. His hair was thick and brown, maybe a little too long. He pushed it out of his eyes whenever he

As a missionary in Korea, David Race Bannon baptized Korean men and women who converted to Christianity.

During the time he spent in Korea, David met Lee Hyung-Jin, a man who would become a colleague in many covert Interpol missions and a lifelong friend.

AP Wide World Photos

Race found himself in the middle of the Kwangju riots where hundreds, mostly students, died before order was brutally restored.

Noting Race's bravery helping the wounded in the Kwangju riots and, later, his daring while in prison, Commissaire Jacques Defferre recruited Bannon for Interpol service.

As an Interpol operative under Defferre, Race used many covers, including being a member of the Belgian gendarmerie.

Before it was discovered that Eunmi was a double agent, she was a friend and colleague of Race and Hyung-Jin.

French DST agent, Sidelle Rimbaud, the woman he loved and planned to marry.

Race's fiancée, Sidelle Rimbaud, was laid to rest in this gravesite in a Lyon cemetery.

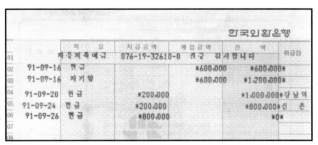

One of many bank statements showing moneys surreptitiously given to Race by Defferre for Archangel missions.

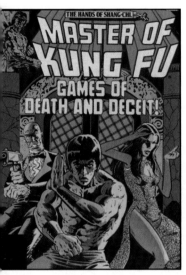

The comic book about a courageous master of Kingfu of which Race and Defferre often spoke.

Shin, a talented performance artist, comforted Race after Sid's death but was kidnapped and brutally murdered.

Race came home to his young daughter, Jessica, whose joy and radiance gave him a new perspective on life.

An article about Race entitled "Deadly Hands: An Interpol Officer's Fight for Justice," depicting the story of Annie, the child Race saved, appeared in a recent issue of *Kungfu Qigong Magazine*.

The magazine article included reenactment photos of the Wonderland club bust. Here Race confronts a video camera operator.

The reenactment showed Race storming into a hotel room and encountering an armed man (left). Then he uses a hapkido maneuver to efficiently disarm and take down the criminal (right).

took off his glasses, which he kept wiping down and replacing. He had a little paunch and was trying to hide it.

I sat in back. Waitress/stripper rolled up on me, flirting for a lap dance. I wore an oversized coat and a baseball cap. I'd tossed on some thick-rimmed glasses to add to my lonely guy image. The stripper looked about sixteen. I slid a twenty her way. "For some chit-chat," I said. The twenty disappeared and she started to peel off her top.

"No, really. Just for some talk."

"You want it dirty or what?" she asked. Longshoremen had sweeter voices. Probably weren't as tough, either.

"I want you to sit here and treat me like a regular, okay?" She shrugged and told me that the twenty got me about ten minutes of whatever I wanted.

I told her I wanted refills on my Coke every time. "Even if I ask for something harder just bring back a Coke, okay? I'll pay like it's the hard stuff—plus tip." Then I pointed at Roades and told her, "I want to meet him." She didn't even ask why. When people say, "Sixteen going on forty," about their teenagers, I just laugh. No one alive is as old as that kid.

"I'll tell him you're my best regular and a stand-up guy," she promised. I slid her a hundred.

Roades wandered over after his favorite dancer crawled off the stage. He was on his third beer and wasn't walking as straight as he thought. I hated drunks. "You want to talk with me?" he asked. Not surly. My waitress had done her job.

"I'm looking for something special," I said. "I could use a friend in town." I waved over my waitress and ordered my guy another beer and something hard for me. My waitress had a new twenty in her tight shorts for the trouble. Roades noticed the jack and how the waitress treated me.

"Friend? Got lots of friends. What sort you after?" He was on the make. I laid out the type of kiddie stuff I was looking for. Ages, sex, positions. He ate it up. We talked a few hours: he got good and drunk and I kept drinking Cokes. By the time the club closed, he thought we were kindred spirits. Roades was eager to talk more, so we caught a cab back to his place. He never stopped talking, wiping his glasses off whenever he said something that really excited him.

At his place, Roades laid out how much it would cost for a specialty tape. "Say $2,000 for a kid doing two grown-ups," he said. I nodded. "But if you want a kid for yourself, that's more. Unless you go find the kid on your own."

Roades went on about how he had snagged a kid once. He said that he had spent "some time with a guy in London" and was convinced that violence was the only way to teach kids a lesson. "I've loved them and loved them," he confided in me, still drunk. "But they always leave me. Some even want to tell! After all I've done!" He looked like he might cry, so I pushed for more information.

"You tried the violent approach?"

Roades gulped back his near-tears, took off his glasses and wiped his sweaty palms on his jeans. "I drive over to Jersey, right? And I wait outside this mall. I'm not the most aggressive person; so I had to find the right sort." Roades watched until he spotted a kid about twelve years old walking way ahead of his parents. Roades opened his car door and said in his best teacher voice, "Get in now."

The kid didn't know what to do. He got in. Roades drove away fast and took the kid to an alley behind a closed supermarket.

He forced the kid a few times, made the kid do some things for him. Then he took the kid next to a dumpster, bent him over, and while he was forcing him again, lifted a baseball bat and knocked him out.

I stood and acted like I was stretching. Roades was so excited about his story that he started to fondle himself. I fought back a retch. "How many kids you do that way?"

"Just the one. I tried it again on a kid in Harlem, but he told me to kiss his ass. I told him that I wanted to and he laughed at me. His friends walked up, so I drove away." He flicked hair out of his eyes and took a long drink of beer. "I haven't had the nerve to try it since."

I nodded like I understood his pain; then asked where he stashed his goodies. I laid out about $3000 and told him that his story put me in the mood to buy. Roades replaced his glasses and took the jack. "Follow me," he said.

His place was decorated to be a kid's paradise—filled with cool music and posters and even a foosball table—all in exchange for doing a few favors. Selling the torture/rape/death tapes brought him to the attention of Archangel. His story about the kid at the mall nailed the coffin shut.

I waited until Roades opened his secret cubbyhole in the back of his bedroom closet. It was filled with photos and tapes. I extended my telescoping baton and caved his right leg. As he sank to his knees I straddled him from behind, choking with the baton until he passed out. His bladder released. "Just when I thought you couldn't get any more disgusting," I murmured, stripping him. He had a cupid tattoo on his upper left thigh, pointing a little arrow towards his crotch. I found some remarkably strong nylon rope in his cubby—wonder what he used that for? I trussed his hands and legs and rammed his head into his cubby. He'd stay tied-up there until the cops arrived to find his hole of goodies.

"Roach Hotel," I said, connecting that over-played commercial to Archangel's Bug Hunt. "They check in but they don't check out." For some bizarre reason this struck me as silly and I fought back a crooked smile. The Eagles' *Hotel California* came to mind: "You can check out anytime you like, but you can never leave!" Tune wouldn't leave my head, so I hummed it while I finished the job.

I snagged all the cash I could find and wiped the place down. It looked like a kiddie porn seller took a customer home and got mugged. Roades wouldn't know any different. The stripper would remember a lot of cash and a big coat, big glasses and a baseball cap. If Roades' lawyer let him talk about it at all, that is, and if the cops bothered to check the club, and if Stripper bothered to tell them anything. Archangel had a lot of friends in the New York Police Department.

I switched legends. With a passport and other identification that set me up as a Canadian national traveling to Korea on holiday, I caught the next flight to Seoul.

Defferre was going to give me hell about not cleaning the guy. Jergens had raped, tortured and killed small children. Roades had seduced and raped middle school boys—but also sold Jergens' sleaze. I wasn't sure what the difference was, but I hoped the New York legal system would sort Roades out. I was in my own country, where I trusted Archangel wasn't the only answer.

fourteen

SEOUL MAN

I arrived at Kimpo Airport in a dark brown suit, white shirt, no tie and a travel bag. I didn't bother with luggage. Eunmi was waiting for me outside customs.

"Chanyoung-*si!*" She moaned deeply and wrapped her arms round me. This type of public display wasn't customary in Korea and we got a few stares, but foreigners in airports got a little slack. "Oh, my dearest friend," Eunmi said in Korean, tears soaking my suit, shirt and neck. "Oh, I am so sorry about Sid."

I thanked her and returned the comforting hug. It was my first since Sid died. She dried her eyes. "I tried to call you so many times, Chanyoung. Did they give you the messages?"

"Where?"

"At Archangel, of course."

I hadn't received a single message. As we walked to the taxi stall, she told me, "Hyung-Jin is on an NIS assignment in Inchon." I asked her if Hyung-Jin had tried to phone, too. She nodded. "But it is not only Sid, it is about him and I."

This caught me off guard. "How so?"

"We broke up." After Sid died, Eunmi and Hyung-Jin had a falling out. She wanted to fly to Lyon; Hyung-Jin saw the writing on the wall. Defferre nixed Eunmi's planned trip, but the damage was done.

We were in Changan District, north of the Han River in Seoul. I had the taxi pull up to the Taeyujang Inn. It was just another faceless, common inn. In Korea, the inexpensive hotels— called *yogwan*—are pretty much for the locals. Hardly any English is spoken and—except for those yogwan near military bases—the accommodations were entirely Korean. Eunmi came up to my room with me. It was small, with a television and bed, and a bathroom adjoining. Yogwan bathrooms had a tub with hand held shower hose and either a western-style commode or a Korean "squatter"—a completely sanitary but slightly uncomfortable toilet buried in the ground. Business is done without ever touching the porcelain. Thank God this yogwan went in for western-style.

"Defferre told me about the villa," Eunmi said. As soon as I hung up my suit coat, she opened my bag and began unpacking for me. Bold, but oddly comforting. It was nice to have someone show me tenderness that didn't have death or threats attached to it. Archangel was not a wellspring of human sympathy.

When she'd finished, she hugged me again, lightly brushing her lips over my cheek. "You know I have always had deep feelings for you," she said softly. I tensed and she added in the same heartfelt tone, "Do not concern yourself. I care about you too much to be anything other than your friend. There's too much work to do and too little time for even that simple comfort."

We sat in silence for a while on the bed, empty flight bag between us. I flipped on the television. "*Columbo* reruns aren't on all week. I checked." Nice to have someone looking out for you.

Our target was a musician named Pak Seyong. Eunmi had tagged him using the names we got from Jergens. "He was easy to find," she said. "He's something of a star for other performing artists." She had snagged some tickets for a fancy little show that night.

Korean dinner theaters usually charged a flat rate for a two-drink minimum with dinner and an elaborate musical review. We dressed up and headed to the Café *Sarang* (Café Love) in Kwanhun District. It was near Insa District, where Seyong had set up his musical performance art studio. Insa was famous for its antique and art stores.

Café Sarang was one of two Sanchon Restaurants. A Buddhist priest oversaw and blessed the strictly vegetarian menu and the entertainment was exclusively Korean music and dance. Café Sarang had recently ventured into the art world, hosting weekly performance pieces.

After the meal, the show began. Most of the short performances were "re-interpretations with modern influences" of Korean *sijo* and *pansori*, the first a unique Korean poetry form with strict meter requirements, the second a Korean oral tradition of singing exhaustive folk tales. Seyong infused post-modern synthesizer rock with the pansori singer. It was an intriguing blend, but didn't seem to offer anything new to make the ancient singing tradition "relevant to modernity," as the brochure proclaimed.

The *sijo* performances were dramatic readings. Most of the artists stuck to the rigid form requirements of the short poems; others tried improvisations to achieve an "air of spontaneity," seeming to miss the point that simplicity in art takes years of training and work to attain. During the *sijo* performance, one artist asked for audience participation. A few members stood up and offered miserably bad *sijo* to the general entertainment of all. Seyong's music wove a synthesized blend of tones that were never quite background music. It was almost as if he were improvising incidental music to the audience's live performance. The *sijo* artist tossed out a joke about the foreigner in the audience.

"Perhaps our American guest has something to offer!" Koreans often assume every Caucasian is American and every American can't master their language. "Maybe he knows something deeply artistic, like" he mimed an Elvis leg wiggle— "Michael Jackson or Prince!" It was an obvious attempt to insult American culture at the expense of someone he thought didn't understand Korean. It got a few laughs, but most of the audience members were quietly shocked at such rude behavior.

"Please pardon me," I said in perfect Korean. "I am Canadian, not American, but I would still like to offer my own small effort." *Sijo* had been my favorite form of Korean poetry since the first time I heard it as a neophyte missionary. I had been attempting to master its subtleties and deceptive beauty for two years. I stood and cleared my throat:

> *Twenty years of mountain snow*
> *Drift west, drift low*
> *A tired leaf floating by*
> *First wet, then dry*

Under the snow it has lain
Gone to the fresh earth again

Café Sarang erupted in unanimous praise for the *sijo*, which I had recited according to the tones and delivery tradition of the form. The artist on the stage was taken aback but quickly caught which way the patron wind blew and joined in his praise. After a few explanations of why I wrote *sijo* and my business in Korea—Canadian on holiday—the performance moved on. Eunmi squeezed my hand under the table. "That was beautiful, Chanyong-si. Full of *han*," she whispered, referring to the Korean sense of unrequited sorrow. "But also very hopeful. When did you write it?"

I sipped my tea. "After."

"*She* was the leaf?" Eunmi used the two terms from my *sijo* poem: *ipseh* for a fresh leaf on a tree and *nakyop* for a fallen leaf.

"No. I am."

We were interrupted by a bright light bursting from the stage, followed by complete darkness. Seyong's music filled the room. It was time for the main event. A single spotlight fell on center stage. A Korean woman in her late twenties crawled slowly into the light, her black leotard giving the impression that she was materializing out of darkness. Just as she was almost into the light, it shut off and reappeared to her right. She screamed and pounced into the new light, standing slowly, body undulating with the quickening music, eyes filled with insistent sexuality. The light played on her in such a way to reveal her supple body under the thin black leotard, feigning an anguished nudity.

"Do not take me," she chanted. "Do not hurt me. I am your daughter." She lifted her hands and by a trick of light, an orange circle appeared above her head. "I am the father who lusts for his child." The circle of light turned deep red. The music changed with each hue. "I am the child who seduces her teacher." Circle turned blue. "I am the mother who hates her son." Green circle burning bright, brighter, as she pulled it down from the air and placed it on her bosom. The reflective surface of her leotard showed a countryside scene: rich waving hills, deep meadows. She clutched the image to her, moaning, "I am yours alone, do not rape me." The stage lit in dull orange. Mannequins dressed as farmers, housewives, children and soldiers surrounded her. They were prone, beat-up in death poses, as though after a great battle. A tall battered crucifix loomed to her left, positioned so its heavy shadow obscured the faces of the bodies. "Do not take me. Do not hurt me. I am your daughter." The stage blackened.

The audience was so overwhelmed that there was no sound for a few long moments; then they stood and roared their approval. The lights rose and the artist and Seyong took the stage, bowing.

Café Sarang stayed open late that night as audience members and artists shared drinks and small talk. We stuck around, hoping for a chance to make friends with Seyong. He was holding forth with a group of admirers at one of the larger tables. They had even set up a board of *changi*, a Korean game similar to chess but faster and more ruthless. Seyong wore a black beret. Probably to hide a bald spot, which was thought of as grotesquely ugly by many Korean women. He was easily in his early sixties and wore black slacks and a red mock turtleneck covered by a black vest. He put on glasses to play *changi*, but took them off whenever chatting with his admirers. The more he drank, the louder he got.

"Maybe I should challenge him to a game," I suggested to Eunmi. "I'm not so bad and we could all make pals. You flash him those pretty eyes the way you know how to do." I said this without even a hint of flirt. For me, Eunmi's attractiveness was just another tool for the job and we both knew it. We were about to order drinks for Seyong and friends when the star artist appeared at our table.

"I enjoyed your *sijo* very much," she said in coy, perfect Seoul dialect. She had lost the leotard for a *hanbok*—the traditional Korean dress that was sometimes worn for special occasions, such as an important art reception. Hers was white and flowing, the tiny vest and large folds lightly decorated with blue and jade swans. It was a complete antithesis to her earlier image. Her name was Shin HyeKyung. "May I join you?"

We didn't get to talk with Seyong that night, but tagged him the next day. He liked to loiter at McDonalds and bakery shops—popular hangouts for kids. He'd watch them, maybe strike up a conversation. If they didn't seem to have much of a home life, he'd invite them back to his studio. He'd rave about how they were special, had hidden talent, the usual line. That was just his spiel at home. He saved more elaborate scenarios for trips to Thailand.

We watched him pick up a hooker—a boy of maybe fifteen—and get a room at a little dive yogwan south of the Han River called Highway Inn. An hour later, the kid came out a couple bucks richer. We almost took Seyong then, but he sprinted out of the yogwan and hailed a cab right away. Back to his studio.

Over the course of a week, we watched him intently; we noticed that most nights he worked late at his studio. The Seoul police, *kyungchal*, passed Insa every couple of hours. As each night ended, I returned to Taeyujang Inn and Eunmi went to her hotel. I didn't ask where.

I swung by the South Korean National Medical Center and asked for Director Kim Cholkyu. It was my second week in Seoul. I had on the brown suit with a dark maroon tie. The clerk gave me the once-over, unimpressed. He didn't seem keen on letting me in to see the doctor, so I let on that I was expected. He jumped to that. Little putz.

"I was expecting you?" asked Dr. Kim after the clerk let me in. "Since when?"

"Hey, we archangels need check-ups!"

He sighed, smoothed his tie, and smiled softly. "*Cham*, that is entirely true."

We caught up a little; then I got to the point. "Defferre said you might have an update for me." Dr. Kim nodded and flipped a switch on the small box on his desk. White noise. "William has completed his assignments. Apparently the Saudi target was visiting his German contact when William got there. Defferre said that it was two for one. Margaret's target left Tokyo for a sex tour in Thailand. You are to join her there."

I took it all in, then asked if he could call Defferre. Dr. Kim said it was about 3:00 A.M. in Lyon. Like I cared.

Defferre answered on the first ring. Didn't even sound groggy.

"Jacques, why didn't you tell me about Eunmi's messages?"

"She is not all she appears," Defferre said. I grunted in disgust and he continued. "But, as you hate the mystery, I will be blunt. She has associations with North Korea. We do not know exactly the nature of them, but we must be careful that she learns no more of our little group. And we might try to discover more about her associations if possible."

"You want me to play her?" I asked. So much for my last friend.

"Never play, *mon ami*. She adores you. Treat her well." Defferre paused, then added, "But find out what you can."

We rang off and I stared at Dr. Kim. He handed me a lollipop from his desk drawer. "It always makes me feel better," he confided.

The same day, I left Dr. Kim's office and headed to the Silla Hotel in Changchung District. On the top floor was La Continental, Seoul's most charming and expensive restaurant. The view was great. Shin Hyekyung showed up right on time. She wore a fashionable gray skirt with a matching sweater that hung off the shoulder and was very beautiful.

At Café Sarang she had hinted that we meet. I jumped at the chance to do something normal. "*Sobak hage?*" I asked her, using the Korean term for simple and pure—like the way two high school kids might grab a hamburger or old friends reunite to catch up. Shin understood that I was saying romance wouldn't be on the menu. She smiled the way artists often do, completely in the moment. "That sounds nice," she said.

A small crucifix dangled from a delicate gold chain around her neck. She tended to touch it whenever she was delighted or surprised. During the meal I dropped Seyong's name, testing the waters. Shin shuddered almost visibly. "He is a truly talented musician," she said; then studiously worked on her *pulkogi* marinated beef.

"But?"

She looked out the window, then back at me, hard. I recognized the artist I had seen on stage: impassioned, demanding, angry. She seemed unaware that she was clutching her crucifix. Each word was dull and lifeless. "But he likes to go to Hong Kong with boys." I nodded and let it drop. "Going to Hong Kong" was a Korean euphemism for orgasm. Shin's uncompromising views on sexuality were part of what made her art so challenging. It was clear that Seyong's personal tastes were not hers.

We changed the subject. She didn't have any information about Seyong that would help. We whiled away the afternoon chatting about nothing; even went to Lotte World and caught some rides.

Nice and normal. A tonic.

That night, Eunmi and I hit Seyong's place. We watched the police walk by two hours after midnight. Seyong was still in his studio. I had changed to black jeans, sturdy boots and a dark sweater.

Eunmi positioned herself behind a Bongo van—Korea's answer to the VW van—and poured some liquor out of a bottle onto the street. She dabbed some behind her ears like perfume. "Treat me right and I might let you get drunk later," she flirted, practicing her routine. If the cops came by she'd flash her smile and crash the bottle on the street. Cops would be enjoying this tasty drunk's tight mini and open blouse while I took off another way. If there were no problems, I'd give her the sign as I left the studio and we'd go our separate ways.

Seyong was practicing some pyrotechnics on his keyboard that sounded like Emerson, Lake and Palmer. Had to hand it to him; he definitely had the musical chops. No wonder he worked in his studio: his music was too loud for a neighborhood. I realized that there was no way I could hear Eunmi breaking a bottle on the street, but I was already in the studio.

Seyong didn't hear a thing. I had wrapped a garrote around my leather-gloved hands, but his posture was so perfect at the synthesizer that the stiletto made more sense. It was over quickly.

It would seem strange if Seyong's studio were quiet; so I rummaged through his tapes. H.R. Giger's eye-popping cover to ELP's *Brain Salad Surgery* had always been one of my favorites. I slid it into Seyong's cassette player and pumped the volume. Karn Evil 9 filled the studio.

Seyong had plenty of pictures around the place. He hadn't bothered to hide most of them. Personal photos of Seyong with Korean boys were on each wall. He had stashed a binder behind his tiny fridge. It had pictures of his sex tours in Thailand, including Seyong having sex with an infant, another with two boys no older than six or seven. There were dozens of "proof photos," a term used by Koreans for pictures that weren't aesthetically pleasing but clearly showed Seyong posing in front of brothel signs. I flipped through them casually until one caught my eye. Seyong standing in front of the popular and cosmopolitan Kiddie House. "Oh, Margaret's gonna love this," I murmured and stuffed the picture in my pocket.

Next stop: Thailand.

fifteen

FREE MARKET

I was in a horrendously long queue through immigration at the Don Muang Airport, about twenty-five kilometers north of Bangkok. Because Thailand offered free, short-stay visas on the spot, the airport was notorious for its anonymous visitors and endless waiting.

"Excuse me, sir." A customs official took my elbow. "This way please." He and his partner led me away from the line to a side door. My Canadian legend was still good and I had the rap down from Seoul. They escorted me down a long hall to a large office. Margaret sat inside.

"No more lines for Race," she said with her grim little smile. One of the customs officers had worked with Archangel before. Although Thailand was not an active participant in Interpol, some of its officials were sympathetic to the idea of international law enforcement cooperation. Others could be bought.

We slipped out of the office and to a taxi stall without a second look. No one even inspected my bag—which always held nothing more than clothes and toiletries. After a slow and dangerously reckless ride into Bangkok, we took a breather in Margaret's room. It was a cheap guest house outside of Patpong, Bangkok's notorious sex district.

Margaret tossed me a bulky over-sized black leather jacket—used and ragged—along with a KA-BAR and a Beretta.22 caliber, just like Bennet recommended. "You can't shoot for shit, Race," said Margaret. "But I figure it might look impressive in a tight spot." She was right, of course. I could hold a pistol real good. I slid into the jacket, which covered up my weapons nicely.

We walked to Patpong. Margaret wore dark conservative slacks and blouse under a thick gray wool jacket. The neon-lit go-go bars of Patpong district loomed like rides in a sexual theme park concentrated into a small area between the eastern ends of Silom and Suriwong roads.

Patpong was only a muddy stretch of riverbank when Bangkok was founded, but now it had grown into a flashy district of clubs for the Thai elite. Chinese millionaire godfather Patpong named the area after himself. In 1969, an American refitted a tea-house into a nightclub for Westerners and GIs, and Patpong's sex trade was born. It was a rough and violent area, despite its glossy front as Asia's sex reservation. Only the facade had changed.

The center of the skin trade was on the two interconnected *sois*, Patpong 1 and 2. Go-go bars shared their patch of land with regular restaurants, bookstores, supermarkets, even a Kentucky

Fried Chicken. Street corner salesmen were pitching knock-off watches and cheap T-shirts. We strolled along Patpong 1, blinded by the blazing neon signs spelling out names of bars like Love Nest and French Kiss. In front of the bars, girls cajoled us with a bored, lifeless sensuality while hawkers handed out one-sheets listing the goods for sale.

Margaret waved at one place and the doorman greeted her like an old friend. "My guy from Tokyo hangs out here," she explained in a low voice. "I've been here almost every night for two weeks." She passed some jack to the doorman and he cleared a table for us, to the side in a dark area. They figured she liked to sit in the dark and enjoy the show anonymously. "I've been paying well for the privilege."

Bikini-clad and topless women gyrated to Western music, playing hostess to the male-dominated crowd. They were almost all Thai, with a few Koreans in safari-type outfits tossed in. Korean businessmen on sex tours preferred the khaki look. Most of the Japanese trade was on Thaniya Road, a few blocks away.

We were the only Caucasians—and Margaret was the only woman customer. However, white skin was not rare in Patpong and no one gave us a second look. A table of Thais noticed Margaret's red hair, but quickly turned away. Even their penchant for foreign, or *farang*, women wasn't enough to approach the wrecking ball. She settled into her chair, short, heavy, tightly mus-cled bulk making the cheap wood creak. "Sometimes it's a blessing being so ugly," she said, sipping her Coke. "None of these guys bother me." She said it in the same tone Eunmi used to describe her attractiveness: a practical aspect of the job, nothing more. But I wasn't playing.

"You'll never be ugly, Margaret," I said, sincere half-smile close to her ear. "A mother and friend is the most beautiful person in the world."

Margaret turned to me slowly, head tilted. "Call me Peg." Then we went to work. "That's my guy," she said, subtly nodding in the direction of a Japanese man sitting with some Thais at the bar. He was so completely non-descript that it was easy to miss him.

"His name's Tsunashima Masahiro, a VP with Minolta in Tokyo, a '*salaryman*.'" She pronounced the title in the Japanese version of the American phrase. "He's got a wife and two kids in his expensive little condo. Two kids, right?" Margaret snorted in disgust; then resumed her banal description. "The guy's so ordinary, it makes you want to puke."

Margaret had followed him in Tokyo for a few days before he headed to Thailand. Masahiro kept a little locker near the subway, where salary men sometimes slept in coffin-sized hutches if it was too late to get home or they were too drunk. Margaret saw him poring through the locker the day he was leaving. "After he caught the subway, I let myself in," she said. "Full of the worst stuff. Children from every country, adults from every race and plenty of Masahiro *with child*." Margaret's voice was even, but her hands were red—then white—as she gripped her glass of Coke.

Masahiro stood and wandered up the stairs in the back of the bar, a hostess encouraging him. I waved over the doorman and laid out some jack. "We want a better show," I said, pointing at the one-sheet's promise of live sex. He nodded and had a hostess lead us upstairs.

The live shows were grotesque mockeries of human sexuality. Whereas Shin's performance art had desperately expressed her intimate core, these shows were jaded displays of bored couplings. There were a few rooms where groups could watch girls perform together or with men. Other rooms were private affairs. Our guy had gone into one of those; so we pulled up some chairs, paid the fee for the group room and waited.

Masahiro came out with two Thai girls, one about ten and the other maybe twelve. They smothered him with gratitude at the extra cash he paid as he left, a smug look of contentment on his face. He was the perfect farang sucker: well-behaved with plenty of jack to spread around.

We picked him up outside as he headed east of Patpong 2 to the dead-end alley, Silom 4, where Bangkok's hippest nightclubs thrummed their endless bass beat. "After he has a kid or two," Margaret explained, "Masahiro meets a guy at the clubs and they party all night. Usually they wander over to gay street." Two blocks over, Silom 2 offered a wide range of homosexual venues. "I followed Masahiro's friend last week. He's a bouncer at Kiddie House."

The light dawned in my mind. "That's why Defferre had me join you."

Margaret kept her eyes on the bouncer, partying with Masahiro. "Defferre must figure Kiddie House is a two person job," she said. Unlike many of the brothels in Bangkok, Kiddie House specialized in photos and tapes of foreign children—preferably Caucasian. We knew that Jergens' ring supplied them with a lot of the porn—including the photos of Margaret's son. We were going to find out the names of their other suppliers.

I handed the picture of Seyong posing in front of Kiddie House to Margaret. "Souvenir," I said in the same tone I might use to hand her a stick of gum.

She looked it over and pocketed the print. "Masahiro's the last one. Then my little darling can rest."

Our guys partied until the wee hours; then parted. Masahiro stumbled in the dark back to his hotel. On a deserted stretch, Margaret took care of him.

We decided we'd watch Kiddie House for the next few days. Over breakfast, I picked up a copy of the highly respected *Bangkok Post* to check the weekly column on the sex industry. The Thai sex industry pulled in over a billion dollars a year. That was big business, definitely newsworthy, so the paper listed hours of operation, special offerings and gossip. The paper appealed to the two million farang males that arrived every year to visit the Patpong district; some German and Japanese companies even organized sex tours as rewards for high productivity.

We nibbled on some obscurely bread-like substance, watching the daytime atmosphere of Patpong. Like someone with a mellow hangover, the district was sluggish in the light. Bar girls dressed in respectable clothes hung out at the food stalls and cafes. Their faces were strained from the heavy diet of antibiotics and heroin they used to ward off venereal disease, boredom and misery. Kiddie House was on Patpong 2, where during the day *farang* tourists slumped at bars and watched videos, waiting for evening to come.

The farang sex industry was relatively new, starting during the Vietnam War as a way to entertain GIs from the seven bases in Thailand. When the United States secured rights to ferry soldiers on R&R from Vietnam to Bangkok in 1969, the industry began booming. Sex tours became an established part of Thai culture and still are.

Prostitution and polygamy had long been intrinsic to the Thai elite way of life. Until Rama VI broke with custom in 1910, Thai kings always kept a retinue of concubines. Some may have been elevated to wife or royal mother; the rest were kept in harems as sexual playthings. Status-hungry nobility aped the practice and newly rich merchants followed suit in the early nineteenth century.

The Thai monarch was monogamous after 1910, but upper-class Thai men continued the custom of owning a *mai noi* (little wife). This was rationalized by the popular affectation that an official wife (*mai luang*) should be respected and elevated on an altar, like a temple's main Buddha image. The little wife, on the other hand, was seen as an amulet to be taken out and shown off. Men without the cash to own "a little wife" followed the socially accepted tradition of hiring hookers. About 97 percent of sexually active Thai men used hookers once or twice a month. A night out wasn't complete without a trip to a bar or massage parlor.

On paper, prostitution had been illegal in Thailand since 1960, but the government actively promoted sex tourism. Advertisements in popular foreign magazines featured prepubescent girls entreating the reader to visit Thailand soon for "sensual love." Brothel owners got round the paper laws by simply naming their houses bars, restaurants, barbershops, massage parlors or nightclubs. A little grease to the local cops and they were on their way.

Sex workers—women, men, girls and boys—had no legal rights and often endured horrible abuse and violence from pimps and customers. If they complained, a heavy-handed pimp or sadistic customer paid no penalty; it was the sex workers who faced imprisonment and fines for any disturbance.

The majority of the women working in the Patpong bars came from poor rural areas in north and northeast areas of Thailand. They were easily drawn into an industry where they could make in a single night what took months to earn working in rice fields.

Rural families expected all family members to contribute equal shares to the family income. Many women chose to spend a few lucrative years in Patpong to assist in paying off family debts and improve the lives of their families mired in poverty. Some just shrugged their shoulders at the *karma*—one's lot in the present life dictated by misdeeds in past lives—that led them to work in this industry and earn next-life merit for helping their families.

In some Isaan villages, money sent home by prostitutes in Bangkok far exceeded government financial aid. To avoid poor people banging on the door of the agricultural subsidies department for assistance, the government actively encouraged poor rural parents to sell their daughters into prostitution. The women who willingly entered the brothels had at least some small idea of the work and conditions. Children did not.

Child slavery was a reality of Thai life. Over a quarter million of the prostitutes were between ten and fourteen years old. Some houses specialized in much younger children. The teahouses of Bangkok's Chinatown offered prepubescent virgin girls for thousands of dollars to the first customer. Sex with them was thought to restore vitality and ensure long life.

Desperate parents sold their children—girls and boys—as bonded slaves to pimps and agents like Narit Chaiyasut. Margaret had interrupted just such a deal when she nabbed Chaiyasut in Phetchaburi. Some investigators suggested that parents didn't know the nature of their child's indentured service and—if they found out—didn't have the means to locate their child in far-off Bangkok. That was a crock of shit. Margaret had watched parents bring their children to the door of brothels all week. We saw it twice one morning while we were watching Kiddie House.

When there weren't enough willing candidates, pimps kidnapped children outside of Bangkok and sold them into slavery. Inside the houses, the kids were ruthlessly beaten and fed drugs to ensure compliance. Those who had been sold by their parents were kept locked up until they had repaid the money fronted their mothers and fathers. It usually took two to five years. Brothel fires often spelled death for the children, who were locked into small basement rooms or chained to their beds.

The whole district enraged us. "We could spend the rest of our careers just cleaning these skells," Margaret said fervently.

"Or following the foreigners back to their home countries and taking care of them there," I agreed. "Pretty good chance they're abusing kids at home."

"And buying and selling kiddie porn."

Archangel tried to break up international child porn rings: to hunt and punish those who raped, tortured and killed children for profit—and thought themselves above the law. But what could we do when it was legal? We stood on Patpong 2, disgusted over the whole dirty business. Next to the Kiddie House was another brothel in a long row of such houses. We looked up at the neon sign, now dimmed in the noonday sun: The Baby Shop.

This street could never be cleaned enough.

Night fell on the Kiddie House. They might remember Margaret from when she tore her son's picture off the wall with barely controlled rage; so I sauntered in alone. Margaret waited across the street at a café. I walked into a small foyer with a blackened glass door leading to the lounge area. I could feel the dull throb of the bass beat in my bones. The foyer had pictures of children on every wall. I stared at them for a few moments, my anger rising. The picture of Margaret's son had already been replaced.

"You like the white boys?" asked an elegantly dressed Thai woman in her late forties. Her hair was held up by a long ivory pin in a becoming coiffure. No doubt it could be used as a lethal weapon. She had seen me perusing the pictures and luckily been unable to read my thoughts.

"Pictures of them, yeah. I want to buy some, maybe get some tapes." I tossed her some cash to grease the deal. It disappeared.

"More than pictures, yes? We have much more." She pulled my arm and I pretended to resist, then acquiesced and let her lead me into the lounge area. Thai girls of about fourteen or fifteen were gyrating grotesquely to the Western rock-and-roll. Men from all over the world were watching them, pawing through photo albums of children. Europeans, some Americans, Asians, old, young, men, women—the place was packed with customers. Madam Elegant sat me in a comfortable love seat and called over a teenage girl in a high-slit dress. "Show the gentleman our catalogue," she said and returned to the foyer.

The girl smiled sweetly and caressed my thigh. She was maybe thirteen. I resisted pushing away. Skells in this dump were supposed to like it. Instead, I leaned forward to a small table and pointed at the book. "Anything younger in there?"

She got the hint and removed her hand. We looked over the photo album. "This is a catalogue, right?"

"Catalogue, yes," the girl replied, nodding and smiling. It was clear she hoped I didn't want conversation. Her English was almost non-existent. I pointed at a picture of a little boy. "This boy," I said; then pointed upward. "He's upstairs?"

She smiled, relieved. "Yes. Upstairs. All upstairs."

I continued looking at the catalogue. They must have had thirty kids for sale. Near the back I hit the international section. Caucasian kids. My hands were shaking. My "hostess" interpreted this as excitement and smiled, pointing at one blonde-haired boy about seven years old. I mimed drinking and said to the girl, "Coke." She walked to the bar.

Despite our revulsion, Margaret and I couldn't do a whole lot about the Thai government encouraging slavery of its own children, but these kids didn't look like Thai nationals. I counted out the pages, reading each "name" in the catalogue aloud: "Tommy. Pearl. Cherry. Baby. Bobby. July." Six kids. All easily under ten years old. Pearl looked to be the youngest, maybe five. Looked like Jergens didn't tell me everything. I should've tortured him longer.

My hostess returned and I pointed to the oldest child, Tommy. She nodded and took my hand, leading me upstairs. Tommy's room was an ugly little hole, poorly lit with a red lamp. But the bed was a four-poster fetishist cliché. Tommy was waiting on the bed. I handed the jack to my hostess. "One hour," she said and bowed out.

Tommy's eyes were strangely alert. He had long brown hair to his shoulders in an effeminate cut. He was completely naked on the bed, posing so I could see him. He watched me look round the room. I stopped at a small window, peering down at the alley behind Kiddie House. Bars on the window. I turned. "How old are you?"

"Five," he said. More like ten.

"Is your name really Tommy?"

"Yes, Daddy."

I nodded. He had spoken just enough to catch some of his accent. I was betting British, maybe Australian.

"There are six foreign kids here, right?"

"Whatever you like, Daddy." His voice was a put-on little baby voice. It was horrifying to hear him do his job. But I knew they'd beaten it into him.

"Are there any more foreign kids?" I asked. He stared at me blankly and I offered an explanation. "Like maybe I want all at once, you know? More the merrier."

He did his posed smile and told me there were six of them, just like in the catalogue. That's what I needed. I didn't tell him anything about Margaret and myself; there was no way to tell if he had been completely brainwashed and was loyal to his captors and abusers. It happened sometimes. I told him to get dressed. "I like to see you in clothes," I said.

"Yes, Daddy."

I felt like puking.

One hour later, I paid some extra money to the house owner, saying the kid was just perfect. That might spare him a beating. I strolled across the street to the café. Margaret was in the back.

"This you won't believe," I said and laid it all out. We knew that there was a booming business for "white slavery"—the kidnapping of Caucasian children for slavery in Thai brothels. Defferre's board of missing children and his skell list of those who traffic in human beings were testaments to the reality of this global problem. But we had never seen it face-to-face. We talked it over as we headed back to Margaret's cheap guest house. Once there, we called Defferre.

"Jacques, we need more weapons and six legends," I said as soon as he picked up.

Defferre didn't miss a beat. "Ages and sex?" he asked. I told him, guessing on most.

"*Mon Dieu*," Defferre said, voice filled with emotion. Margaret got on the phone and Defferre filled her in on where to get more weapons and a car. She had worked with the same contact on her last trip. Margaret tossed out the idea of backup, but didn't want to wait for anyone to arrive. Defferre told her that two cleaners were enough. She handed the phone to me.

"Margaret and I need new legends, too," I said. American family on vacation with six kids. Defferre set the time and place to pick up the new identification.

"There was a whole group of poor Thai kids as well," I offered, knowing what he'd say but wanting to voice their plight anyway.

"Race, understand that we cannot help the Thai children. There is no law to help you. No way to get them out of the country." I said that I understood. Defferre told me a boat would be waiting for us at the tiny fishing port of Laem Ngop. The customs agent there was an Archangel contact. Our boat would be posing as a tourist vessel. "Your small family should hire it to take you to Ko Chang Island. The boat will take you down the Gulf of Thailand to Kuantan in Malaysia, where you'll drop off the kids with another Archangel team."

Defferre's voice suddenly lost his usual control. His breath was deep and harsh. "Clean them, *mon ami*. Clean those animals and at least you'll save six of the children."

sixteen

PADLOCKS

I spent the next three nights posing as a paying customer at Kiddie House. I looked over the upstairs as best I could. On the third night I ordered a girl named July. She was about ten years old, like Tommy, but infinitely more talkative. She had long sandy brown hair and hazel eyes shadowed by long lashes. She described the rooms they slept in downstairs. Two of the kids didn't speak English: Pearl was German and Bobby was French. July and Tommy were British; Baby was American and Cherry was Australian.

"They keep us together in one room, with two other Thai girls. They're older." July explained that the two older girls watched and protected them. The other Thai kids resented the white children. "We get better treatment 'cause they can charge more for us." She said it like she was explaining how good grades got her a higher allowance. I figured she wasn't as far gone as Tommy, though, so I took a chance.

"Want to get out of here?"

"You'll buy me?" she asked, batting her eyes demurely like she'd been taught.

"Something like that," I said. I didn't want her talking to the owners about me. "But I'll get you back to Britain. Maybe see your folks again." July looked at me a moment. She'd heard promises before. "Whatever you say," she said in a dull, pseudo-coy voice, "Daddy."

Margaret and I decided to make our move the next day. Just before dawn she returned to the room with our new legends. I looked them over. The Reverend Mr. Williams and wife with six kids. Margaret had picked up a bible in a Patpong all-night bookstore. We wrote in it and bent the pages. Well-worn for the preacher.

Defferre's contact provided us with a van and clothes for the kids. We put our preacher-and-wife clothes in the back: my suit and a Sunday-go-to-meeting floral print dress for Margaret. We planned on hitting the place around 7 A.M., which in Patpong was like the dead of night. Everyone would be asleep.

Margaret dressed in good boots and loose, sturdy dark blue pants. She wore a long-sleeved shirt of the same material over her Kevlar vest. She had two SIG Sauers in shoulder holsters under each arm and a KA-BAR knife strapped to her lower back. While loading the pistols, she apologized for dressing light. "Defferre's contact couldn't get anything bigger."

I watched Margaret, thinking how dangerous she had become. Her small mouth was pursed in a grim line, thick, stubby fingers nimbly caressing the pistols, confident and knowing. She had always been the best shot of the three of us. "One of the best I've ever seen," bragged Bennet, who was usually stingy with compliments.

I kept the smaller caliber Beretta that Margaret had given me when I arrived in Bangkok. It was quiet and lethal, perfect for close work. Margaret would have to handle the heavy firepower. The Beretta fit snugly in a back holster; the KA-BAR sheath hung on my belt.

"Don't worry about me, Peg," I said. "If things get rough, get the kids. Don't open yourself up to flying bullets."

"Sid was doing her job," Margaret said evenly, eyes locked in mine. "She did the right thing." There weren't many secrets left when you spent as much time together training as hard as we did, sweated blood and pain together. I'd learned all about Margaret's husband and son; she'd heard about Sid. "Stray bullets are no one's fault." She slid a long, loose jacket on, covering her pistols and the knife.

I put on a pair of durable black jeans and a black T-shirt under my Kevlar. Damn stuff itched like hell. Over that I buttoned a dark gray, long-sleeved shirt of strong cotton. Inside the Kiddie House it would be dark while they slept. We hoped our clothes would make it harder to see us in the first few seconds. I strapped on a small leather backpack that lay flat just below my shoulder blades. Its main pouch was filled with extra rounds. The front pouch was empty. I slipped on a loose jacket, charcoal gray. We both wore tight-fitting black leather gloves.

At 7:00 A.M. we drove over to the alley behind Kiddie House. A back door led into the kitchen area. Margaret picked the lock and we stepped inside. She had both SIG Sauers drawn. I held my blade angled down against my forearm. Kitchen was clear. Lounge was clear. Stairs were clear. I led the way downstairs, hoping to quickly clean anyone we met. I kept my body sideways so Margaret had a clear shot.

A thickly built guy with a matching belly was sleeping face up on a sofa at the foot of the stairs. Knee on his chest, hand full of hair, I slid the knife into the side of his throat and pulled it toward me, slicing the vocal chords. A wheezing hiss filled the hall. He wouldn't wake up.

July had said their room was right next to the bathroom at the end of the hall, one of the privileges for being high dollar goods. The floor was cement, so we moved down the hallway with barely a sound. Next to the bathroom were two doors. The right door was steel and secured from the outside with a heavy padlock. We knew the kids would be in there.

The second door looked out of place. Heavy wood with a decorative braid hanging from a hook. Margaret took covering position in the center of the narrow hall and I tried the knob. It opened noiselessly. Whoever was inside didn't worry about visitors. I figured it was the elegant older woman in the foyer—she had control and didn't need locks.

She was in bed with a younger Thai, well-muscled and wrapped round her employer. There was a steel box on the dresser. Margaret nodded at me, then at the sleepers. I shut the door, crossed to the bed, and used the quiet .22 caliber.

Madam Elegant had a key dangling from her bracelet. It fit in the cash box. My first glance told me that just in yen, won and pounds there were thousands of dollars, not counting the other international currency. I dropped the long jacket, slid open my backpack and filled the front pouch. It might provide some needed grease on the drive down to Laem Ngop.

Jacket restored, I joined Margaret in the hall. She shook her head, pointing at the padlock. All the other doors in the hallway were padlocked. I leaned close, lips touching her ear as I mouthed, "All kids down here. The other skells are on the top floor." Margaret nodded and handed me one of her SIG Sauers. I walked down the hall, checking each door; then took position at the foot of the stairs. Margaret opened the bathroom door, stepped inside behind the door and aimed at the padlock. Ricochets could be nasty business. One shot and the lock was a crushed mess. The report was loud and we knew we wouldn't be alone for long.

Margaret opened the door. The two Thai teenage girls started screaming. I heard two dull thuds. Margaret had knocked them out. The other kids just stared. "Time to go. Don't get dressed," Margaret said. They obeyed. It broke our hearts how quickly they obeyed.

I ran up the stairs, stopping at the head. There was creaking above us. "Peg," I said and tossed her the pistol. "They're coming." She might need both high-powered pistols to watch our backs. I still had my Beretta and knife.

I ushered the children through the lounge, into the kitchen and out the back door to our waiting van. Not a peep from them, even Pearl, the five-year-old German girl who spoke no English. All their eyes were glazed, waiting to see what happened next. Margaret was right behind us. "They're on the way," she said, sliding behind the wheel. She'd been driving in Bangkok longer than me.

As I closed the doors in the back of the van, a bristling Thai ran out of the Kiddie House kitchen, machete lifted high in his right hand. Margaret took aim from the driver's seat, but he slid out of her line of sight behind the van.

He swung the machete down at my head. I stepped in and to the right of the attack, blocking the blow with my left arm. Then I swung my arm out over his; after that I twisted my forearm and hand back under his elbow, locking his arm against my body. He flinched in pain and yelled as I jerked his arm down. He lost his balance, head forward. I stepped and twisted forward, driving the heel of my right palm into his chin. He fell back against the van. I rammed a thumb into his eye.

"Race." It was Margaret. I stepped back as she pumped a round into him.

We had to get out of there fast or they would get us—and the kids. I heard the thud as we drove over the body as we backed out.

The silent, seemingly dazed kids obeyed when we told them to change into the clothes we had brought. They fit okay, a lot of pastels and loose pants. The contact had even thought to include ribbons for the girls' hair.

I switched into white shirt and slacks, blazer hanging on a hook in the back. I emptied the cash from the front pouch of the small backpack into my flight bag. We took Highway 3 down the east coast, a five hundred kilometer stretch of dismal beaches and obnoxious family resorts. We could smell the stench of the oil refineries for the first one hundred kilometers. The kids didn't seem to notice. Tommy started to weep quietly. The others simply stared.

We stopped at a small town on Highway 3, just outside of Pattaya Beach. Margaret was in the back of the van, changing into her floral print. Momma Preacher. We were standing by the back doors. The children got anxious and July finally spoke—the first one to do so since we left Bangkok. "Are you taking us to Pattaya, Daddy?"

"We're pretending I'm your father for this trip," I said patiently. "But I'm not your Daddy. You'll never have to call another man Daddy."

"We've been to Pattaya before," she said simply. Pattaya was the ugliest strip of gray beach in the world. Visibly polluted sea, trash-filled narrow beaches and sewage dumped straight into the bay. It also hosted the largest sex industry outside of Patpong, catering especially to Western tourists. "The children have been taken on day trips to 'Patpong-on-Sea' for special parties," Margaret observed, whispering to me.

"Not today, kids," I said. We climbed back in the van. As the Reverend Mister of the brood, I drove. Margaret stashed the backpack and work clothes in a metal box bolted behind the passenger seat.

After we passed Pattaya, our passengers started talking. The French and German children had developed a rudimentary mix of signals and broken English to communicate with the other kids. They had all been at Kiddie House since they were kidnapped from their homes, from holiday trips, wherever they had been alone long enough to be snatched. Bobby, the French boy, had been at Kiddie House for about three months; Tommy had been there four years.

Margaret spent the rest of the trip explaining that we were going on a boat ride, then to Malaysia. "After that, you're all going home," she said. The kids couldn't believe it. Maybe wouldn't believe it. But in the way of even the most battered children, they

couldn't stop themselves from clutching at even the slimmest
chance. Their hopes seemed to grow as Margaret encouraged and
reassured them.

"I told you before, Peg," I said a short while later during a
quiet spell, "A mother is always beautiful."

Finally we reached Laem Ngop. It was little more than a
wooden pier, one main road and a small collection of traditional
Thai houses inhabited by fishing families. Most of them were
Muslim. We locked up the van in front of an open lot off the main
road, a few blocks from the Thai Farmers' Bank. Margaret stuck
her SIG Sauers in a large matronly purse; I had my knife and
Beretta in the flight bag. We herded the kids to the pier head.
Margaret spotted a guy waving to us from one of the tourist information booths. I walked over alone.

"Trip for your family to Ko Chang Island today, sir?" He
was a small, slender seaman with thick black hair and scarred
hands. I guessed his age at somewhere between forty and ninety.

"Defferre," I coughed, hand over mouth, but knew he'd
heard me.

"Defferre said you would have keys for me," he replied.

I handed him the keys to the van and waved over Margaret
and the kids. The captain led us to his craft and we were on our
way.

Just outside Malaysia, Margaret and I dumped the
weapons overboard. Our captain was pained to see such quality
merch lost to the sea. We docked at Kuantan. The immigration
officer loomed over our family passports, frowning, until he
inspected my flight bag. The stolen jack was right on top. "I hate

that ugly bag," I said, turning my back. "Wouldn't care if I lost it someday."

Temporary visas approved.

Two of Defferre's people met us at the bus terminal. I immediately recognized the black leather jacket and close cropped brown hair of the tall Frenchman who had helped Bennet escort me to Archangel on my first day. His name was Jean.

"*Mes amis! Mes amis!*" he cried amicably, planting kisses on both Margaret and my cheeks. Jean was mid-forties and smiled at the kids like he was their long-lost uncle. He handed Margaret and me bus tickets. I nodded toward Bobby and Jean greeted the boy in French. Bobby beamed.

Jean's partner was a woman about his same age. She spoke German to Pearl, English to the other children. They both had a gentle way about them that seemed to comfort the kids.

July walked over to me, hand outstretched. I shook it. "Thank you," she said in her usual matter-of-fact tone. I looked at Margaret, wondering how this was affecting her. Dry-eyed and ready for more work.

We shrugged and headed to the bus queue.

"Wait!"

We turned. July and Tommy ran over, throwing their arms round Margaret's thick, floral-print-covered waist. "Is it really over? Are we really going home?" they asked.

"Yes, my darlings," she said, stroking their hair. "It's finally over."

Margaret and I bussed to the airport outside of Malaysia's capital, Kuala Lumpur. On the way, she turned to me, eyes distant and cold. "We can never change it all, you know. It will never be enough."

I nodded. "I know we left a hallway full of Thai kids in a country that enslaved them. But, Peg, at least we freed six who would still be there." It was a small victory amid the horror of which Conrad had once written with such razor-edged eloquence.

I looked out the window and thought about all the children, tortured and abused, forced to live behind padlocks.

seventeen

Masks

At the airport in Malaysia, I phoned Defferre. "I'm thinking I'd like a break, Jacques. Maybe go back to Seoul."

"To get information on Eunmi?" he asked hopefully.

"Not really."

"Ah, Shin the performance artist," Defferre's smile was easy to feel through the phone. "You could use some female company; the kind smile and tender gesture. You know, I believe our dearest Sidelle would approve." Everyone but Defferre tiptoed around Sid's death, perhaps out of respect and fear that I might fall apart if they mention it. This candor was Defferre's way, an odd mix of violence, manipulation, empathy and encouragement. "Enjoy some R&R."

After arriving in Seoul, I checked my account. Defferre had dumped in some extra cash for my leave. I still was using the Canadian businessman legend. I phoned Shin and we arranged to meet downtown that same afternoon. I wore a plain white long-sleeved shirt and gray cotton slacks, just like anyone meeting a pretty girl. As I was walking, I caught a glimpse of myself in a window. My hair was a nightmare; so I combed it right there on the street.

"I can't believe you!" Shin stepped up beside me, all smiles and remonstrations, speaking in Korean. Her conservative blue slacks and matching vest complimented her petite figure. The vest had a row of gold buttons that matched the tiny gold crucifix peeking from beneath her ivory blouse. Her long dark hair glistened in the late afternoon sun.

"Oh, yeah, right," I said. "Combing my hair in public is all rude and stuff. Sorry." Korean custom forbade such vanity.

She laughed. "Barbaric uncivilized Canadian!"

"Wait a sec, if combing my hair in public is rude, then why is it okay to urinate on the street?"

"That's only in the country!" Relieving oneself on side roads was a reality of life outside of Seoul.

"That's okay," I said, laughing. "In Canada it's rude to pick up your bowl and sip soup." I mimed the Korean method of cupping a bowl close to the mouth and shoveling in the food.

"Then how do you eat noodles?"

I held my arms low, slightly tipping an imaginary bowl away from me; then pretended to lift a shaking spoon to my lips. "Mostly we just spill a lot." We laughed at the oddities of different cultures.

Deciding on a nearby coffee shop, we walked around a corner and saw the street was full of college students in the middle of another riot. The students marched forward a few steps, most of them wearing headbands pronouncing the cause for this particular demonstration. The line of police, behind heavy shields and wearing Darth Vader helmets, announced through a megaphone in courteous formal language: "You may demonstrate here. Please do not advance forward."

The students advanced a few steps. The police moved back, repeating their injunction. "You may demonstrate here." Students moved forward; police stepped back. Finally the students reached the American embassy on Sejong-no, named after Korea's most famous and honored king. Sejong was credited with important civil reforms and the creation of the Korean alphabet, *hangul*, praised by linguists as the simplest and most scientific in the world.

At the embassy, the students planned to demonstrate against the presence of the thirty thousand United States troops in their country. Once again the police told them to move back. But this time as the students advanced, police fired tear gas, and there was an inevitable clash. The students screamed and tossed malatov cocktails; the police advanced with batons. Watching from a side street, I could tell many of the police were only half-hearted in their duties. The riot was dispersed; some of the students were arrested.

Shin and I hurried away, holding our breath and keeping our eyes closed until out of tear gas range. Our throats were sore the rest of the day.

"I know I'm a foreigner, but I have to ask." We sat at a small wooden table in a coffee shop, sipping tea. "Why didn't the students just demonstrate down the street? The cops said they were fine if they didn't move forward."

Shin stared at me like no one had ever asked that before. She shook her head. "I'm not sure. Perhaps because they can't throw firebombs from down the street."

"Fair enough," I nodded. "But why throw the firebombs? Why not just demonstrate, get a little attention from the newspaper, maybe get some signatures from citizens." By this I meant the middle class, who held more political power in Korea. College students may have pictured themselves as champions of civil rights, but without middle class support their voices were ignored. "After all, they riot every year. It's always something: democracy, anti-Americanism, reunification with North Korea. Those are all very important gripes— really I mean that. But it might be hard for people to take them seriously if they push the police so hard. Why not try a little cooperation?"

Shin bit her lower lip. "It's not the way they do it," she sighed. "I'm not really sure why."

I told her that as an outsider I could never really understand all the social factors that led to clashes like the one we just saw. "I'm really just asking, because I'm curious. I'm sure the students have good cause for what they did."

"It's all we've known for years," she said, smiling sadly, hand subconsciously toying with her crucifix. "First the Japanese, then the Korean War." Japan had annexed the entire peninsula from 1910 until the end of World War II in 1945. After just a few years of recovery, the Korean War began in 1950. "Since that war ended, the Americans have been here and our government has been corrupt. We've always had war and riots." Shin was sad; her deep brown eyes filled with passion and weariness. "It's seems like we'll never have any peace."

I suggested that her performance art might be about that very topic. She smiled, blissfully showing off her irregular but becoming teeth. I had long ago been told that, according to Korean tastes, my own irregular teeth were my most charming point. "It's my own small protest," she said, leaning close. "It's less violent and no one fires tear gas at the stage."

Shin and I saw each other almost every day for a couple of weeks. I attended her performances; we caught some local events, movies, dancing. A little romance flourished. I couldn't mention my day job or Sid, since I was using the Canadian businessman legend. So I tried to be pleasant and friendly without the whole heavy-duty, gasping, wanton *can't-live-without-you* routine. Shin didn't seem to mind.

Twice I tried to reach Hyung-Jin, but he wasn't around. He didn't have an answering machine and his mother—who always treated me with great kindness and respect—only knew that he was working out of town.

One day Eunmi and I met for a late lunch at the Gardenia restaurant, part of Hotel Lotte where I was staying. Her hair had recently been cut in a way that framed her face, random locks trailing casually across her rich, deep eyes down to lips tastefully dabbed with subtle mauve. A pale pink blouse complimented the overall affect. She didn't know how to reach Hyung-Jin, either. "But I hear you've got a new friend," she said a little harshly, then added, "She's Catholic, you know."

"Someone completely outside this dirty business, Eunmi." I ignored the Catholic remark. Eunmi knew that Sid was Catholic and that I had divorced myself from organized religion. Perhaps she was hinting that it would never work between a believer and someone like me.

Eunmi softened. "Is she sweet to you?"

"That's the word. Nothing more than that. Sid is still my whole world. Making friends with Shin is just" I shrugged lightly—"healing, I guess."

"Have you...?" Eunmi's voice trailed off.

"I wouldn't tell you if we had." Eunmi took that like a slap. Because she had always been a good friend to me, I added, "We're

just making friends, sort of romantic, too. We're just seeing how it
goes, nice and slow, right? *Sobak hage.*" Pure and simple.

Eunmi nodded. "That's the best type of date in the world,
Chanyoung." Her eyes lingered on mine. "How could she resist?"

"Hey, dozens of women have resisted me. Hundreds!" I
laughed, but it was true. Not that I felt like counting them. Eunmi
smiled wanly, pointing at her chest. "Not this one. I've never had as
good a friend as you."

Nice of her to say; it was perhaps true. Good friends were
hard to come by in our line of work.

Shin had a weekend gig in Osaka. "I've never been to Japan.
Want to come?" Before my return visit to Seoul, she had recently
finished a tour of southern Korean cities: Pusan, Masan, Taegu,
Kyongju. She had passed out fliers of her future performances in
Seoul and Japan during the tour, trying to stir up interest in her
work. Our few weeks together were as much a vacation for her as
they were for me.

We were in her apartment, an endearingly small place in a
high-rise north of Seoul. Shin's long hair was wrapped in a ponytail,
bouncing playfully over her ridiculously baggy shirt and mismatched
but equally baggy shorts. We had spent the morning re-arranging
her living room to hang a framed print of Pablo Picasso's *Le Repose*
that I gave her the night before. Picasso's works often touched me
deeply and the heady, swirling images of *Le Repose* seemed to exude
the effortless hope and unaffected sensuality that I sensed in Shin's
performance art.

She had decorated her apartment with traditional Korean
masks and fans. In the hall hung a small shadow box containing

coin-sized replicas of the wooden masks used in one of Korea's most treasured and ancient plays, dating back more than a thousand years: the *Hahoe Byolsin Exorcism*. It dealt with everyday people and the bitter irony of unrequited passion for love and art.

Shin had life-sized replicas of the masks on her walls. She took the shadow box from the hall. "The masks represent stock characters," she said. "And aspects of everyone's personalities." She pointed to each mask, describing the history of the play.

According to oral tradition, the Heo family settled in Hahoe village during the Koryo Dynasty, which lasted from 918 to 1392. A son of the Heo family was commanded by the gods to craft Hahoe wooden masks—a commitment to his art that forbade the love of women. He fell in love with a village maid that peeked into his workroom and—stuck in an impossible situation—poured all his deepest passions into the masks before dying of a broken heart. The mask dance and exorcism are performed to console his spirit, the ghost of an unfulfilled heart. The wooden masks used are housed in a sacred shrine and identified as National Treasures, along with the drama itself.

"When you travel," she said, presenting the shadow box as a gift. "You can remember these masks in my home and think of us."

I declined her offer to go to Osaka with her, saying I might catch some bookstores and museums on my own. I was in search of a Korean translation of my favorite novel, Tolstoy's *Anna Karenina*. "I'd like to read it, too," Shin said, then nestled close. I felt her crucifix press against my arm, her breath warm on my neck. "Maybe when I get back," she sighed, "we can read it together in bed."

Okay, maybe this was getting more serious than I thought. I resolved to think it over while she was in Osaka and either break it off when she returned—which didn't sound so good—or find a way to broach the nature of my occupation. I had been too selfish or too immature to accept that either we would get tired of each other—that happened often enough—or the time would come when our friendship would deepen and the truth had to be told.

I told her I'd make a point to get two copies of the book. "Reading them together sounds nice," I said sincerely. It did, too.

"I'll only be gone a few days," she smiled.

After a week, I started to worry. Shin hadn't come back. Defferre called, saying it was time for me to go back to work. I wanted to at least say goodbye to Shin; so I phoned the studio that represented her. They hadn't heard a word from her since the weekend performances. I got the name of the theater in Osaka and called there.

Shin had performed three times, as scheduled. The owner raved about the "raw power of her impassioned artistry." I agreed, then asked, "But have you heard anything from her?" He said no, but tossed out the name of her hotel. I called, saying in perfect Korean that I was her studio agent. They put on the hotel's Korean translator.

Shin had checked out the previous week. Five more days had passed since then. I phoned Defferre from my hotel room, spinning my mask shadow box on the slick bed comforter. "Missing person, maybe," I said. "How about someone in Osaka check it out for me?"

Defferre agreed, but was philosophical. "I'll send someone snooping around, but perhaps she found a friend and they are touring the countryside." He was being tactful. "These things happen, after all."

I looked at the masks, so many faces that each of us showed the world, always keeping our secret hearts hidden. One of my Japanese friends had told me that each of us has three hearts: the heart we show the world; the heart we share with our family, friends and lovers; and our secret true heart—the one the world never sees. "That could be, Jacques." I shrugged and said, "But I have an idea that she's not the type."

We rang off and I flipped through the channels on my hotel television, dozing off to some crappy historical drama. Later that night the shrill ring of the phone woke me.

"*Mon ami*, it is bad news," Defferre said. His voice was genuinely concerned.

"Did she get married or something?" Suddenly I felt a little jealous.

"*Non, non.* She is missing."

"*Muallago?*" I asked in Korean. *What did you say?*

"You're speaking in Korean. Get up, splash your face with water," advised Defferre. "You need to be awake for this."

Defferre laid out what his man in Osaka found out. Shin had returned to her room after her last performance. During the night she had received three calls before asking the concierge to block her line. Next morning she checked out, chatting with the doorman about how she loved flying as she waited for a taxi. The doorman remembered her good looks and vivacious personality. He helped her in a cab. She never arrived at the airport.

"That's it?" I asked, feeling helpless. Japan had 104 million people and Koreans were generally second-class citizens. Japan's sex trade—*Mizu Shobai*, or Water Business—was filled with Japanese, Thai, Filipino and Korean hookers—not all of them willing. It was run exclusively by the Japanese mafia, the *yakuza*. I told Defferre I wouldn't know where to start.

"There is an archangel deep in the yakuza, Race," Defferre assured me. "He asked around. No one has seen her. The Korean girls are usually imported hookers or kidnapped kids. Not famous artists."

Shin wasn't that famous yet, but I was hoping we wouldn't be seeing her in any Osaka headlines soon. Defferre said there was one small break: an abandoned Osaka cab just outside of the sprawling port city of Kobe. "It was reported stolen last week," Defferre added. It was impounded at Kobe. "Our man can get a peek inside."

"I'll join him."

A few hours later Eunmi knocked on the door, black leather jacket cinched over hastily thrown on clothes. "Short notice, but I think we've come up with something that will work." There was a boom market in Korea for smuggled Japanese torture porn—about the only porn they produced. The really rough stuff was illegal; so naturally people like Kon and Chong were selling it. I was on the outs with Chong, but Kon might be a possibility. I phoned him shortly after breakfast.

On hearing my name, Kon's man connected me right away. Kon greeted me like a long lost son. I laid it on thick. "My own stuff hasn't been paying so well," I lied. "I'm visiting a girl I know in Osaka and hoped you might have something you needed brought back."

"You still using the missionary routine?" he asked, all business.

"It never stops working. Do you perhaps have another suggestion, honored sir?" Kon had always liked my cover, that I was a missionary gone bad. He said he needed some videotapes brought in.

"If they don't need their original covers, I can slide them into

Christian video sleeves," I said. "Customs never plays them—probably don't want to hear the preaching."

The value dropped without the sleeves, but Kon would make numerous copies anyway. We discussed my share and the deal was set.

"When you going over?" he asked.

"Today."

"Can't wait to dip it into that little Japanese girl, huh?" Kon chuckled. "They say Japanese is the best for good health."

I endured a little more of that talk and we rang off.

Eunmi had my old missionary legend ready. She sounded genuinely upset, explaining that she hoped I might break up with Shin sooner or later, but not like this. "Too many Japanese are perverts," she said with unconcealed contempt. "Kill a few while you're over there." The centuries-old racial tension between Korea and Japan ran much deeper than her passing jealousy of Shin.

Archangel's man met me at the airport. He was about 5'4", stocky with a close-shaved head and one eye that was glazed white. His arms and neck were covered with tattoos. Yakuza traditional. "Call me *Musashi*," he said in English.

"No shit?" I laughed. Musashi was a seventeenth century swordsman famous for winning over seventy lethal duels. He had written a treatise on his philosophy of fighting and living so close to death called *Gorin no Sho*, *The Book of Five Rings*. I'd read the book and loved it. Archangel's man used Musashi as a nickname. "Then you can call me Osugi!" I said, naming the embittered old hag that made Musashi's life hell in famous fictionalized accounts of his life. The characters were well known to Japanese audiences.

On the way to Kobe, I mentioned my errand for Kon.

"I know the guy that supplies him," said Musashi. "Gimme some cash."

Musashi would say that I had been eager for some Japanese sweet stuff when I arrived and he met me while delivering a girl. When he brought her, I told him why I was in town. The cash did double duty as proof that I paid for the girl and respect money before the meeting. "This way I'll be there if things go sour." Musashi had a girl that would say anything we needed. I laid out some extra jack for her pockets, too.

Musashi spoke fluent English—much better than my Japanese. "College at UCLA," he said; then pointed at his tattooed arm. "Before these." I asked if he could get me a good knife. "We'll find one in Kobe," he said.

At Kobe, we ate at a little restaurant that specialized in private booths. It was on busy Hamabe Street, just down the road from the Municipal Building. Musashi's cover in the yakuza provided lots of contacts with the police. An off-duty cop walked by, dropping a bag next to Musashi's seat. We ignored it until the cop was out of the building.

"This is the stuff they found in the taxi," Musashi said. We closed the curtain to block off our booth and poured these items out: the remains of a roadside *yakitori* box with some chunks of chicken and bamboo skewers left inside, a bus ticket stub from Yonago to Osaka.

And a tiny gold crucifix.

eighteen

COMMUNION

Musashi and I sprinted to the depot the minute we connected the crucifix with the Yonago bus ticket. We arrived in Yonago by bus later that day.

Yonago surrounded a patch of sand called Sakaiminato, the north side of which faced the Shimane peninsula. It was near the *Kaike* thermal spa, which boasted saline springs as warm as 180 degrees. On the west, Yonago overlooked the Naka Umi lagoon and on the east, the spa overlooked Miho Bay. It all rested under the majestic Daisen Mountain.

Musashi asked around. Taxpayers didn't care for his tattoos, but we weren't looking for a solid citizen. At the spa, one of the lower *yakuza* ran the local brothel. He knew a guy who was saying he had a Korean girlfriend. Seemed that the guy was hinting around about selling some sex pictures to the brothel customers.

"She wasn't with him, but the guy is from around here," Musashi related to me. "Stays at a farm a few miles down." I hoped that I wouldn't be in Japan if the yakuza ever wanted me. No one could hide. We walked over.

The guy's farm was about three acres of rice land terraced into a hillside. At the bottom was his house, a small box-like cement shack. We waited a while; then the guy wandered out to his rice fields. He wore a tan long-sleeved shirt and work pants rolled up to his knees for wading in the rice paddies. His hair was thick, black, hanging in his eyes.

"Go talk to him, see what you can find out," I suggested. "If he isn't forthcoming, slap him around a little." Musashi's one good eye squinted, hard and ready. He stripped off his shirt, tightly muscled body covered with tattoos. The guy would probably faint when he saw him.

Musashi wandered over, stopped the guy on a patch of solid ground at the foot of the rice terraces. I tested the house door. It wasn't locked. Inside, there was a kitchen with fridge and freezer, small table and a wooden chair. The main room was dominated by a large television with VCR. A single wooden chair from the kitchen table faced the television.

Quickly I covered the rest of the place. Two bedrooms were filled with religious icons—crosses and pictures of Jesus on the walls. There was lots of sports stuff, like ball bats and mitts, pictures of Japanese players. I knocked on the walls, pounded the floors. Cement. The place was empty.

"*Aiiiya!*" A male voice screamed. I looked out the window. The guy was on the ground, holding his arm at an odd angle and Musashi was fending off a huge dog. It was a mix between big and bigger. Musashi's right pant leg was ripped open, blood flowing. He kicked the dog on the snout. It skittered back, yelping and snarling, keeping its distance. I grabbed a wood baseball bat and ran out.

Up close the dog was matted and had blood on its lips and

fur. Seeing the bat, the dog ran up the hill and out of site. I got to Musashi just as the guy stood up. He leapt, kicking Musashi across the chin. Unbelievably fast, he didn't telegraph it at all.

Musashi fell, dazed. Blood was pouring from his leg where the dog attacked him. He shook his head and tried to stand. The guy kicked him again. His one arm was clearly broken—Musashi had done that much damage—but his feet were a blur of pain. Musashi hit the dirt face down and was trying to rise just as I spun the bat at his attacker's legs.

The guy dodged and backed up. I weighed the bat in my hand, waiting for him to come in my circle. I'd never seen anyone so fast. His knees were bent slightly. Suddenly he jumped up at me, rotating his hips, right knee cocked. His foot slashed out. I pulled my head to the side and his heel crashed onto my shoulder as his foot came down. I stumbled back, bat poised. My shoulder screamed at me.

He gave me an opening and I swung the bat low at his left knee. Just as I closed the arc, his leg flashed out sideways, hitting the bat insignia. The wood broke in two.

I shifted my weight, adapting to the new shorter weapon. The guy lifted his right knee and I shifted sideways as he landed a heel in the side of my stomach—it had been meant for my chest. In the same movement, he squatted, turned counter clockwise on his right knee and rammed his left foot into my shin. If he had hit my knee, it would have snapped like the ball bat. My shin kicked out from under me and I fell to my knees, dropping the broken bat handle.

He stood and rushed forward. I reached up, grabbing his broken wrist with my left hand and his upper sleeve with my right. My right foot kicked outside his left leg. I yanked his hurt arm to the left, tripping him over my foot. His arm was loose and squishy. He fell with a hard thud.

I scrambled to the broken bat handle, standing and turning toward him. He was already on his feet, facing me. He angled in for a quick sidekick. I stepped into it, taking the brunt against my left side and grabbed his belt. I pulled his waist toward me as I rammed the handle's broken tip into his throat, pressing his neck back and forcing him to the ground.

The guy lay gasping, throat bruised and swelling, but not ripped open. He was still alive. Musashi stumbled over, shaking his head. His good eye looked clear. "Kill him," he said.

"In a minute. You wrap up that leg." Musashi looked down, seeing the dog's teeth marks for the first time. The blood had already started to coagulate around the tattoos on his leg. I shook my head. "You're gonna need a shot for that."

Musashi nodded and plopped his butt down on the guy's chest, causing an aching groan.

"Good thing you broke his wrist." I stripped my shirt and handed it over. "I couldn't have taken him without an edge."

Musashi wrapped my shirt round his ankle. "Pervert. Farmer. Asshole," he muttered, punctuating each word with a kick to the guy's broken arm. The guy's breath was getting short. Musashi stood up. I leaned over the guy.

"You know a Korean girl?" I asked.

The guy's eyes flicked to a steel shed at the other end of the rice field, then back to me. He didn't move. I ground his broken arm with my foot. "In the shed?"

His mouth moved but no sound came out. His throat was still swollen from the bat handle blow.

Musashi ran to the shed, stepped in the door for a few seconds, and then sprinted back. "She's over there," he panted. "I think."

Musashi grabbed the guy's bad arm. I took the other and we dragged him to the small building. A meager wood frame supported the shed's thin steel walls. Farm tools and rope hung on large hooks. A tripod and video camera in the corner looked oddly out of place.

A thick wooden trap door lay open, a padlock beside its heavy latch. I dropped the broken handle and looked down. A short ladder led into a cement square room, maybe eight-by-eight. Inside were some freshly gnawed bones, what looked like a human leg and bloody clothes. I recognized the gold buttons on Shin's blue vest.

I scrambled up the ladder.

"Where is she?" My voice was more of a desperate groan than a scream. The guy just stared. His throat was returning to normal. Musashi took a hatchet from the wall and swung it at the guy's crotch. He squealed. His throat was working fine now. Blood spread quickly.

"Nowhere!" he screamed. "Nobody! Nowhere! Nothing!"

I ran to his house, leaving Musashi to keep working. Inside, I tore apart the bed, the closets, everything. In the kitchen, I drew up short. The fridge was huge; next to it was a horizontal freezer about the same size. My teeth ground in bitter anguish and my head was dull, throbbing with terrible certainty.

I opened the fridge.

Shin was there. Head and arms in metal pans. Her eyes were gone. I slammed the door and gagged. Nothing came up. I lifted the heavy freezer lid. The rest of her was chopped and wrapped up inside. The freezer door fell as I stumbled outside and retched until my throat bled.

Musashi patted me on the back, lifting me up. I told him what I found in the house. He waved the bloodied hatchet toward the shed. The door was closed and the huge dog was back, whining and pawing at the wall.

"He wouldn't talk," Musashi explained. He mimed hacking the guy's legs. "He was bleeding really bad, so I tied off his legs with some rope. Be dead within an hour, probably."

"Down in that room," I gasped. My throat was raw, words a harsh rasp. "You think those were her legs?"

"He must have fed the dog what he didn't want," Musashi said in a low monotone. The dog had found a hole on the lower part of the metal door, pushing his bulk through a small opening. He was halfway there.

"Dog's hungry," I said. The animal's hind legs gave one final heave and disappeared inside the shed. The screams went on and on. Then they stopped.

"Yeah, snack time." Musashi said.

Musashi and I looked over the guy's house. The fridge and freezer loomed like a dark sore oozing into my mind, but we had to find out what happened to Shin, what else this freak had been up to.

His name was Shingo. A top row in the cabinet next to the large television was filled with homemade videotapes. There were over a dozen. The side sticker of each tape had an obscure, convoluted Japanese name, month/day and a number. Musashi translated some of the names: "*Cherry Blossom Falling On Oil Slick. Monkey Crawls Into Hell. God Sees the Thorny Cavern.*" We slid one tape with an older date into the VCR. The title read, "*Happy Hands Opening Demon Candy Wrapper,*" and had a number 12 in the corner of the sticker. It was a girl of about twelve or thirteen, shivering naked in what looked like Shingo's little cement room in the shed. We turned it off.

"Why is it always the *kids*?" I asked, so far beyond disgust that my whole body was numb. The fridge sat grim and accusing, almost taunting me.

"It's our karma," answered Musashi. "Everyone at Archangel has the same karma."

We spotted a tape dated a few days before. "*Screaming Whore of Light*," and the number 26. My hands didn't even shake as I slid it into the VCR. It was a bootleg of Shin's performance at an Osaka theater. Bad sound and you could barely see her, but there was no doubt. Then the camera zoomed to her face and the image started shaking. Fuzz filled the screen. A new picture rolled into view: Shin standing naked in the cement room. She was screaming in Korean for God to save her. Shingo came into view, wearing a black mask. Musashi went into the bedroom.

I watched the whole thing.

When it ended, I stared at fuzz. Musashi gripped my shoulder. "Look at this," he said, lifeless. It was an envelope addressed to the groundskeeper of a catholic church in Taegu, South Korea. Inside was a tape with a plain sticker that read, "*Holy Communion*." Musashi slid it into the VCR. Shin's tape.

"Too bad I can't take the dog with me to Taegu," I said, and horribly, we laughed, a dark and bitter release. We took the envelope with Shin's tape and left.

Musashi would come back later with a cleaning crew. The tapes would be sent to Archangel and finally to Interpol for the painful process of connecting the images with missing persons in Japan and other countries.

Musashi and I met with Kon's supplier and made the deal without a problem. We wrapped the tapes in Christian videotape sleeves and I flew into Pusan the same day. After stopping at my condo for a good knife, I took the late bus to Chunju. First thing in the morning, Kon took the merchandise and paid what he owed. After what happened, the Japanese porno tapes should have burned my hands, but I was moving in that nebulous world of non-feeling that Archangel had drilled into us. Kon asked if I was interested in more work.

"Right now I have to go to church," I said.

I hopped a bus to Taegu. The envelope was addressed to Choi Sangki, Groundskeeper, care of a medium-sized catholic church in north Taegu. I took a room next to the bus depot. Next morning, I dressed in a conservative suit and found my way to the church. Taegu had some Caucasians, but not enough to stop using some sort of legitimate cover. An American or Canadian in a suit gave the impression of a missionary or a businessman.

I entered the church and genuflected, then sat down in a pew. A large crucifix loomed over the room, reminding me of Shin's performance and the gold icon she always wore. I still had it in my pocket.

Signs listed the hours of confession and the priest's office hours. It was mid-morning and the church would be almost empty for the next few hours. A blind Korean woman was sitting close to the front, old, gray hair wrapped in a scarf. I moved to her side.

"Pardon me, Honored Grandmother," I said. "Do you know how to reach the priest when he is not in his office?"

She smiled, showing only a few teeth, but pleased to talk. "*Cha* and aren't his hours posted?"

The woman assumed I was Korean. I told her I was visiting from Yosu—a small coastal town—and didn't know the diocese. "Perhaps the groundskeeper can help me get in touch with a priest?"

"Groundskeeper Choi lives here; he's always around," she said, tilting her head as she listened. "*Aigo*. Where could he be?" She took a moment, sliding her finger on the smooth wood of the pew in front of her. "Well, and so. And so again. Where then? He's either cleaning inside the building, outside tending the flowers, which I just love and smell every time I come to visit, or he may be in his personal apartment." She pointed up, wrinkled finger waving. "In the upper rooms."

She let me in on all the gossip. Seemed that the local priest was well respected in South Korea. People came all the way from Seoul and Japan to meet and pray with him. "He is the confessor for many great people in Korea. Businessmen, government officials, singing stars and artists."

My throat caught. As with many of the blind, she noticed a change in my demeanor that sighted people might have missed. "Are you all right, brother?" she asked.

"I'm overwhelmed with a need for confession," I said.

She patted my arm, concerned and supportive. "Then you've come to the right place."

The confessional was closed. I slipped inside and looked around the dark interior. In the upper corner I spotted a tiny black piece of plastic, no larger than a dime. I pulled. A slim black wire was attached. It was a cheap microphone that cost about three dollars at any electronics store. Outside the confessional, a slim black wire led through a barely discernable hole in the wall. Easy to miss.

The other side of the wall was a hallway with offices. There were no wires that I could see. I slid my finger along the smooth wall surface, near the floor. There was a slight ridge, like for a cubby. I pressed. Nothing. Slipping my knife from under my suit jacket, I pried at the ridge. A section of wood about one-foot square slid out of the wall. Behind it rested an inexpensive tape recorder. It was a large older model that loaded tapes at the top, with large buttons on the front. It was empty.

To record confessions, someone had to open the panel and press the record button. The whole setup—no matter how cheap the equipment—took someone with time, tools and legitimate access to the church. Like a groundskeeper.

I replaced the panel. At the end of the hall, a stairway led to the upper floors. I took the steps two at a time to the third floor. There were a number of doors, most of which were unlocked. I peered in: storage and heavy dust. Near the back of the hall there was a door that had a cheap, framed picture of Jesus. Beside the door was a hand-written sign: "Groundskeeper's Quarters."

I picked the lock and stepped in. Empty. The room was spare: a small television, VCR, medium-sized bed and small writing desk. A full bookcase was mounted to the far wall. By the window was a worn easy chair, its padding sticking out on the arms and back.

A cassette player, similar to the cheap model I'd found downstairs, sat on top of the desk. There were no cassettes. I rummaged through the desk. Groundskeeper Choi's address book was filled with names and places of churches, local hardware and grocery stores, nothing I recognized. When I got to the Korean equivalent of "P," I noticed an entry under Pusan. Chong's little black market shop. I tore out the page and stashed it in my pocket.

The bookcase held mostly Korean paperback novels of the self-important, artsy type. A few mysteries. No cassettes. Floor was spotless under the bed. Old chair cushions held no surprises.

A small hall adjoined the main room. The bathroom with squatter was on one side. Opposite the bathroom was a small compartment. The floor was stacked with books. Most of them were used paperbacks and covered with dust. In the middle of the room sat a wooden chair with a broken leg supported by more books. Against the wall, a massive tome inscribed with Chinese-Korean characters caught my eye. It was covered by the other less-ornate books and seemed out of place. I pushed the cheap books away and opened the large book.

The inside pages had been hollowed out. It was filled with cassette tapes. I flicked through, noting that some were blank and others had stickers with names scrawled in sloppy handwriting. Small groups were rubber banded; some singles were taped to photos. One cassette was wrapped inside a sheet of blue paper. I unfolded it.

It was Shin's flier promoting her future performances in Seoul and Japan. An image of a Korean War battlefield was juxtaposed behind Shin's lithe figure in a black one-piece body suit. The photo must have been snapped while she was performing—her face was alive with passion and commitment. I hadn't seen this flier before. Seeing the image tore into my heart, but it was how I wanted to remember her. I tenderly folded the paper so the creases didn't mar her face and slid it into my suit pocket.

I popped the cassette in the player on the desk. Shin's voice filled the room. "Forgive me..." I clicked it off before hearing another word. Her confession was sacred, a very private devotion between herself and her God. I had watched the videotape of her brutal death, because I hadn't been there to help her. She had asked me to accompany her to Japan and I declined. Guilt and a need for vengeance drove me—two emotions that had long been my companions. But listening to her confession on tape would have been a violation of her spiritual being—another form of rape for which the groundskeeper must answer.

Removing Shin's cassette from the player, I ripped the delicate tape from its plastic housing and flushed it down the squatter. I dumped the remaining tapes on the floor in the side room. Easy to find.

The apartment had a conspicuous absence of holy items. I took Shin's crucifix from my pocket and tenderly kissed it. Popping the tape of her murder into the VCR, I let it run a little with the sound off. When I got to the part I wanted, I shut off the television. I removed my tie and jacket, sat in the corner—and waited.

Late that night I heard the latch twisting. I turned on the television. An image of Shin being brutally cut flickered in the dark room. Choi, the groundskeeper, entered. He was full bellied, tall, with slight graying at the temples. He shut the door behind him and was taking off his sturdy work jacket before he noticed the television.

"Shingo?" he asked the dark. He recognized his pal's work. That was enough for me.

I stepped from the heavily shadowed corner and held the thick handle of my knife to his throat. He gasped, mouthing words without sound, hand raised. He turned to the door. I tripped him onto the bed, his face buried in a pillow. My knife sliced the tendon of his inner right arm. A tiny squeak from the pillow. I flipped him over and stuck the blade into his mouth.

"Look," I said.

I used the knife to guide his head toward the television. Made him watch a little; then guided him back to look at me.

"You knew her?"

He nodded.

"You told Shingo to nab her?"

Nod.

"Why?" I slid out the knife.

His tongue was bleeding and his eyes roved up and down, looking through me, terrified, uncomprehending. "Whore," he said.

I cleaned him slow.

Two days later I walked into Chong's black market shop, through the glass door, all the way to the back. He was with his bodyguard. Chong's guy may have been tall or short, fat or skinny. At that moment, I didn't pay attention. I popped two rounds into his head with my Beretta 92FS, so close that even I couldn't miss.

Chong stood, cigarette dangling in his hand. I caved his knee with a sidekick and he fell onto his little sofa. I rammed the barrel into his mouth.

"Choi Sangki," I said slowly. Chong stared back, confused. I said the name again, slower, emphasizing each syllable by pressing the pistol deeper into his throat. He gagged and I pulled it out.

His leg was swollen and he started to rub it. "Kon sent you?" Tears were streaming down his face.

He wasn't getting it. I kicked his twisted leg again. He screamed.

"Choi Sangki. He paid you for something. What was it?"

"Girls. He had me send hookers to Osaka. That's all. He'd pay big bucks; so they could work over there."

I thought of telling Chong that he was too evil to live. Instead, I shot him three times.

I took the train back to Seoul and stumbled into my room at the Hotel Lotte. The phone rang.

"You are back at last?" asked Defferre.

I laid it all out, talking in the vague way we always did.

Defferre let me finish, then said, "Musashi told me some. He thought you might go to Taegu." He sighed. "Did you leave something for my contact in the Taegu police?"

"Groundskeeper was taping confessions and setting up victims for his boy in Japan. Shin's trip was just a lucky break for them. I left the cassettes on the floor."

"Did he have any other videos?" asked Jacques.

"Couldn't find any. I left Shin's in the VCR. But they should look in the walls." I explained about the secret panel and the confessional setup. "It should be enough."

"*Oui*," Defferre said. There was a long pause. "We can use Chong's poor appearance to improve your standing with Kon."

"Good idea, Jacques." I wasn't being facetious. I had become everything Archangel trained me to be. Defferre sighed again, as unable as me to find the right words. "My friend, some very bad men are gone. You have done your job well. Come back soon."

"Thanks. Will do."

We rang off and my eyes fell on the shadow box full of masks. I clutched it to me, pressing the smooth glass to my face. *Exorcism Masks*. Would Shin's soul rest in peace? "Oh God, oh Sid, Shin, God help us all." Moans and tears poured from me: an unanswerable flood of loss.

Seconds or minutes later, there was a knock on the hotel door. I stumbled over, listening. "Let me in." Eunmi.

I opened the door and she fell into my arms, beautiful eyes weeping. "Jacques told me everything."

We held each other all night, skin and tears blending deep, deeper, until our sorrows intertwined.

nineteen

FORGOTTEN SEASON

Back at Archangel, William, Margaret and I continued advanced training for new, more dangerous and complex missions. William said I was crazy and avoided me; Margaret thought I was the best partner imaginable. Maybe they both were right.

We practiced on man-shaped dummies and targets. My shooting improved a little. When Archangel first trained us, they used words like "engaging" the target—meaning "kill." Now the phrasing didn't matter. Kill. Clean. We rehearsed every aspect of killing, visually, physically and psychologically conditioning ourselves even more.

Denial and shutting down emotions were my defense mechanisms for dealing with everything since Sid died. Now we rehearsed the act of killing another human being until it became a process. With realistic mimicry and practice, death lost meaning. The actions were performed automatically, in the state of "no-mind" that constant training provides. "No-mind" was a term coined in the real Musashi's *Book of Five Rings*. It was a concept we understood all too well.

Defferre and Bennet pushed us harder and harder. They emphasized that those we cleaned were "evil beasts" that preyed on helpless children. Their removal was completely justified and should be performed without regret. This form of induced contempt—coupled with denial, training, and moral repugnance at the acts committed by these devils—was reinforced every time we "killed" a dummy or man-shaped target.

Defferre joined us in training at times. "We work under Archangel's authority," he said, completely sincere. "We have civil and moral authority." To emphasize this, we also practiced with targets of children mixed in with the male figures on the shooting range and we were severely sanctioned if we hit the smaller targets.

Defferre came into my room late one evening after training. I was sipping lemonade, listening to *Karn Evil 9 1st Impression* by Emerson, Lake and Palmer.

I had tried thinking about nothing, but it always turned into uncontrolled memories of the woman I had loved. So I tried to deal with my loss in my own way—a bad idea, but it was all I had. Most nights I spent reliving every moment of my eight months with Sid up to the last few seconds. In comparison, listening to music that evoked memories of Shin was a relief. *Karn Evil* didn't remind me of Seyong and the horror I had witnessed; the progressive music took me back to the beauty of Shin's performance.

"*Do not rape me,*" she had said.

Defferre and Archangel were riveted on their goal. Their reaction to psychologically traumatic events which occurred in its enactment was to train us to dispense justice whatever the cost. They encouraged emotional blunting to personal tragedies and a heightened sense of moral outrage within the Archangel structure. Recurrent nightmares, due to the horror of past experiences, even when these involved the brutal death of a loved one, were, according to Archangel to be subjugated to the ultimate goal: ridding the world of these menaces who had no respect for humanity and preyed on the innocent. One's emotional traumas were utilized to remove societal inhibitors against killing, thus turning us into better cleaners. Music and not purposefully recalling gave me fleeting moments of peace away from the inner battle I waged with my agitated conscience.

"This is progressive rock," I informed Defferre. He listened but had some trouble with the lyrics. I wrote them out and he read them carefully, pocketing the sheet of paper. He appreciated the relevance.

"Who's your favorite writer, Race?" Defferre asked suddenly. He did that when he wanted to shake me out of a mope.

"Tolstoy," I said. "Dickens, Edgar Rice Burroughs, Shakespeare. That's who I read the most."

"What, no Dumas?"

I'd read *Three Musketeers* as a kid. *Man In the Iron Mask. Count of Monte Cristo.* I enumerated them for him.

"Ah! Then you know all about revenge!" Defferre beamed, proud of the greatest writer that ever lived—in his opinion.

"We don't need Dumas for that, Jacques."

Defferre nodded. "True, true, but from Dumas we can also learn about justice." Defferre walked over to the Master of Kungfu poster, considering the word. "You see how this character is fighting for justice? He is valiant and noble and each month can find an answer to the problems before him." Defferre turned, face suddenly weary, eyes deeply shadowed. He slid his hand through the only part of him that didn't sag—his Bogey cut. "But for us there are no easy answers. Our friends and loved ones die. We may die. And the beasts will still go on."

"Not if we clean them all," I said. I didn't care if it was impossible. Archangel owned my soul.

"*Bon*," said Defferre, looking up into my eyes. "So it shall be."

Defferre set up our assignments with local police, intelligence agencies, any group that was willing to work with Archangel. We either sneaked into a country under false legends or were escorted through immigration by Defferre's contacts. After we rid the world of one menace, the local contacts stepped in to ensure that damning evidence was all around the bodies. These skells liked to collect pictures of themselves with the kids, so evidence of their heinous crimes was plentiful.

When I asked him, Defferre explained it like this: "Except for a few countries, no one wants these animals within their borders. But they are very hard to catch. They keep their secrets locked away; they obey the laws so police cannot search for their hidden treasures of pornography. They nurture connections high in their own governments. They cross borders to take children in other countries. They play their tricks so cleverly. Our contacts are glad to see them disappear from their cities—and glad to have someone else do the cleaning."

Next I went to Marseilles. Marc, our target there, had spent his life following children home and pleasuring himself outside their bedroom windows. Finally, he started taking some kids back to his house, using them, taking pictures. He sold the photos.

Two missing children were last seen near his apartment, but nothing could be proved. I tagged him talking to a child at a park near the Vieux Port. The little girl took his hand and walked around with him. He took her behind some bushes. She was maybe nine.

"Go home, sweetie," I said, smiling and looking so like a young puppy that Marc took a swing. I dodged and the girl ran away.

I shoved the blade through his eye and then deeper. He screamed, but I was long gone.

In Ghana, fat Christopher was a buyer for a United States aluminum corporation. He liked African children and had no problem buying them on his trips, too. He sold the tapes of their rapes to all his pals back in California. Two of the tapes showed up at a skell's place that William cleaned. I made pals with Christopher as a fellow buyer; I even had my certification. We toured a raw alumina mine. Christopher slipped and fell on the track, right in front of a cart loaded with ore. Perhaps it was divine justice or he was just unlucky. He spent a week in the hospital before he died.

William was on an assignment in Germany when Christine pointed at her seven-months-pregnant belly and begged for mercy. William paused and she pumped five rounds into his head and chest. Christine ran a daycare center where men could come during the day and use the kids for high prices. Christine liked to join in. An archangel caught some of it on camera through a side window. It took Margaret and I months to catch up with Christine in Switzerland after she killed William. We played rock-paper-scissors for the privilege. I won.

In Brazil we singled out a pimp who dressed up little boys as women. Bras with padding and everything. Kiddie transvestites for sale. I boosted a van and picked him up on a street corner. He smelled like sour milk, giggling over his pictures. He had them cross-referenced with little tags and dividers. He was easily pushing 275 pounds. Defferre had hoped that the guy might roll over on his customers, but I just couldn't stand breathing the same air with this freak a second longer. I cleaned him quick. Brazilian nights are hot and his sour milk smell quickly turned to *eau de putrid-trash-heap*. When I finally dumped the van with him in it, I had to burn my clothes.

My next stop was to be Korea, where Hong Kihwan, a doctor, used a small bag of surgical tools to deform children without killing them. He had almost exclusive access to kids in an ignored orphanage outside Masan. Most Korean orphanages were ignored. He examined a child, pronounced him deathly ill with cancer and amputated away. All over their bodies.

Before going to Masan, I stopped in my Pusan condo. I was cooking dinner when I got the idea to try to call Hyung-Jin again. He answered this time.

"Long time," I said.

"I've been hearing about you."

"Guilty," I said without humor.

"Yeah, you are." Hyung-Jin let a long second drag between us. "We've been following Eunmi. I know you slept with her."

"She said you broke up."

"Yes," Hyung-Jin laughed, bitter. "Unfortunately we found out she's cozy with some North Korean spies. At least, that's what it looks like."

I told him that I didn't know anything about North Korean spies. "Last North Korean I saw put holes in Sid." We talked it over a little. I tossed him a nibble about Defferre's thoughts on Eunmi. Then I added, "Eunmi and I—our friendship—it's pretty messed up."

"Just don't get in the way when we take her down."

We rang off and I headed to Masan. Dr. Hong kept a little cot in his office at the orphanage so he could sleep there when he worked late. It was a balmy night, so he had his fan running high and the window open. No locks to pick. I slipped in and almost cleaned him in his sleep; then I spotted an ether mask. His sleep got a lot deeper. I strapped him onto his table and went to work.

Back in Pusan, I took inventory: need milk; sharpen knife; write the folks. I thought briefly about calling Defferre, maybe Eunmi or even Hyung-Jin. Once again I was wracked by guilt and uncertainty over all that I had become. Was all this justified? Had Archangel made me as bad as those I was eliminating? Who would help these poor innocent children if not those consumed by this mission? I pushed my thoughts down by popping in a favorite tape and cranking the volume. Lee Yong's *Forgotten Season* always took me down the streets of Marseilles, into the arms of Sid:

Even now I remember October's closing eve:
When we were forced to part,
And only words we couldn't say were left between us.

The lyric speaking of the coming autumn and lonely dreams brought back my loss.

I cannot forget.
My heart is broken.

I dozed as the song played and dreamed of Sid. And begging God to forgive me and bring her back. The phone woke me. I had to remember to turn it off when I wanted sleep. Which was never. It was Defferre.

"It is confirmed," he said, assuming I knew what he was talking about. "Good job. Well done."

"What?" I said, still half in a dream state.

Defferre paused; then the light dawned. "Ah! I must explain. I'm speaking of Eunmi." It seemed that Defferre and Hyung-Jin were right all along. Eunmi was helping the North Koreans. "The NIS taped a phone conversation in which she and a known North Korean intelligence operative let slip a meeting place. The NIS team then bugged the meeting place and Eunmi's guilt was without question," Defferre said.

North Korea's National Intelligence Committee of the Central Committee of the Korean Workers Party (NIC)'s primary agency for foreign intelligence gathering was the Research Department for External Intelligence (RDEI). The RDEI had four subsections assigned to as many geographic regions, including North America. The largest subsection was devoted exclusively to South Korea. The NIC controlled some 1,500 agents; it was estimated about 200 were in South Korea at any given time. In the 1970s, North Korea began clandestine tunneling operations along the entire Demilitarized Zone (DMZ) between North and South Korea. Three tunnels were discovered by the South Koreans. Twenty-eight more were suspected.

North Korea primarily relied on human source intelligence for gathering of data in South Korea. They had limited capability to intercept communications and electronic transmissions and so depended on intelligence gathered by agents or informers such as Eunmi. Usually they recruited agents by appealing to the overwhelming sympathy for reunification between North and South Korea. Eunmi's family was split during the Korean War and there were uncles and grandparents she would never meet, because they were living above the 38th Parallel. I suspected they had manipulated her natural inclinations into assisting them with intelligence activities.

"Where do you think I fit into the picture?" I asked slowly.

"She is an Interpol officer, Race," Defferre said. "She knows of Archangel. I want you to bring her here."

Simple enough. I had the feeling she'd follow me anywhere if I just asked nicely. I packed an overnight bag and reserved a quick flight up to Seoul for the next morning. I rummaged through my night stand until I found the letter old Woo Yonggak—the Taejon political prisoner since 1958—had asked me to deliver to his son in North Korea. If Eunmi's pals cornered me, the letter might be handy to buy some time. Or after all the smoke cleared, maybe we could trick, bribe or coerce one of Eunmi's contacts and use the letter to our advantage. Defferre or Hyung-Jin might have some ideas on how best to exploit the situation.

I sighed. Old questions of good and evil collided in my mind for a few moments. Once again I pushed them away and readied myself for another mission.

My father was a Korean War veteran. As I rode in the taxi from Kimpo airport to Seoul, the coincidences of our times in Korea struck me with acidic irony.

Looking out the window, I saw a farmer with a modern tractor beside another tract of land being plowed by an old man behind an ox. My dad had written of a similar scene that he witnessed over thirty years before: "One night during one of the interminable air raids, we were all in holes in the ground surrounded by sandbags. While across the fence an old Korean man couldn't sleep with all the racket so he hoed in his garden." My dad became friends with the gardener's son, but lost other friends. "After the 'armistice,'" he wrote, "I saw a good friend shot to deaths as we were moving to Osan-ni from Seoul." Even as I was riding in a taxi to Seoul myself, there were still 33,000 American troops in South Korea. *Which armistice was that?* Dad may have wondered.

"Black market. Illegal," Dad wrote of his time in Korea during the war. "US dollars and Brut LB Stirling were the only currency worth anything. Sell them and you could bet they would come back in the form of bullets from the North." Two North Korean bullets took Sid from me. Dad and I both shed tears and sweat in Korea, perhaps linking us, father to son, son to father, in a terrible way that was beyond words or expression.

I thought about the deaths I'd seen in South Korea, the friends who had died in the war Defferre and Interpol had dropped me into the day I walked out of Taejon Prison. And before that, my own hopeful beginnings as a missionary turned sour because of all I'd seen in the Kwangju riot. Now I was back in Korea again, fighting for Archangel in a war that would never end.

My father and I both fought wars—mine dark and cold, his bright and hot—that seemed to carelessly use up life without the satisfaction of a clear resolution. The Washington, D.C. Korean War Veterans Memorial's dedicatory plaque reads: "Our nation honors her uniformed sons and daughters who answered their country's call to defend a country they did not know and a people they had never met." We chewed the same dirt and shed the same family blood, years and miles apart.

I wondered, with my dark thoughts, my memories, would I ever be able to find peace? Questions gnawed at me as I took a room at Songnyu Inn in Chongdam district south of the Han River. Eunmi's apartment was in the same area. I called her.

"I've been thinking about us," I began. I had rehearsed my impassioned lover's plea on the flight up. She cut me off.

"Me, too. All the time. Can we talk about it later tonight?" Her voice was strained. "I need to go out in a little while."

"How long is a little while?"

"I'm leaving in about a half-hour. Be back before dinner. Want to come over then?" She sounded like she was about to cry.

I agreed and we rang off. Then I armed myself, sprinted outside and hailed a cab to Eunmi's block. I got there in time to grab a Kin Cider at a corner market and watch her apartment. She came out about twenty minutes after I arrived. Lucky for me she was running late.

She had a large bag thrown heavily over her shoulder and a light green jacket. She hopped on a bus downtown. I hailed a cab. "You're not going to believe this," I said, crawling in and pointing at the bus.

"Follow that bus?" The driver laughed, shaking his head. "Americans. Always just like the movies." The driver knew where the bus was headed. "It runs through downtown. It runs up to City Hall Plaza; then follows Ulchi Road past Myong Dong Shopping Area and loops back down through Mt. Nam Tunnel."

My heart skipped a beat. *Mt. Nam.* The ANSP (South Korea's Agency for National Security Planning) offices were there. And I had never seen Eunmi carry any kind of bag before—especially a big heavy one. She had sounded so strained on the phone. My brain kicked into turbo and I jumped to about eighty or so conclusions at once—none of them good.

"Take me to Mt. Nam," I said.

We got snagged in traffic and I watched anxiously as Eunmi's bus pulled lazily out of view. As my taxi finally pulled up to the ANSP offices, I desperately looked up and down the street for any sign of Eunmi. Maybe I was wrong. If so, I would still meet her tonight. I walked to the parking garage. If Hyung-Jin's car was there, I'd invite him to lunch and try to patch things between us.

His car was parked next to the ANSP building on the first level. A green coat was underneath it. Eunmi slid out from under the car as I approached.

"Chanyoung-si," she whispered hoarsely, eyes watering.

"Don't do it, Eunmi. Whatever it is, just leave with me now."

She looked behind me. I turned. At the far end of the garage two men were watching us closely. She held up her hand toward them in a halting gesture. "There is no leaving, Chanyoung. I'm sorry."

"What are you going to do?"

She lifted her bag. It was empty. "When Hyung-Jin started his car, it would have blown up most of this building," she said, tears freely flowing. "He wanted to arrest me. To kill me." She turned and got into Hyung-Jin's car, using the keys she had kept after they broke up. "Now I can't wait for him. Run away now, Chanyoung." Her voice turned shrill, helpless. "Run! Or stay and hold me and we'll die with them all!"

She inserted the key.

Without reason, my brain flashed to an image of Eunmi hugging me the first time she saw me after Sid died (*"Oh, my dearest friend. I am so sorry."*). I could not allow myself to think of her that way. She wasn't an agent supplying North Korea with information. She was a North Korean terrorist. Just like the guy that killed Sid.

Now she was going to kill Hyung-Jin, me, hundreds of others.

I plunged the blade into Eunmi's neck before she could turn the key. She looked at me. Her hands fell to her side and she sagged forward. Her eyes glazed and blood spurted over her. Her jaw opened but only bubbles came out.

I stepped back as the two men from across the garage fell on me. I felt a dull thud on the back of my neck; then blackness.

twenty

CAPTIVE IN
NORTH KOREA

The same day that Eunmi placed a car bomb outside the ANSP offices in Seoul, three North Korean terrorists detonated a remote control bomb at the tomb of Burmese hero General Aung San in Rangoon. It was an attempt to assassinate South Korean President Chun Doowhan on the first stop of his tour of six Southwest Asian and Pacific Region countries.

The bomb exploded in Burma at 10:27 A.M. local time, 12:57 P.M. in South Korea. President Chun was late and escaped unharmed. Seventeen South Korean officials were killed, including Deputy Prime Minister Suh Sokjun, four cabinet members and thirteen other delegates. The blast also took the lives of four Burmese personnel and injured fourteen Koreans and thirty-two Burmese.

Burmese and ANSP investigators tracked the Belgian Browning pistols found on the scene to Swiss arms dealer Hans Joachim, a resident of Hanover, Germany and a known supplier to North Korea. Investigators also found an explosive device similar to one used by North Korean terrorists when they failed at an attempt to assassinate Korean officials at the Republic of Korea National Cemetery.

Hyung-Jin was attached to the team that investigated the car-bombing attempt in Seoul. The overall findings concluded that both incidents were part of a North Korean terror campaign against South Korea.

When the Burma bomb exploded at about 1:00 P.M. South Korean time, North Korean agents were positioned to detonate car bombs at the two ANSP offices in Seoul. Eunmi and her two companions were assigned the *Mt. Nam* ANSP offices; another group of North Korean agents (probably three in number) parked a car loaded with explosives outside the ANSP offices in *Imun* District, eastern Seoul. The ANSP team found the second car bomb unmanned with a faulty remote device on the detonator.

Both car bombs were scheduled to explode shortly after the Burma attack, killing ANSP personnel and inflicting heavy damage on South Korea's intelligence organizations.

The two North Korean RDEI agents worked me over after knocking me out. They rammed needles into me, ensuring complete unconsciousness. I woke briefly on a boat, then again on a train. Finally I came to full consciousness listening to the roar of a truck. I was sitting in back, two North Korean guards facing me. My hands and feet were shackled.

Taejon Prison lesson number one, I thought grimly. *Shut the hell up.*

We pulled into a large compound. It was a prison camp in North Hamyong province, North Korea. I saw piles of rocks in rows just outside the gates. Wild pigs and hawks were gnawing at corpses trapped under the heavy stones.

As we drove through the gates into the camp, I was stunned by the large number of inmates. The elderly, children, women and men—all skin and bones working in loose, tattered rags. Many of them suffered from tremendous malnutrition and averaged no more than four feet eleven inches. Eyes and mouths were scarred, misshapen or missing completely. Many of them had been beaten so severely that they had no ears. As they worked, a large percentage of the prisoners stumbled on makeshift crutches.

We pulled up to a large building—one of many cement edifices that held the inmates. I was dragged through a side door and down a series of halls. They tossed me into a dimly lit room with a small chair, a slender metal table against the sidewall and two more North Koreans. My truck escorts left while the two new guards used sharp knives to strip away my clothes without removing the shackles.

"Ugly monkey, isn't he?" one asked the other in Korean. Their dialect was difficult to make out. I feigned non-comprehension. The guard cupped my genitals. "That's why they're so big down here," he said, squeezing painfully. "'Cause they have no moral values at all. Just animals."

"Fuck like monkeys," agreed the other guard. They didn't worry about how much their knives nicked and cut me as they worked.

They shoved me into a chair, chaining my shackles to its legs. An officer came into the room, placing a large briefcase on the table. "Has he spoken?" he asked in Korean. The guards shook their heads. The officer slapped me hard. He walked behind me and slapped the back of my head; then in front of me again.

"You liked that little whore?" he asked in English. "She was just another filthy slut that fucks Americans to you, eh?" He slapped me again. "But she was a hero of our country!" Slap. "She endured your sweaty, hairy, ugly body, because it was her duty." He drew a long, slender blade from his belt sheath and tapped it on my genitals with each word: "And. You. Killed. Her."

The officer crossed to the table, opened his briefcase and held up a handwritten note on a thin sheet of rice paper. Woo's letter. Time for me to speak. In English.

"Sir, I was in a cell across from the Honored Woo Yonggak. He is in solitary confinement in Taejon Prison. The South Koreans treat him like an animal. He is old and gray. He begged me to deliver this letter to his son in North Korea when I defected."

The officer slapped me again.

"Honored Woo's wife is dead. His son has been notified of this letter." The officer leaned close, screaming. "That's why you're still alive!"

Woo's son wanted to talk with me about his father. Apparently, he had enough clout to get a stay of my imminent execution. The officer might not kill me just yet, but he wasn't done. "Why did you say, *defect?*" the officer spit out the words.

"You were right, honored sir. I did have carnal knowledge of the woman. She convinced me to join her in serving the Great Leader Kim Ilsong in your blessed country" and here I feigned choking with tears, as though the thought of Eunmi's death were too much to bear. It didn't take much acting: she was my friend, my enemy, my lover—and this man had me terrified.

The officer waved to one of the guards, who stooped in front of me and broke some toes. I screamed in agony. He lifted my right leg and twisted the shinbone until it popped out of my knee socket. I passed out.

When I woke—minutes? hours?—the officer demanded to know why I killed Eunmi. I said that I didn't kill her. The two RDEI guys in the parking lot jumped me for no reason. It was lame and made no sense, I knew, but Woo's letter and my story of wanting to defect with my secret lover Eunmi were all I had. I stuck to them.

To add to the horrors of physical torture, the North Korean officer wanted me to see even greater miseries that lay ahead. Despite the way my right leg hung at an angry angle, swollen and throbbing with pain, I was dragged out of the room to another area of the camp. Other prisoners ignored me, not even shocked at the sight of a naked Caucasian helplessly flung about by the guards. Many of the inmates wore only rags or no clothes at all.

I was taken to an open courtyard and witnessed the killing of three prisoners: one with a bullet and two with sledgehammers. "You will get the sledgehammer," the officer told me in a bored but malicious voice.

North Korean prison camps were places of the most grotesque tortures. Prisoners routinely died of starvation and disease. My guards forced me to witness another execution. A woman prisoner was stripped naked of her rags and attacked by ravenous, feral dogs. "Perhaps that will be you," teased the officer. I thought of Shingo in Osaka. Perhaps Musashi had been right: there was such a thing as *karma* and my fate was coming back to me.

There were thousands of prisoners at the camp. Many were convicted of political crimes, but they were thrown in the population with murderers, rapists—and American enemies of the state. North Korean prison camps held over 200,000 inmates.

The officer also forced me to witness various forms of torture—all on my first day. I saw one woman's stomach filled with water via a tube forced down her throat; then the water was pushed out by a guard who stood on a board across her stomach. A man was forced into a heated kiln as we passed. There were children everywhere, the unfortunate relatives of convicted "class enemies." Two were fighting over the right to eat a dead frog, much to the amusement of my guards.

"We bury bodies in groups here," the officer told me, wrenching my head back and forcing me to watch as a truckload of corpses roll by. "We won't kill you. We'll bury you alive with them." The guards on the trucks couldn't have been more than sixteen years old.

The guards then dragged me into the infirmary, instructing the doctor to keep me lucid for further questioning. The doctor went to get some materials to treat me. Around the dirty medical facilities, I saw amputees on cots, screaming for anesthesia that would never come. They bit on rags or their own hands to stifle the wails. One chart near my cot listed experiments conducted on a healthy patient as part of the guards' inner-camp medical training. The doctor returned and gave me a shot. As I slipped into unconsciousness, I could feel him bandaging my broken toes.

I woke up confined in a little box. I couldn't move, so tight and cramped was the space, curled up without an inch in which to move. Completely dark. I was on my knees, forced by the walls of the box into a fetal position, knees under chest, buttocks on heels, arms bent, head pushed low. The walls were heavy steel, black, with tiny holes covered in dark cloth. I could hear and breathe, but when they shut off the lights in the outer room, I could not see.

My legs cramped. My bowels cramped. The box smelled of my feces and urine. I couldn't move. Even the act of scratching my nose was a blessed relief, such a tiny movement. They opened the hole near my face and fed me something through a straw. I gulped.

Vinegar. My stomach rolled and I vomited on myself, barely avoiding choking on my own bile. The officer's voice was my only companion, and that only for brief intervals.

"Tell us!" he screamed over and over.

I didn't know what he wanted me to tell. I repeated my story about defecting and Woo's son like a litany. To keep myself talking and the officer listening, I rambled about prison life in Taejon.

"Tell us!"

My whole body was cramped, by swollen knee screaming, and I felt my sanity slipping away.

"Tell us!"

I had nothing to tell. They shut the lights off in my tiny coffin and left me alone in the dark.

My mind wandered back to Pusan and the numerous tests performed by Dr. Kim when I was first recruited for Interpol. "You have nothing to sense or feel except panic in a small place," his comforting voice reminded me. "Concentrate on breathing, on your own pulse, but never on the time. You cannot count minutes in that situation. When you feel your mind slipping… try singing or reciting poetry or going over favorite movie scenes. This will keep your mind focused."

I wouldn't let myself think of anything real. The horrors of Sid and Shin, Eunmi and Archangel were too near, too deeply felt. I recited poetry, sang, focusing on the words and my breathing. They were all too short. I was soon left with only the dark and my awareness of the walls holding me in. "God, I'm so thirsty," I said aloud. I had long since stopped worrying about listeners. Company would have been a relief. "Me throat's gone dry."

I laughed at my bad Irish brogue, cackled maybe, losing my grip. The quote was from Barry Fitzgerald's character, Michaeleen

Oge Flynn, in one of my favorite movies, John Ford's *The Quiet Man*. "*Do-doot-do-doot-dittydoodoo-do-doot*," I started half singing, half humming the main theme and lost myself in the plot line. John Wayne. Maureen O'Hara. A filmmaker's nostalgic look at an Ireland that only existed in the movies.

The Quiet Man had played every St. Patrick's Day on our local television station when I was growing up. I watched it each year and knew the lines by heart. I played the film over and over in my head, the only thing that was long enough, simple and positive enough, to keep my mind off the cramped horror of the box.

"Tell us!"

I rambled when they wanted, sipped water if they offered—no more vinegar for a while—and when the lights went out, tried to hold onto hope that they would let me out someday.

"Me throat's gone dry. *Do-doot-do-doot-dittydoodoo-do-doot*..."

Later they pulled me out of the box. I have no idea if I was inside it for a single day or week. When they stood me up, my cramped muscles screamed and I couldn't walk. My right knee was swollen and crooked. My whole body quivered. I gagged and vomited only bile. As they dragged me out of the room, I looked back at my prison. A box no larger than a filing cabinet. I was still naked. They flung me into the back of a truck.

Lying flat on the hard floorboards, bouncing with every hole and rock in the road, my body outstretched in a blissful agony of freedom, I thanked God for this short time outside the box. Even if I was on my way to death.

The truck stopped. A guard threw back the flap and pulled me onto the hard dirt road. He pointed to the front of the truck. I hobbled forward.

Ahead was the Demilitarized Zone between North and South Korea. The guard pushed me forward. I stumbled into the dirt. He pointed down a road that stretched between the two countries.

I stood on my left leg and started across. Naked, hopping on one leg, body and soul completely without hope, I crossed that bitter pass. Near the South Korean side, Hyung-Jin and Defferre rushed forward to catch me and wrap me in a blanket.

My friends had saved me from hell.

I spent the better part of two weeks sleeping and recuperating at the National Medical Center in Seoul under Dr. Kim's watchful eyes. Because the director had taken an interest in me, I had an individual room—a real luxury in Korea's crowded hospitals—and two doctors with a platoon of nurses that checked on me every few minutes. My toes were healing slowly and they had reset my knee.

No one sent gifts or flowers, but Defferre came by and brought me the television schedule. "Next time we need to track you down," he joked, flipping through the pages, "I'll just find out where *Columbo* is playing and *voila!*" Defferre ruffled his hair—a first!—then searched through his coat packets in a bad Peter Falk impersonation. I really needed to find a new favorite show.

Defferre and Hyung-Jin had filled out a few hundred reports and did whatever was needed by Interpol, ANSP and a few other organizations to wrap up the whole mess. I was glad I slept through it.

"How did you find me?" I asked. I really didn't care; being free was enough. Hyung-Jin and Defferre were sitting in padded, straight-back metal chairs—standard hospital discomfort. Hyung-Jin was wearing a tight, white T-shirt and loose chinos; Defferre wore a tailored double-breasted gray suit.

"Thank Captain Wolper," Defferre said. After the Rangoon bombing, counter-terrorist groups around the world were on the alert. Henri Wolper's DST team was deployed along with many others to watch known or suspected North Korean agents and monitor communications from other intelligence services. The French *Direction Generale de la Securite Exterieure* (General Directorate for External Security—DGSE) issued a classified notice to the DST teams that indicated the North Koreans might have captured an American smuggler.

This intelligence report came from the Japanese National Police's infamous "modern ninja," a euphemism for what would later become Japan's elite, counter-terrorist Special Assault Team. Trained by the French Intervention Group of the National Gendarmerie (GIGN) special operations unit, the Japanese team was part of a pilot program that endured a rigorous schedule of combat shooting, close quarter battle, hostage rescue, counter-espionage and surveillance of know belligerents—such as North Korea.

The special relationship between the Japanese National Police and the GIGN encouraged free exchange of information. One tidbit was this hint of an American in a North Korean prison.

Captain Henri Wolper was a thorough professional who did his homework. His DST team had worked with Interpol in questioning Shoaib Akram—the Pakistan citizen who sold kiddie porn to fund terrorism against neighboring Middle Eastern countries. Wolper again found himself working with Interpol to nab North Korean terrorists that were smuggling child pornography and drugs through Marseilles. That assignment led to Sid's death—one of Wolper's team members and a valued friend.

Wolper made it a point to learn what he could about my background and Interpol's role in combating international crime as it related to his team's objectives. He quickly realized how frequently Defferre's officers posed as smugglers. He phoned Defferre, asking if the Japanese intelligence report was of any interest.

As soon as Defferre got a copy of the classified notice, he called Hyung-Jin and they put two and two together. They worked with Interpol's contacts in the ANSP and other South Korean agencies to locate me. Defferre even asked Dr. Kim to lend his considerable clout in coordinating the discreet efforts. Archangel was not something to broadcast to standard police organizations in South Korea—especially with the last cleanings in Taegu and Pusan still hot. The bombing attempts made everyone edgy.

"Eunmi's role with the North Koreans was more than even we imagined," Defferre told me one morning in the hospital room. Hyung-Jin winced at the mention of her name.

"She was a terrorist," I replied. They nodded in unison, having discovered this fact during the bombing investigation. Defferre rearranged himself in the chair, looking out the window. "Hyung-Jin and I talked it over and realized her death must have been your doing."

Hyung-Jin stood, unable to rest while talking about Eunmi. He was grim but efficient. "Hapkido knife work has a unique signature. So when Commissaire Defferre informed me that you were following her—to take her back to France, which we would have never allowed, by the way—it wasn't too hard to figure out that you had saved my life." Hyung-Jin's small lips held a brief hint of his quiet smile. "Again."

Defferre said that he had "exactly one contact" in North Korea. "That wasn't enough to get anything done, but the ANSP had their own agenda."

"We uncovered a mole a few years ago," Hyung-Jin said, referring to an RDEI agent that had posed as a loyal ANSP employee for years, all the while sending intelligence reports back to North Korea. "We've been feeding him false intelligence to pass back to Pyongyang, but he stopped coming to work after the bombing attempts. The idiot didn't even call in sick on the day they planted the car bombs—just didn't show up. He must have been pretty sure they'd succeed." Hyung-Jin paused, finally stopped pacing, and sat down. "We nabbed him booking a flight to Hong Kong."

The mole had intended to meet his contact in Kowloon, then, with Chinese assistance, return to North Korea. "When we detained him, he rolled on the bombing attempts, but we didn't want to make it public," Hyung-Jin explained. "Moles are bad press." The guy was buried so deep and for so long that everything else he knew was obsolete.

"So you traded him for me?" I asked.

Hyung-Jin looked sideways at Defferre, then carefully studied his calloused hands. Defferre cleared his throat. "There was no trade, Race. Because both governments state that this mole never existed." Official denials aside, the ANSP had recorded the mole's confessions and—with a little creative editing—made the tapes easily accessible to other known North Korean agents. They also planted some smuggled goods in his condo: French liquor, Playboy magazines, decadent Western black market stuff.

"As an Interpol representative, I contacted North Korea," Defferre continued, "expressing our deepest hope that they might consider deporting a known smuggler and vicious criminal that they held in North Hamyong province prison. I assured them that this despicable lawbreaker faced the most severe punishment in France." Defferre stood and hung up his jacket, loosening his tie and smoothing the Bogey cut.

"They said I was a smuggler, officially?" I asked.

Hyung-Jin shook his head. "There's nothing official here. But saying you were a criminal saved face for everyone." Hyung-Jin shrugged, smiling softly.

The North Koreans went along with Defferre's suggestion that I was a smuggler caught inside their borders. I asked "Do you know how I was taken out of the country?"

"They packed you in a little case," explained Hyung-Jin. "Then they just loaded you into the back of a van, onto a boat and back to North Korea."

"Was it that easy?" I asked, massaging my swollen knee.

"Nothing is easy in this business." Hyung-Jin shook his head. "But they had an escape route all set for three people after the bombings. You made number three."

"Instead of..." I began; then paused, throat tight. *Instead of Eunmi.* Hyung-Jin and I stared at each other for a long moment.

"Right," he said.

Defferre let the silence linger, then continued his explanation. "I also suggested that Interpol was unconcerned about the troubles between north and south; that we would gladly assist in deporting a known smuggler of Western goods back to North Korea where he belongs. As you can see," he waved his arms expansively, "no one wants smugglers in their country."

Hyung-Jin laughed, deep and long, almost doubled over, his thin T-shirt heaving. "The mole was just a dead asset," he said, gasping and wiping a bit of water from his eyes. "Defferre makes it sound like world governments dance to his tune!"

"*Oui. C'est vrai,*" Defferre agreed with a slow wink. *That's true.*

"So the guy goes back to North Korea," I said, "and they think all the ANSP knows about is one mole with obsolete intel. In the meantime, you play dumb about the other North Korean agents that you're still feeding with false information."

"He's catching on," smiled Defferre.

"It's the Korean food." Hyung-Jin tapped his temple. "Good for the brain."

"Speaking of which…!" Defferre reminded us that it was almost lunchtime. Hyung-Jin headed for the cafeteria to bring back something for Defferre and himself. After he was gone, Defferre stood and took my hand. "Don't be fooled, *mon ami*," he said quietly, leaning close. "It was all Hyung-Jin's idea. Mole or no, he would have found a way to save you."

They visited me each day until I was well enough to leave the hospital.

ANSP never caught the North Korean terrorists that set the car bombs in Seoul. Burmese teams and ANSP agents tracked the three North Koreans that detonated the Rangoon bomb. Two of the terrorists were arrested—Major Chin, the leader, and agent Kang Minchol. The third agent resisted and was killed during a gun battle. Chin and Kang received death sentences from the Burma High court.

Twenty-seven days after the explosion, Burma officially announced that the incident was part of a carefully orchestrated terrorism attack by North Korea. Burma severed all diplomatic relations with the communist country. As a result of the terrorist attack, Western Samoa, Costa Rica and Morocco soon did the same. Sixty-nine other countries issued official condemnations and exercised diplomatic and trade sanctions.

Woo Yonggak's letter bought me precious time in North Korea, but I never met his son.

twenty-one

REVERENCE

After I was released from the hospital, Hyung-Jin insisted I stay with his mother and him at their home in Seoul. His mother was about five feet tall, late fifties with prematurely gray hair and—like her son—had a quiet smile and gentle demeanor. Hyung-Jin told her an abridged version of our friendship, including Taejon and Taegu prisons, ANSP, Interpol and the North Korean camp. Her husband—Hyung-Jin's father—had passed away many years before. She kept a tiny Buddhist shrine dedicated to his memory housed in an alcove. She treated me with patience and fondness, uncompromising about my many failings but also deeply grateful. "For the life of my son," she said sincerely. "And the friendship between you." She visited the Chogyesa Temple twice while I was there to beg for heaven's blessings on my behalf.

Just before I left Seoul, Hyung-Jin and I joined his mother on one of her visits to the temple. Although Hyung-Jin professed Christian beliefs, he told me it was his filial duty to respect his mother's wishes and occasionally accompany her there.

Chogyesa Temple was the headquarters of the official *chogye* sect, serving some 1,500 affiliated temples throughout Korea. The temple was in the middle of Seoul in the Kyunji district. An alley on Ujonggukno, northwest of the Poshingak belfry, led to the temple grounds.

Sunho's mother stopped at a row of shops in the alley to purchase a candle. We all wore slacks and dress shirts, comfortable but appropriate for the sacred edifice. I noticed a row of people shuffling toward another entrance to the temple. They were in rags and old, unkempt clothes.

Like most Buddhist temples, Chogye housed an area designated especially for the city's poor and unfortunate, where they daily received food and counsel. Hyung-Jin's mother was in the habit of avoiding this area—wisely, as an elderly woman alone—so she left to speak with the monks while we wandered over.

"We have missions in the worst parts of town for homeless people," I told Hyung-Jin. My toes and knee were on the mend, but I still walked carefully. We had plenty of time to talk. Chogye Temple was nestled between Chongno and Yulgokno streets, a busy downtown area. Monks were passing out bowls of soup and bread to the homeless, some of them sitting on the steps and teaching groups how to read and write. I saw a list posted of the monks' rotating schedules for working with the poor, including the chief abbot. Looking around, we saw maybe one hundred and fifty or two hundred people that day, many of them filthy and repulsively pungent. I stood there a minute staring, shocked at the full measure of human charity. A monk handed me a bowl with bread and patted my shoulder, muttering a blessing in a warm but stern smile.

I turned to Hyung-Jin, who was already sipping his soup. Breaking bread, I continued, "If the homeless need places to sleep or helping hands in America they can't go to most cathedrals or large churches. Many of the pastors would call the cops."

"Then what good is the church?" asked Hyung-Jin, genuinely puzzled.

"Place of worship, sense of congregation," I said, shrugging. "For the local community. But if you're poor and smell funny," I shook my head, cocking a thumb back over my shoulder, "out you go."

"I don't remember reading that part in the Sermon on the Mount."

"It must be in a new translation," I joked and we laughed. "But it's not Christianity's fault. After all, look at Mother Theresa. Her whole life is helping the poor." I chewed the fresh bread, thinking. "Maybe some churches are just scared of the poor or need a Mother Theresa to show them how."

Meanwhile, I was still wrestling with my own moral conscience. I felt violent, embittered and vengeful toward others, worried that the pride I felt ridding the world of evil made me the antithesis of what a Christian should be. Despite that harsh reality, I was embarrassed to know that the church in which I grew up did not welcome unfortunate people every day, week after week, year after year, like the monks in this temple.

The soup was pretty good, too. It had a lot of vegetables and spices, none of which I recognized. *Monsters-of-the-Sea soup*, we called it. Yummy.

There was a lot of activity as we entered the main temple grounds. A gilded Buddha in the worship hall was sheltered in a glass case, surrounded by acolytes. Hyung-Jin's mother was near the piano to one side, conferring with a young monk. She waved us over.

"This is a new member of the temple staff," she said, bowing low. "He asked to speak with you." I bowed and caught myself, eyes lingering on the monk's open, sad face. He was perhaps mid-forties with a shaved head and thin lips. He pressed his hands together, the folds of his traditional gray robe flowing as he fell to his knees before me.

"Forgive me," he whispered, and beat his head against the wood floor. Hyung-Jin was shocked, stepping back with his right foot as though attacked—a reflexive defense stance when surprised. His mother smiled warmly, her hands wrapped round her prayer beads, a tear flowing out of the corner of one eye. The monk's palms were flat on the dusty floor, then he gently touched my boots, entreating, "Forgive, forgive, forgive."

I knelt and lifted his shoulders. "Do I know you?" I asked. He stared into my eyes, wiping tears with his dirty hands, leaving gray trails along his temple and cheeks. Then where I had seen him before hit me. Solitary confinement in Taejon Prison. This was my talkative guard.

"Please forgive me!" he wailed again. I lifted him up and we embraced, long and heartfelt, while sobs wracked his whole body. At last he stepped back, bowing low. "I have many debts in this world," he said. "I must repay them all."

"Me, too," I said sincerely.

We went to an antechamber and sat on the small wood chairs, sipping tea. The monk found a soft cloth, wet it and cleaned his face. "I left Taejon about six months ago and joined the temple as a novice, committed to a life of service as penance for the many wrongs I committed while working at the prison of which I feel guilty." Hyung-Jin's mother was overwhelmed with joy, watching the reunion of prisoner and jailer.

"Buddha provides all answers," she said devoutly. Hyung-Jin patted his mother's hands, silent and watchful.

"When we fear a thing, we invite it," the monk agreed. He had feared meeting old prisoners, but felt he must face them as part of his penance. "Because I dreaded this day, it came quickly."

I nodded slowly, not quite sure what to say. This man had slapped, backhanded, punched and bludgeoned me with his baton—all part of life in solitary confinement. Forgiveness was not a virtue I had cultivated; God knew Archangel didn't place it high on the priority list. The monk sat quietly, allowing time to pass between us.

"What's your name?" I asked.

"My old name is forgotten. I am now Popun." He had taken the Buddhist name of King Chinhung of Korea's Shilla Dynasty, lasting between 57 B.C. and 918 A.D., who was known for his devotion and active promulgation of the religion. After Chinhung's reign, several Shilla kings were ordained and their queens and families often entered monasteries. The guard's new name meant "Dharma Cloud."

"Popun," I muttered slowly, taking in life's changes. I thought of the cruelty of the North Korean guards who tortured me for stopping their attempt at mass murder via car bomb. I felt tremendous guilt over Eunmi's death, but believed I had done the right thing. Unlike when I went on assignments for Archangel— which provided cleaners with constant affirmations of moral authority—I felt no ambiguity about what happened in that parking garage in Seoul. My mind wandered back to the crime that sent me to Taejon in the first place. "I'm not so sure there's anything to forgive, Popun," I said at last. "I have my own debts to repay."

"I was cruel. I must seek forgiveness in this life," he repeated, a mantra of guilt that was completely heartfelt.

"We are all guilty in this life," I offered, to which Hyung-Jin's mother nodded sagely.

"But you have also helped those who were desperate." He looked up at me, uncertain but hopeful. I glanced sideways at Hyung-Jin, who nodded. "Do your vows bind you to silence if I share a confession with you?"

Popun leaned forward, clasping his beads. "I serve only the Buddha," he said. As a guard, he had also served South Korea and learned how to keep a secret.

"Let me tell you about Woo Yonggak's letter," I said and laid it all out. North Korea, the letter and Woo's son finally hearing from his father.

Hyung-Jin's mother listened intently until I finished, then added, "Even the smallest kindness may save a life."

"As you say, Honored Mother," agreed Popun.

"I lack the wisdom to judge anyone," I said solemnly. My knee still ached and my toes were tingling from sitting in the small chairs. "To say 'I forgive you' would mean that I have the right to judge and offer mercy." I shook my head slowly, eyes locked in his. "I'm out of the judgment business."

Popun was a little confused, but felt he was helping to perform a type of absolution. He straightened, transformed from penitent to sympathetic monk. I leaned forward, hand on his shoulder, and wondered for a moment if seeing this man and his transformation was not a kind of divine lesson for me. Then I pressed the thought back into my subconscious. "We all have done things of which we are not proud, for which we must pay in this life and the next. Maybe it's part of being human. I don't have the moral authority to 'forgive' anyone. But if you will accept it, I offer my understanding, from one human being to another."

"I thank you," Popun whispered, patting my arm, eyes smiling. "Human to human."

Hyung-Jin stood and walked behind my chair, kneeling next to Popun and me. His voice was low, filled with deep thoughts. "You're right, Chanyoung," he said, using my Korean name as Eunmi had always done, in a form of language reserved for intimate friends. It was the first time he had used it since he and Eunmi broke up, since she and I slept together, since she died. "Only God can forgive," he said. "The best we can do for each other is try to understand." We stood and embraced.

Popun intoned a soft prayer. Hyung-Jin's mother wept openly. "Praise Buddha," she said, wise and uncompromising. "For in this life we need each other."

After leaving Hyung-Jin and his mother, I took a train to Mt. Naejang. I had promised Sid that we would go there, "to watch the leaves burn in the air." Hyung-Jin and I once walked on Naejang, comparing leaves. Now, sorrow passed through me and I felt he had been right: leaves that fall from the trees may be gold and beautiful, but people walk all over them.

I had mentioned to Hyung-Jin's mother that I hoped to write a few more *sijo* sonnets. She told me, "You must become 'as a spirit' to capture the effervescent beauty of true emotion—the goal of the poem." I strained to understand the forces of life that led me to this moment. How to be a spirit? I found a quiet place off a path on Mt. Naejang. The leaves were falling and all sounds were like water and wind in the pines. They slipped by in lines and curves; the silence of time moving and not moving. The cry of life's cyclic struggle.

> *This stout pine chuckles as its gray hairs*
> *Wave in spring winds and delights*
> *In the growth of a calm chrysanthemum*
> *Is it only a dream that these two live in peace?*

In that moment of insight, I came to see time as more and more precious. The lives of friends in the United States were passing in my absence; my life was passing. The beauty of Naejang and the emotions of the life I'd led far from my own family made me think of home.

I decided to take a long-postponed return trip to Yosu, the port of Admiral Yi Sunshin. Eunmi and I had taken a weekend holiday there forever ago. It was a place where rivers came together, with bridges and river islands. As soon as I crossed the first bridge, I remembered images from accounts of the great battles with Japanese General Toyotomi Hideyoshi's fleet in 1592. I saw in my mind the river clogged with bodies, people dragging themselves from among fallen comrades. Thinking of Archangel, of friends and loves lost, I recalled the heroic and violent Admiral Yi Sunshin's poignant *sijo*:

> *Alone at the tower on moonlit Han San Island,*
> *My sword and my anguish beside me*
> *The distant whisper of my enemy's flute rends my heart.*

The memorial park was almost empty, so different from the bustle of the day Eunmi and I had spent there, laughing and snapping pictures when we were best friends. It was nearly closing time. Not much grass, lots of open space, empty benches. Times like this made me want to go home, made me want to know how to forget all the blood-clogging vengeance and pride and fear that made me unable to just love the people I loved. Our lives were all passing with each moment, dying quietly with time. Like those Yosu people who were going to work or putting out laundry or tearing down houses to make firebreaks when the battles started. Like the children we avenged, the poor tortured children we had saved and failed to save, of whom the world remained unaware. Like the evil men who feasted on them, now dead at the hands of Archangel's cleaners. I tried another *sijo*:

> *The blistering storm is nothing to crows safe at home:*
> *Scholars! Experts!*
> *Ignorant of poor starving fish!*
> *Posing as white herons in the shallows will you also feast on these?*

What remembrances of my friends and loves would I get to keep? Were there any not poisoned by memories too bitter to endure?

Before leaving Korea, I bussed to Pusan and looked over my condominium. The lease would be up after Christmas and I hoped there would be no reason to renew. I phoned Defferre. "I need to talk things over with you," I said without preamble. "Get me back to Archangel."

"Just one small thing before you leave," he said. "Pay your respects to Kon. Our contact in Chunju says he's most pleased that you helped clean Chong. He wants to thank you personally."

"He can send me a card," I said. "I'm not going that way this week."

Defferre sighed. "Call him, then. And hurry back."

When I called Kon, he was ecstatic. I told him I was heading out of the country indefinitely. "That's a long time," he said. "If you make it back to Chunju someday, call me. I pay what I owe."

I woke the next morning and strolled along the beach. The light was yellow and green, clear. The water was the heart of all colors, no two days the same. As I returned to my condo, from the distance I saw a man standing by the door. At first my reaction was defensive, but as I drew closer, I noticed his stance, his slow lingering smile. Hyung-Jin.

He had a gift for me: a temple lamp his mother bought at an antique store thirty years ago and had kept in a closet since. "She says you need a temple lamp more than her," he said. "She carries her own light."

We laughed, because she was so candid and because it was true. He handed me a wooden box with a single crane on the lid, carved with rare delicacy. I opened it, unwound the long white cloth from around the lamp. It was plain and white, no larger than the palm of my hand, chipped on the lid through which the cloth wick ran. The small handle on the side seemed made for a child's hand.

The lamp seemed to breathe with its own life. It had a slight imperfection, made beautiful with age. It had shone for many people, seen humanity's constant struggles by its small light. It seemed ripe with knowledge.

"It's a haunted lamp," I whispered reverently, turning it slowly in my hands.

"Yeah, I think so, too," Hyung-Jin said. "My mother told me to give you this note with it." He handed me a carefully penned letter on thin rice paper.

"Dear Second Son: This lamp is a complicated gift, a responsibility. It knows that choosing to love something means losing something else. It is old enough to know that the world has too much paradox in it to let the heart rest in one place. The heart must forever be dreaming, growing, moving beyond the pain it has suffered. This lamp knows the pain of *han*, but still it endures and offers light to others."

I felt the weight of the lamp, sensing the meaning behind it. "Please tell your mother that I accept her gift and will forever cherish it," I said.

His smile was genuine, subdued and slow. "Will do, younger brother."

Then Hyung-Jin and I lit the lamp once, letting the silence linger.

Lyon. As soon as I unzipped my bag in my room at Archangel, there was a knock.

"Knee inspection!" Margaret burst into the room, wearing dark jeans and a blue silk blouse. She hugged me and demanded to know everything. I laid out the short version while unpacking. She sat on the bed and listened. When I finished, she shook her head. "Damn, Race, you really should become a priest."

"Why's that?"

"Your relationships end badly." Margaret, Ms. Subtle.

"I noticed that."

"As if the church would have you!" she said with a deep Irish chuckle.

"Peg, I'm thinking about getting out." I sat next to her on the bed, both of us staring at the poster of Shang Chi, Master of Kungfu. *Games of death and deceit,* I had quoted to Defferre. He took the comic seriously, always referring to it as a "book," in keeping with the French and Belgian respect for the medium. It didn't surprise him at all when Art Spiegelman's comic novel, *Maus: A Survivor's Tale,* won the Pulitzer Prize.

Margaret pointed at the poster. "Defferre said this is some super tough kungfu guy. He showed me the comics. I didn't read them."

"Nice dodge, Peg. Did you hear me?"

She nodded slowly, eyes still on the poster. "This guy, he was some sort of pacifist that was forced to be a spy, right? In the comic books, did he ever make a difference?"

"Sometimes, I guess." I thought about it for a while. "Not really."

"Well, we do." She patted my knee, using it as leverage to lift her bulk off the bed. She slipped a picture out of her blouse pocket. It was July in a long pretty dress, white with flowers and a sash round her waist. Two adults stood beside her at what looked like a church bazaar or picnic. "She's in Wales," Margaret said. "That's her family. I had an archangel check up on her and he snapped this picture." Her hand trembled slightly as she pointed at the little girl. "Her real name's Elizabeth. Goes by Lizzie."

I held the picture with reverence and felt the closest I'd been to God in a long time. "Is she…" my throat caught, emotion-filled. I tried again. "Have you heard how she's doing?"

Margaret shook her head. "Just that she's with her family and going to some sort of therapy." She took the picture back, returning it to the pocket over her heart. "With her family, Race." To Margaret, the reason for Archangel's existence was summed up in that photo. She would never want out.

Defferre didn't seem to mind my announcement that I was leaving. "You are done with cleaning? Of course!" He walked 'round the desk at his Archangel office and embraced me, carefully avoiding my knee, although it was pretty much back to normal. "I'm not surprised that you want out, Race. Most of the cleaners don't live out their first year."

I thought of William and grimaced. "I'm serious, Jacques. No more. I'm out."

Defferre didn't skip a beat. "Perfect timing, *mon ami*." When he used his exaggerated Frenchman routine, I could sense something was coming. He slicked back his hair and adjusted the long-sleeved work shirt he usually wore around Archangel. "There is something that is perfectly legitimate that I need from you."

Defferre wanted me to go back to Brussels. "You're apartment is still in good order. The gendarmerie has been asking for their instructor." He had been bragging about my association with the Korean ANSP and a gendarmerie contact suggested that I might participate in a new training program for the Belgian ESR (*Equioes Spécialisées de Reconnaissance*—Specialized Reconnaissance Teams).

Belgian ESR units were organized in 1961 to gather intelligence on deep reconnaissance missions. Euphemistically referring to themselves as "Shadow Warriors," ESR teams soon took on other roles, including counter-terrorism. Their existence was sometimes praised, but more frequently denied, by the Belgian government. Twelve ESR soldiers were deployed in Kinshasa to defend the Belgian embassy against rioting Zaire rebels: a role that saved the lives of their countrymen but was denied officially by their government. The ESR was fairly active in Africa, especially in places such as Congo, Rwanda, Burundi, Zaire and Somalia where missions ranged from peacekeeping and territorial defense to citizen evacuation and hostage liberation. In Somalia, twenty-eight ESR fighters gathered intelligence by monitoring General Mohamed Said Hersi and other leaders. They participated in the joint "Silver Back" operation, rescuing European hostages in Kigali, Rwanda. ESR soldiers were assigned to bodyguard Belgian General Briquemont, commander of the "Blue Helmets" in Sarajevo. They worked closely with the Belgian Long-Range Reconnaissance Patrol Detachment (LRRP) commando teams.

Defferre handed me a notebook of Belgian contacts and my gendarme identification. "The ESR has a new edition of their training manual coming up," he said, sitting on the edge of his desk. "The sections on close quarter battle include assassination techniques. Do you know anything about that?"

I spent a little over a month contributing to the ESR manual and training several teams on Archangel cleaning techniques. Afterward I planned on going home to the United States. Before I left for Brussels, however, I had one last important trip to make.

I bought some orchids, rented a car and drove Route N8 through Aubagne to La Treille, a small town in the hills behind

Marseilles. It was built on the first buttresses of the western slope of the Garlaban Massif.

Near La Treille a fresh river flowed. Receding layers of hills surrounded the village. Each time I visited, I saw the way the light fell on those hills at different times of day and times of year: it was never the same. Sometimes mists hid the hills or pocketed into the folds between them.

Pulling into La Treille, I parked and strolled in the bright morning light. A tiny fountain ran in the village's central square. I caught a trickle of icy water in my cupped hand. It tasted as fresh as the river running through the nearby hills.

I came from the central square onto a bridge and the whole valley opened up before me in its chosen light for the day: gray and clear. I was aware that the mountain range was always there, never the same colors or degree of clarity, but always there, even when it was invisible behind a low cloud. I walked along a worn path under bare trees and climbed up into the hills surrounding the city. I looked down, listening to the sounds of autumn. I was absolutely alone on earth, on the edge of invisibility. I could turn sideways and, like a spirit, disappear.

I walked the streets of La Treille, the Garlaban Massif running before me and after me. Filled with love and sadness, I watched the light change on the surrounding hills. I loved this place, even though I knew that I would disappear, that I would leave it. I spent those few hours letting the village imprint its shape and colors on my inner landscape, so the memory would be pressed and preserved for the future. I spent the time like one who knows he is dying: everything was precious because everything was disappearing. I thought of Sid in Marseilles and tried composing another *sijo* poem:

In the night, silently, silently a bird taps at your window
Awakened, tightly, tightly you press him to your breast,
Oh! That blissful moment!
Slowly, slowly I awake from my dream.

I had to go home to gain perspective and be alone with my conscience. My life with Archangel seemed like the life of a spirit: fluid, uncontrolled, vicious and lonely. But now the spirit needed company, family, a sense of belonging to the world. It was time to go back to a place where I was not a foreigner, where the language was mine, where old friends waited, where I could be part of a community. Above even my love of these hills and the dear heart that lay in them, the knowledge that it was time to leave kept floating to the surface.

In these hills everything seemed clearer. I knew that I wouldn't always be there, but found it hard to imagine not being there forever. I was no spirit. Only a human could feel such sadness.

There was a pale half-moon waxing over the trees, even though the sky was still light. Thin clouds moved slowly across its face. It disappeared for a moment, but I knew it would appear again.

At a small cemetery I carried orchids up a wandering knoll. Old flowers rested at the foot of an angel statue, dead for days from the evening chill. I knelt and cleaned away the dried arrangements, setting the orchids I'd brought on Sid's grave. It was close to the anniversary of her death. She had died on October 21—now it was the eighth of November.

"Sorry I'm late, my love."

twenty-two

HOMECOMING

Back in America, I tried to live a normal life. As I traveled between the continents, I went to college. Then, in the states, I married a woman of great beauty, insight and candor and lived poor. We had a daughter, who taught me, just by being herself, that life is rare and beautiful, to be treasured every moment and always my assignments for Interpol intervened.

I was impossible to live with. Trying to embrace some sort of peace, I read all I could about pacifism. Talk about denial. A few therapists later, it was clear why my marriage was failing. I hadn't told my wife about Archangel or Interpol; so how could a relationship based on such false foundations possibly survive? I wronged her terribly by not trusting her with the truth, but at the time I was tormented by the fear of losing her. After all, my luck had been bad with lovers prior to meeting her and I'd turned into Mr. Abandonment Issues. Inside, I expected it to end badly, and, as Popun said about all expectations, it naturally turned out the way

I most feared. Later I was diagnosed with post-traumatic stress disorder. I wasn't handling my life very well. Bad dreams, intimacy problems, fear of the truth and fear of losing loved ones. The usual.

One morning, Defferre called me from his office in France. "You have heard of the bombing of the Korean Airlines jet?"

On November 29, 1987 at about 2:00 P.M., Korean Airlines Flight 858 flying from Abu Dhabi, UAE, en route to Seoul, exploded over the Andaman Sea near Burma, killing all 115 passengers and crew members on board.

"Sure, I heard about it," I said. I tried to keep current with Korean news. "Sounds like North Koreans to me, Jacques."

"*Oui, mon ami*. I agree. We need you for a straight assignment." Defferre paused and I heard the shuffling of papers. "It seems that the bombing was planned by two North Korean terrorists. Interpol is helping to look into it under our new directive to assist in counter-terrorism." In the spring of 1983, Interpol had hosted a terrorism conference in which sixty nations participated. Nations often claimed that one country's terrorist was another country's freedom fighter, so Interpol's approach to international cooperation with this politically volatile subject seemed to make sense. The issue was raised later that year in the Interpol General Assembly in St.-Cloud, France. A majority of delegates voted to change the Interpol charter, empowering the organization to coordinate communication between international agencies, receive investigative requests and post wanted notices for terrorists. Interpol had been officially involved in the fight against terrorism since 1985.

Defferre cleared his throat, getting to the point. "Based on your experiences, ANSP asked if you might help with the investigation. Sort of an advisor role." A long pause, then, "Hyung-Jin asked for you especially."

I sighed, long and heavy. Advisor role? Didn't sound so bad. "Will do," I said, and heard Defferre chuckle across the sea.

The Overseas Intelligence Division of the North Korean Workers Party trained agents Kim Hyunhee and Kim Sungil to bomb the KAL jet, reportedly under direct orders from North Korean leader Kim Jongil to "throw a wrench into the two-Korea policy and preparations for the Olympics." Sungil posed as a father on holiday with his daughter, Hyunhee. Under Japanese names, the two terrorists traveled to Moscow, Budapest, Vienna, Belgrade and Baghdad.

On November 29, they boarded KAL Flight 858 leaving Baghdad. They placed the bombs—which were cleverly disguised as a portable radio and liquor bottle—in an overhead compartment. The bombs had a delayed detonation mechanism. Sungil and Hyunhee disembarked and transferred to Bahrain at Abu Dhabi. KAL 858 continued its flight and exploded nine hours later over the Andaman Sea, killing all on board.

Interpol quickly coordinated efforts with the Bahraini authorities. ANSP agents flew in and Interpol officers were on hand as the North Koreans attempted to escape shortly after the explosion. They were captured by the Bahraini and Interpol teams. Sungil and Hyunhee tried to commit suicide with poison capsules hidden inside cigarettes. The old man, Sungil, succeeded. Hyunhee was arrested.

Hyung-Jin and I worked together going through the clever items of concealment the two terrorists carried. The cigarettes were filled with normal tobacco; the poison capsules barely visible. They also had a deck of playing cards that appeared normal, but when the face of each card was peeled back, maps were revealed. The cards could be placed side-by-side, revealing detailed maps of mainland China, should the two terrorists need to find their way home on foot and by rail through that country.

After capture, Hyunhee posed as a Chinese national, tossing up a false legend about her childhood, complete with documents she had hidden in the fake bottom of her makeup case. Recognizing similarities in the bombing and methods used in previous North Korean terrorist attacks, the South Korean National Security Planning Agency requested and was granted the right on December 15, 1987 to take Kim Hyunhee and the body of Kim Sungil back to South Korea. Sungil's suicide method was common among North Korean RDEI agents. The South Korean interrogators got the truth out of Hyunhee shortly after she arrived in Seoul. The 1988 Seoul Olympics went ahead as planned.

My involvement in the investigation was only peripheral at best. Defferre hadn't lied; they just wanted to pick my brain about my experience in the car-bombing incident. A number of ANSP agents made it a point to shake my hand. "I was here that day," one said. "My wife was coming by for lunch when it happened," said another. Their thanks were genuine and touching.

Hyung-Jin and I spent a few days rambling around Seoul, taking in movies and generally catching up. "Don't let Defferre trap you again," he said in a quiet moment. "He's a good man, but a driven one, too."

"Yeah, he's Mr. *Yin-Yang*," I said, smiling but mostly serious. Defferre inspired love and fear all at the same time.

The level and intensity of international crime were increasing and Interpol was attempting to live up to its expanding public image. Interpol now aggressively presented itself as a legitimate coordinating body for its member country law enforcement agencies.

My marriage broke up in 1990. By then, Archangel had been disbanded and Defferre now had another Interpol role. I took an assignment in Chunju, South Korea. I had dinner with Kon only once, at which he presented me with a small gift and genuine thanks. His sister didn't come along. I mentioned that I was going straight and he just laughed. "Aren't we all?" he said. Kon had cashed in and moved to the background of his organization long before.

Moon Jongjin and Yoon Myungju, my friends from the riots, joined me for a reunion dinner in Kwangju. We'd kept in touch haphazardly over the years, but our bond was still strong. Moon found he actually liked the military service. Yoon had never married.

In Seoul, Hyung-Jin finally left the ANSP, went to the university and earned a doctorate. He met a nice woman and got married. She was from a small country village, which was thought of as rustic and backward by many Seoul citizens. Hyung-Jin asked me how he should present his marriage to his mother.

"Tell her that the girls in Seoul are too fast and modern, that this girl has good solid traditional values," I said, remembering how dearly his mother adhered to Buddhist ethics. "It'll work like a charm."

It did, too. Hyung-Jin told me his mother and wife got along famously. They all lived together, as Korean culture required of a loyal son. They even adopted two shitzu puppies. Hyung-Jin swore to me that he hated the dogs, but still insisted that a second pair of chopsticks be laid out at the dinner table so he could feed them treats. Mr. Tough Guy.

In 1991, on assignment in Seoul, I called my daughter. She was two years old and living in the States with her mother. "I'm coming home in a few months," I told her, reveling in the sound of her soft breathing through the phone.

"Maybe," she said, voice tentative and quiet.

Next day I bought a ticket back to the United States and my daughter. I took a long sabbatical from further missions. Eventually I traveled back to Korea to attend graduate school and earned a Ph.D. Home in America, I became a professor, fulfilling my promise to Sid. I hope I didn't get too terribly fat, though.

I spent as much time with my daughter as possible, often keeping her at my place three or four nights a week. One late summer evening, we bounced a ball against the side of my house. She turned to me and laughed, curly hair tossed in careless abandon.

"You know, Dad, you and I are a lot alike!" If true, then I am a lucky man.

twenty-three

THE WONDERLAND
CLUB

Defferre called me occasionally for legitimate and not-so-legitimate assignments. I was trained to be a cleaner and—no matter how desperately I clung to my life as father and average citizen—my past and my mission followed me.

In 1989, Marc Dutroux and his wife were convicted for the rape and violent abuse of five young girls. The youngest was eleven. Dutroux was the key player in an international child prostitution and pornography ring that included kidnapping, rape, sadistic torture and murder. He got thirteen years, but was freed after serving just three. After his release, girls started disappearing again. Dutroux was unemployed, but owned six homes. The houses had undergound dungeons where he tortured his kidnap victims. The jack for all of this came from his business in child sex slaves, child prostitution and child pornography.

By 1996, the Belgian gendarmes' suspicions were sufficiently aroused to demand further investigation. Dutroux's client list spread across the globe. Interpol was called and the list landed on Defferre's desk.

"*Hello, Kitty.*" Defferre's voice echoed on the phone across the miles.

"I don't do that any more, Jacques."

"Just listen, Race," he said, voice grim and imposing. He laid out the story of Dutroux, the "Belgian Beast." On August 13, 1996, four years after the disappearances began, authorities arrested Dutroux, along with his wife (an elementary school teacher), a lodger, a policeman and a man identified as Michel Lelievre. The gendarmes found a soundproof dungeon. Two fourteen-year-old girls were chained inside, starving. They had been used as prostitutes and the stars of Dutroux and friends' videos. The police found more than three hundred similar videos.

On August 17, gendarmes unearthed the bodies of two eight-year-old girls at another of Dutroux's homes. They found videos of their nine-month imprisonment, multiple rapes and torture. The children were starved to death. One of Dutroux's many accomplices was buried with the girls. His name was Bernard Weinstein, a houseguest who participated in the videos. When he lost favor with Dutroux, he was buried alive. At another of Dutroux's homes, two more dead girls were unearthed. The corpses of two women and parts of a third body found in a Lebanese restaurant in Brussels were connected to Dutroux.

While the Belgian citizens were enraged and the gendarmes struggled to investigate the enormity of Dutroux's actions, Interpol assigned Defferre to quietly start tracing the tentacles of the beast's vast global network of child abduction, rape, torture and porn. "There are many names and dates, Major Bannon," Defferre said. "They have been reported to the proper officials, it is all aboveboard and legitimate. Arrests will be made."

"But?"

"But not all will be arrested. The worst of them, they always go free, *non?*" Defferre's voice was raw, revealing the long hours without sleep he had spent on this case. "Archangel is no more, but there are men in France and Belgium who wish it existed again. Just this one last time."

"Not me, Jacques." I paused, trying not to think of what Defferre had told me. Dutroux wasn't the first and wouldn't be the last. The problem was too huge. "Not me anymore. Get one of your other cleaners. What about Peg?"

Defferre was silent. Ten seconds. Twenty. When he spoke, his voice was filled with hurt and anger, guilt and recrimination. "Our Margaret is dead. I sent her after one of Dutroux's contacts in the United States, near Atlanta. She was the last." Another pause, then, "They are all dead, *mon ami*. Only you and I are left."

Suddenly my mind filled with the image of Margaret standing at a bus station in Malaysia, stroking the heads of two children she had rescued from slavery in Thailand. "Call me Peg," she had told me. I was the only one she allowed to call her that. I cleared my throat, sighing at the hard reality of *karma*. "How many of them can't be caught, Jacques?"

"Seven."

"Lucky number." I caught my reflection in the mirror, standing in my small apartment in a sleepy southern town. The puppy dog was long gone. Older, scarred and not nearly as much hair. "Lucky us."

Defferre and I met in Atlanta and kept Margaret's appointment. Then we did some traveling. It took about three weeks to clean the rest.

My past and present finally clashed in the summer of 1998. Law enforcement agents in the United States and thirteen other countries raided the property of nearly two hundred people suspected of membership in a child pornography ring on the Internet. Over one hundred people worldwide were arrested on suspicion of belonging to the ring known as the Wonderland Club.

The Wonderland Club took its name from Lewis Carroll, author of *Alice's Adventures in Wonderland*, who had a fetish for photographing lightly clad little girls. U.S. Customs Service officials reported that investigators found a database of more than 100,000 sexually explicit photographs of children, including graphic acts with adults and toddlers as young as eighteen months.

The coordinated arrests were planned for Monday, August 31 through Wednesday, September 2. Law enforcement professionals across the globe exercised patience while waiting for the worldwide arrest dates.

"We could have adopted the attitude [that] we would just deal with the people in this country, and we could have done it very quickly. It would have all been done and dusted a lot sooner than it was," said Detective Superintendent (Ret.) John Stewardson of the British National Crime Squad, where the sting was known as Operation Cathedral. "But... every one of these images represents a disaster to a family somewhere and we decided that we would go forward by getting as many countries as we could on board with us so that we could maximize on our evidence."

Waiting was not easy for many. One undercover officer in Great Britain related the ordeal of witnessing a suspect interact with children: "The hackles on the back of our neck all stood up on end and we were all concerned as to what our next course of action should be." The officers knew that the arrest must coincide with the worldwide sting to ensure that the hundreds of members of the Wonderland Club would not be alerted early.

Defferre asked me to assist in surveillance of child pornography film and Internet distributors known to be associated with the Wonderland Club. "No cleaning, *cher ami*, just translation," he said. "It is a legitimate assignment and we need your help. Officers are being used across the world." He was excited at the international awareness of the child pornography problem, which had been so long in coming.

Raymond Kelly, Commissioner of the United States Customs Service, called the American participation in the global sting Operation Cheshire Cat. The goal was to apprehend producers who participated in the Wonderland Club distribution ring. Interpol estimated that as many as 25,000 people were involved worldwide in the production and distribution of images and live child-sex shows related to the Wonderland Club network, Wondernet. Wonderland members shared the codes to the Wondernet. We were assigned to watch producers and distributors of these static and live Wondernet shows, waiting too for our September 1 arrest date.

In July, I was sent to a small town in Florida. The team of officers assigned from the International Criminal Police

Organization (ICPO-Interpol), the U.S. Department of Justice National Central Bureau of Interpol (USNCB) and local law enforcement joked frequently that it seemed like an all-male distributors' convention—one suite held two Koreans, a Thai and four Americans. Our base was in the same hotel, two floors down. Defferre had assigned me to simultaneously translate the guttural Pusan dialect of the Koreans, which would later be compared with the more painstaking transcription and translation of the surveillance recordings.

As often happens, the assignment dragged during the weeks preceding the worldwide arrest date. We bought a cappuccino machine, each becoming expert in the serious business of blending beans. A behavioral scientist, my long-time friend, Toni Brynes, was assigned to the team. Toni and I had met when I moved back to the States permanently. We were neighbors and—having many things in common—grew to be close friends. She knew more about Archangel than Defferre would have liked, but I knew she could be trusted. Toni had been consulting with the FBI Baltimore Field Division's Innocent Images National Initiative (IINI), a component of the Crimes Against Children (CAC) Program, designed to track and apprehend online child pornographers. The Bureau's institutional hate for child kidnappers had all but eliminated ransom cases, which never paid off and always brought the FBI down like the Sword of Justice—only less merciful. Most non-family child abductions were sexual in nature, sometimes related to child pornography. In this case, the FBI CAC coordinators had shared their local informant with the USNCB to help crack the Wonderland distribution ring.

Toni and I bunked together during off-hours; she teased me about my hopeless addiction to *Columbo* while I wondered how one shorthaired brunette could shed so much. The petite psychologist made horrible coffee and was forbidden access to the makers. Local deputies saw this as a plum assignment—wearing sweats and enjoying hours of close quarter battle practice with the Interpol linguist, who also made a mean cup of latte. My secret ingredient was vanilla.

On the afternoon of Sunday, August 30, I strolled in at the beginning of my evening shift. Toni was standing quietly in the corner. The local deputies were in full dress; the younger man pacing while the senior deputy stood with thumb hooked on his Sam Browne belt rig under an ample belly. He had eyes that had seen it all and liked it even less. There was very little noise in the room except for the men at the surveillance equipment, listening.

"Thank God you're here," Toni said, and nodded toward the headphones. "You're the translator. What the hell are they saying?" I put the headphones on.

It was a little girl. I could hear her and the Koreans. The tech guys had filtered out the music in the room well enough to catch most of what was said. She was whimpering in English and the Koreans were talking to and about her in their own language. My chest tightened as my mind involuntarily translated every word.

"How long has she been with them?" I asked.

A USNCB officer with crewcut and brooding eyebrows replied, "About an hour. The principal subject, their producer, is about to arrive."

"The Bureau?" I asked.

"Two CAC guys are on the way. Their informant is in the room so the U.S. Attorney says to hold off." These were professionals who followed orders. They had set a trap and, when the targets brought their own bait, they were told to sit tight. Rash action at this emotionally charged moment might set off a firestorm that would cost lives.

Crewcut removed his headset. "Look, Race, none of us likes it, but now we have to treat this as a hostage situation. That means doing what it takes to keep that little girl alive." He grimaced. "Our primary objective is the same."

I turned to Toni, who held her tiny frame tight. Her hands were shaking. I looked around the room. They had been waiting for me to translate. Strangely, I recalled my many conversations with Defferre about *Master of Kungfu*. The main character, Shang Chi, reconciled his search for inner peace with the violence required protecting innocents: "Peace cannot be attained by walking any ground. It is found only... within." Everything Archangel tried to stop, everything I had been trained to prevent, was happening now to an innocent child.

The deputies were frowning. "Do you two have kids?" I asked.

"Yes sir," they responded in unison.

"Follow me." My unprofessional raw emotions jumped to the surface. Having failed to share what I heard in that room, I was asking the deputies to take a leap of faith. They had a pretty good idea of what might be happening but without a direct translation, no one knew how far it had gone. Except me.

I headed for the door. One of the other officers, a tall swaggering expert in *kungfumovie-do*, helped solve the question about the street value of armchair training. He attempted to prevent my access to the hotel master key card. I should have been written up, but he still says that at that precise moment he tripped and fell.

I sprinted to the stairs, aware that the deputies were behind me, but too angry to wait for proper backup. Realizing too late that I had left my Beretta 92FS 9mm pistol behind, I pulled a Marine-type Ka-Bar fighting knife from my belt sheath. The blade was black except for the gleaming eighth-inch edge. Two floors up, I used the key card and rushed into the suite. "Interpol!" I yelled. My mind screamed, *Archangel!* Four males were in the room: two on a sofa, one in a chair, one standing near the door.

The doorman was tall and overweight, but surprisingly nimble. He drew a Heckler & Koch Mark 23 .45 ACP pistol from a mid-back belt-slide holster. I blocked his weapon with my left forearm and, thrusting my body forward, crossed my knife hand over my shoulder and drove the blade down into his throat. My opponent collapsed. The two men by the sofa stood and drew pistols as we rolled to the ground, the knife twisting from my hand under the larger man's weight.

The deputies yelled a warning and discharged their weapons. The two assailants fell to the floor. The third, by the chair, was the FBI informant. He laced his fingers behind a ratty ponytail and dropped to his knees. He had obviously done this before.

I ran to the bedroom. A short, skinny Thai was behind a camcorder tripod. Loud music filled the room. On the bed lay an eight-year-old African-American girl and the two Koreans. All of them were naked. The Thai lifted the tripod and swung it. I stepped to my right, extended my telescoping baton and drove it low onto my assailant's left knee. The Thai lost his balance and the heavy end of the tripod, with the camera attached, fell on his skull.

A Korean in his mid-thirties, frozen by the sounds of screaming deputies and shots over the music, jumped from the bed when I entered the room. He tossed a chair through the window and began to crawl out. In my attempt to detain him he slipped and slit his neck on the jagged window edge. As I turned to the room, USNCB and local law enforcement officers were detaining the second Korean, a young man in prime condition. He displayed a knowledge of martial arts that required the officers to deploy force to subdue him.

My own daughter was now ten years old. I stared at the young girl, only eight, as she lay spread-eagled and naked on the bed. Her eyes locked in mine. I saw shock, mostly, and terror, and a deadness that chilled me. Someone switched off the music. I took a clean blanket from the closet, covered her and sat beside her. She stared. I said the first thing that came to mind:

"It's okay. Your daddy sent me."

She sat up and hugged me. Tight so I couldn't breathe. Tight as though her life were saved. Her dark curls smelled of child's lavender and the reek of men's cologne. I lifted her and went to the only room that didn't contain blood and death—the bathroom. Sitting on the commode, I held her in the blanket. When my own daughter was very young, I often sang "*Somewhere Over the Rainbow,*" "*Too-Ra-Loo-Ra-Loo-Ral*" and "*Daddy's Little Girl*" at bedtime. I knew nothing else to do, so I sang and rocked her. I told her about my daughter. Toni came in and whispered that they had found the little girl's Sunday dress and tiny purse that held a child's ID card.

"Her name is Annie," Toni said, reaching a hand to pat Annie's head. The little girl pulled away, burying her face deeper into my shoulder. Toni smiled sadly. "You have it covered here, Major Bannon," she said. She knew the story behind my Belgian gendarmerie rank, but used it to establish boundaries and assure the girl. "An EMS team is on the way. We'll find her parents and I'll be right back."

Annie spoke for the first time. "I like that rainbow song," she said softly. I sang it again. And again.

Later, Toni told me that Annie's family was heading to the hospital. The emergency medical professionals had arrived, but Annie could only moan and hold me tighter, so I rode to the hospital with her on my lap in the EMS vehicle. Annie spoke a second time, "Talk more about your little girl." The ride seemed very short.

Annie's mother, father and teenage brother were waiting as we arrived. Annie held me; eyes on her weeping mother—whose full body shook with desperate relief—and her quiet, tense father. "It's okay, Daddy," she said. "This is the man you sent to get me." And she fell into the arms of her family.

Later that day, Defferre got hold of me via phone from his office in Lyon. "*Mon Dieu!* What have you done?"

While I laid it out, I could tell he was trying to remain severe with me. "Don't use me anymore, Jacques. I'm only trained for one thing. I need to retire."

"Retire?" Defferre finally laughed, long and deep. "Oh, Race, I think that is just what you must not do."

I received an official reprimand for endangering an entire team. It said my actions were ill-advised, unplanned and risked the lives of team members who felt constrained to serve as back up.

Annie's story was only one in the chronicle of horrors uncovered in the global Wonderland Club raids. Interpol officials charged that Wonderland and its Wondernet operated one of the world's largest, most sophisticated child pornography rings. To trace members, investigators used wiretaps, surveillance equipment and on-line transmission records. The United States Customs Service worked with Interpol, USNCB, British National Crime Squad, FBI CAC coordinators and local authorities to retrieve computers from suspects in twenty-two states.

Raids occurred in California, Colorado, Connecticut, Florida, Georgia, Illinois, Indiana, Kansas, Maine, Massachusetts, Michigan, Minnesota, Mississippi, Missouri, New Jersey, New York, North Carolina, Oklahoma, Pennsylvania, Texas, Utah and Virginia. Other countries that conducted raids on August 31 through September 2 were Australia, Austria, Belgium, Britian, Finland, France, Germany, Italy, the Netherlands, Norway, Portugal, Spain and Sweden.

"I will have to write a scathing letter about you," Defferre chuckled when he called me with the news of the other raids. "It will say that your John Wayne routine could have cost that little girl's life."

"That may be true." I said, wracked once again with pangs about my actions, my motives, my life.

"What? Since when did an archangel endanger a child's life?" Defferre must have felt my dejection. A mix of pride and anger in his voice. "Our cleaners protect the innocent!"

This summed up Defferre's view of Archangel's role. Was it right or wrong? We rang off and I began filling out stacks of paperwork at a desk that the local sheriff had lent me.

"Major Bannon?" It was Annie's father in the doorway. His slender, straight back held restrained dignity. "Major Bannon, Annie told me that you said I sent you."

I shrugged a half-smile. "Yeah, I didn't know what to say. I'm sorry—so sorry—about…" and his hand was on my shoulder, eyes deep and soulful. He shook his head.

"No. You were right." He sat back. "Since they…" he paused and cleared his throat. "Since Annie disappeared this afternoon at church, we've been praying for God to send an angel and save our little girl. He sent you."

"It was my job, sir. I'm no angel. I don't even know if I believe in that sort of thing."

"But I know, Major. I try to be a good family man and I believe that God has prepared me to be a decent father. But I know that I would die trying what you did today. I wouldn't even know how to start. But God prepared you to save my little girl. The deputies told me that you were the one who…" His voice choked and he put his hand on my shoulder again, this time for support. Then he looked hard into my eyes. "You told my Annie the truth, Major Bannon. You were sent today."

He stood. "Now, how can I thank you?"

"Well, sir, those two deputies have been in some trouble because they backed me. Seems that things are hard on them for discharging their weapons: The usual two-week suspension with pay and an internal investigation. Maybe you could put in a word?"

He smiled slowly. "I think I know how to do that."

It was more than a word. Turned out Annie's grandfather had been a city councilman for more terms than most people in the small southern town could remember and had a standing golf game every Saturday with the mayor. During the investigation, it was concluded that the assailants posed an imminent threat of death or grievous bodily harm to the officers and therefore deadly force was required. The deputies were awarded citations. My own misconduct was investigated and, as Defferre had promised, a letter of censure was placed in my European Interpol file.

Several months later, Annie's parents asked me to visit. Annie, who suffers even now from extreme agoraphobia, wanted me to meet her new dog. Her anxiety about being in places without help or escape prevented her from leaving her home. When I arrived, I was shocked to see my picture hanging in the hall.

"We saw you on that television show," Annie's mother explained, referring to a Discovery Channel documentary on martial arts in which I had appeared. "So we looked it up on-line and printed this picture."

I promised to send a real photo right away.

In the living room was the biggest purebred German Shepherd I had ever seen. She was a police dog who lost two litters and so was ruined for the work. Annie was her new pup; the maternal instinct was strong. The animal eyed me suspiciously until Annie jumped from the sofa, her new white dress rustling as she ran into my arms.

"Major Race! Major Race!" The dog jogged over, circled us, sniffed and sat on my foot.

Annie sat beside me during supper, the dog beneath our chairs. Annie insisted that I eat the corn. "I cooked it for you, Major Race," she explained; so I scooped a mountain onto my plate. She quickly added, "Why did you become *innerpole?*"

The whole family stopped eating to hear my answer. Her teenage brother froze mid-chew. "I suppose I wanted to be a decent man, like your father, Annie. In my own way, it's how I have found peace with myself." I smiled softly. "I want to protect the innocent."

Annie nodded. "That's what my dog does, too. She used to be a police dog, but now she watches me. That's why her name is Racey."

Thoughts of Annie filled my mind as I traveled back home to my own daughter.

The trees behind my house were misted over, the most distant ones invisible behind the clouds. A few yellow leaves were taking a long time in the air before coming to rest on the grass. As I practiced basic Hapkido forms, the day waned and my daughter watched and played along with me. The image of trees reminded me of La Treille, but the memory didn't make the view empty, only deeper. It made my home two places at once. Time was passing again, but now the precious moments were with a young person that inhabited them all with beauty. She wanted to go in and have tea like a grown-up with me. Nothing sounded better.

She ran to the kitchen to make the tea as I closed my bedroom door to change. My eyes lit on the temple lamp Hyung-Jin and his mother gave me. Its power to haunt was gone; I could see its flaws and the wear of years. It was a stranger on my dresser. It belonged to another place, another time. I pulled on jeans and—on a whim—a shirt and tie, fully dressed to sip tea with my child.

I had come back home to find a sense of belonging to something, a community. I have found that with my daughter.

She has taught me to love the world; that time vanishes but love endures. I'm aware of how each day flashes by, but with my daughter I have a wide-awake perception, seeing with the eyes of our spirits. Each day with her carries it's own absolute moment, to be treasured in memory across time and miles. A sigh, a sob, a glance, a swirling cascade of blossoms and laughter, a moment of understanding and grace—my daughter has given me all of these.

I finally hope to become a true human.

EPILOGUE

I'll continue failing to understand with my reason why I pray, and yet I will pray—but my life, my whole life, regardless of what happens to me, every moment of it, is not only not meaningless as it was before, but it has the irrefutable meaning of the goodness that is in my power to put into it!
— Leo Nikolaevitch Tolstoy
Anna Karenina

Here are the perspectives through their letters of four people directly involved in my Interpol past, followed by my own thoughts:

I've been in this business too long. It's horrible to watch the victims. Their responses are all different, but eerily similar. In sixteen years, I've never seen anything like what I saw with Race and Annie. When I waded through the room full of law enforcement personnel, I could see evidence of Race everywhere. He leaves a trail. Then I saw him with that little girl in the bathroom. I'll never forget it. She was wrapped up in a comforter like a cocoon. I tried to talk to the girl, but she threw off the top layer of the blanket and

held onto Race like a lifeline. He was singing to her and she was
rocking. Usually the victim is treated immediately by the EMS
team. She keened. I got the impression that trying to take the girl
from Race at that moment was not a particularly safe agenda. The
bond between them within such a short time, only minutes really,
was something I'll never forget. Race saved Annie's life, but afterward when he comforted her, he saved her for the **rest** of her life.
Right or wrong, in that small bathroom, Race was truly a hero.

Toni G. Brynes, Ph.D., M.D,
Dublin, Ireland

Major Bannon has many years investigating the kidnappers and
the pornographers all over the world. I believe that day was the
one last time for him to endure. His behavior was inexcusable. I
reprimanded him. He has the *Lettre de Censure* for such actions.
Cependant, David is a quiet, polite man. *Il charme*. For years he
worked with me and we all knew his strong points and weaknesses. His temperament is the coals, warm before the fire. We
saw many friends sacrifice to the years *y compris* David's lovely
bride. Because I know him, I should not have assigned him to the
case. We all deserve the *Lettre de Censure* for that day. Major
Bannon was guilty only of being Major Bannon.

Commissaire Jacques Defferre
Lyon, France

How may I talk about my lifetime friend, Race Bannon? We
have seen many troubles and difficult years. When he sent to
me the manuscript, I could not believe his writings. To write his
story is very brave because the world is full of evil. Even now, I
read the story of our close friend, Eunmi, and cry for the

injustice of terrorist bombers. I loved her. I hated Race for her death. After hating, I asked myself very candidly the question, *Would I want to be dead and Eunmi alive after the car bombing?* I knew the truth. Race saved many lives and we at NIS were grateful and I am grateful to be his personal friend. Even so, each day he was losing his soul. He is my close friend and I see the payment he gave to Archangel and to South Korea and to his friends and lovers and to me. Race writes in the beginning: "This story is true and I wish it were not." He told me, "I will never be anyone's hero or saint." He published a personal narrative, "Deadly Hands," in the November/December 2001 issue of *Wisdom for Body and Mind: Kungfu Qigong*. Some readers said Race was not a hero. Race said he only wanted to tell the truth about the children. He said there are no heroes. He said in sad anger, "No one should ever do my deeds. No one must want to live my life."

Working for KNBC (Korean National Central Bureau of Interpol), my team participated in the transport and prosecution of a second Korean male arrested during the incident described in the Wonderland chapter. During the trial, the accused male said: "The crazy American attacked us. I thought we would die. He was unfair. I knew he would kill me." When I heard the testimony, I could not stop a grim smile. A child molester calling an Interpol officer "unfair?" Race Bannon saved my life on the Gamcheon Bay docks in Busan, South Korea. I watched his grace and violence. I have known Race Bannon since 1981. We worked on many assignments together, but I was not with him in 1998. Even so, I believe the accused male was telling a little truth. "I knew he would kill me." Yes, I believe that thing. Child pornographers were never safe in vicinity of Race.

Now I must talk about evil and the human soul. I am a
Buddhist now. I am not Christian. This is to honor my family
and not to insult fellow Christians. I have strong feelings about
evil and the human soul. The advice of all Buddhas is not to do
evil, to do good, and to purify one's mind. I hope Christian
friends will agree with such advice. Evil is that which soils our
minds. In *Race Against Evil* we learn the mind is soiled by vicious
men harming children. Evil causes suffering to oneself and others. We see in the book men hurting children who are innocent
and pure. The roots of evil are lust, hatred and ignorance. In our
work, Race and I saw such things and despised them as evil. Men
lusting children hate children and hate themselves and are ignorant, ugly demons. But Race also said to me, "I was part of evil."

How do we understand Race's feelings? Evil is caused by
deeds, words and thoughts. Three kinds of evil are caused by
deeds: killing, stealing and misconduct. Race is guilty of all three
deeds of evil. He is ashamed for stealing and misconduct. He
paid in prison for these deeds. In Japan, an evil man killed
beloved Shin in a wicked deed that makes him unworthy of life.
I believe the killing of this man was not evil. This way, we learn
that some evil deeds are not evil.

Four kinds of evil are caused by words: lying, slandering,
harsh speech and vain talk. Such men lie to children for their own
evil intentions. They hurt and lie to them and make promises that
are not true. Do we see that all people lie? Yes, this is so. We learn
that telling some lies and using angry words is part of our human
nature. The men who lie to children for evil intentions are pure
evil. To punish such evil Race also lied, slandered and used harsh
speech. He is not evil for doing such deeds against evil men. This
book is not a lie nor vain talk. This book is the truth.

Three kinds of evil are caused by thoughts. They are greediness, anger and wrong views. They say, "We are child-lovers. We are pedophiles." These are wrong views. Race is my long-time friend and I know his feeling. He is angry and greedy to hunt evil men—a world of evil men living their wrong views together. It is ugly demons Race faced in dark demon worlds. Race is a guilty man. He hates evil men and hunts them like animals. We learn in the book that to punish evil men he pays with his soul. Race does not know what is good. He says to me, "I have seen evil. I have seen innocent. I do not know what is good." That which cleanses one's mind is good. Why is anything good? Because it gives happiness to oneself and others. So we learn that via writing this book, Race cleanses his soul for children. The reader may hate Race for his evil deeds. Even so, we learn that the world has hopeful life. We learn atonement for evil deeds. This is happiness to others.

There are three kinds of merit. The first kind of merit is charitable giving or generosity, which pushes away selfishness. To write this story is a brave deed by my friend. He gives it to the world without selfishness. He paid with his soul and reputation for this book. Please read graciously his brave words. They are the truth.

The second kind of merit is morality or virtuous conduct which pushes away ill will or hatred. This merit is difficult for human nature. So we learn in this book that Race Bannon is not a perfect man. Dr. Lee Hyung-Jin is not a perfect man. We are all not perfect men or women.

The third kind of merit is meditation which pushes away ignorance. Now we learn the truth about souls in meditation. This book is a kind of meditation. Writing this book was meditation. Reading this book is meditation. We give up ignorance via learning this book's lessons. My friend Race pays with his soul to fight against evil. With this book, he atones his soul. Please for-give him his evil deeds. Please meditate on the merit of my friend, the hero.

Lee Hyung-Jin, Ph.D.
South Korea

For the first time in three years, my daughter blessed Halloween visitors with candy and her perfect smile. Her pet dog, Racey, was beside her the entire evening. She wore an angel costume with wings and glitter that glows in the dark. In the last chapter, Major Bannon tells how he returned our angel to us. Each day we thank God for blessing us with Major Bannon. We know that he received many trials for his actions that horrible day. His career was damaged and he is still uncomfortable talking about that day. His spirit is deeply shaken and I see the crisis of faith in every con-versation. We do not see him as perfect, but we know that God chooses many tools for His work. The Lord sent a brave man to save our little girl.

We believe the story shows the workings of the Lord and His perfect Mercy. We know every day as we hold our little angel that Major Bannon is a blessing to us and we are gifted to know him. Each night my daughter pleads, "And bless Major Race" in her prayers before she hugs Racey and crawls into bed.

Annie's father
United States of America

Time ages us all. However, since I'm lucky to be alive—and sane!—I figure the time I have now is pure gravy. Nice family, nice wife, a daughter so significant and rare that I know I'm a better person just for knowing and loving her. Even a relaxing, ordinary job in a pleasant office. I wouldn't have it any other way. But that mirror—like a great jazz song or impassioned opera—reflects the truth. I didn't always look this way.

Because of Archangel—and despite it—I have seen evil. Seen its dark fetid heart lurking behind dozens of different faces across the globe, always there, a hidden seething mass. It finds innocence and vulnerability and pounces until its victim is broken, beaten, helpless. Evil is hurting a child on purpose. Evil exists unto itself. It is known to me. I have faced its lurid smile and would be dead but by God's grace.

Archangel preached the nature of evil incessantly, but their words and propaganda have no hold on me. Perhaps Archangel has been wiped from the annals of Interpol. The cleaners are all gone, but Defferre and myself. He still insists that our actions were necessary and inherently good.

Over the years Defferre gave me dozens of reasons why he recruited me—usually to suit his need at the time. "We recruited you just because you speak Korean," he'd say, handing me a ticket to Seoul. Or, "It's because you are so blindingly fast with those hands, Race, that we approached you in the first place," right after assigning a particularly nasty bit of cleaning. He usually saved that one for when he sent me out alone. Defferre was a master of using Moral Indignation, Flattery, Obligation and Guilt to get me working. I read a book that called it FOG. The "F" also stands for Fear.

Although I still like to pretend that my language skills and close-quarter combat ability weren't entirely FOG inspired, there were other reasons, real reasons. One is of them was that he wanted me in Interpol because I looked like a puppy. My mirror tells a different story now, but back then my appearance, dress and demeanor defined cute-sweet-nice-guy. "I recruited you because looking at you, no one would ever believe you're a cleaner," Defferre told me in a moment of rare candor. Although the FOGhorn was echoing in the distance, I believed him. Recently when speaking with Defferre, I asked again why he plucked me from Taejon prison to work for Interpol. "We used you because we could, *mon ami*," he replied. Then, though unasked, he seemed to want to explain further. "It is the popular story in the movies, *non*? I knew that you might struggle with our assignments in your heart, but you would complete them." Defferre's eyes were bright as he spoke, assured of his own rightness. "You had a unique set of skills that I needed."

I have heard and read many thoughtful, reasoned arguments regarding the existence of good and evil, God and the devil. I lack the philosophical and theological training—as well as the moral authority and wisdom—to judge such things. But I know that we were not cleaners. Evil cannot be killed; it can never be completely cleansed from this world as long as there is free will. There was nothing clean about the vengeance and indignation that deepened our blood guilt with each assignment. However, true evil and its weeping victims, once seen, can never be wiped from our minds.

It wasn't until my experiences with Annie that I could believe in God's existence again. I believe that murdered innocents rest in His arms and that someday, somehow he will help me to understand why there is evil in this world. In the meantime, through Annie, I have learned to accept my past and embrace the future— All that I am, where I am going and where I have been.

David Race Bannon
United States of America

APPENDIX A

Interpol member countries (179):

A   Albania – Algeria – Andorra – Angola – Antigua & Barbuda – Argentina – Armenia – Aruba – Australia – Austria – Azerbaijan

B   Bahamas – Bahrain – Bangladesh – Barbados – Belarus – Belgium – Belize – Benin – Bolivia – Bosnia-Herzegovina – Botswana – Brazil – Brunei – Bulgaria – Burkina-Faso – Burundi

C   Cambodia – Cameroon – Canada – Cape Verde – Central African Republic – Chad – Chile – China – Colombia – Comoros – Congo – Congo (Democratic Rep.) – Costa Rica – Cote d' Ivorie – Croatia – Cuba – Cyprus – Czech Republic

D   Denmark – Djibouti – Dominica – Dominican Republic

E   Ecuador – Egypt – El Salvador – Equatorial Guinea – Eritrea – Estonia – Ethiopia

F   Fiji – Finland – Former Yugoslav Republic of Macedonia – France

G   Gabon – Gambia – Georgia – Germany – Ghana – Greece – Grenada – Guatemala – Guinea – Guinea Bissau – Guyana

H   Haiti – Honduras – Hungary

I   Iceland – India – Indonesia – Iran – Iraq – Ireland – Israel – Italy

J   Jamaica – Japan – Jordan

K   Kazakhstan – Kenya – Korea (Rep. of) – Kuwait – Kyrgyzstan

L   Laos – Latvia – Lebanon – Lesotho – Liberia – Libya –
      Liechtenstein – Lithuania – Luxembourg

M   Madagascar – Malawi – Malaysia – Maldives – Mali – Malta –
      Marshall Islands – Mauritania – Mauritius – Mexico – Moldova –
      Monaco – Mongolia – Morocco – Mozambique – Myanmar

N   Namibia – Nauru – Nepal – Netherlands – Netherlands Antilles –
      New Zealand – Nicaragua – Niger – Nigeria – Norway

O   Oman

P   Pakistan – Panama – Papua New Guinea – Paraguay – Peru –
      Philippines – Poland – Portugal

Q   Qatar

R   Romania – Russia – Rwanda

S   St. Kitts & Nevis – St. Lucia – St. Vincent & the Grenadines –
      Sao Tome & Principe – Saudi Arabia – Senegal – Seychelles –
      Sierra Leone – Singapore – Slovakia – Slovenia – Somalia – South
      Africa – Spain – Sri Lanka – Sudan – Suriname – Swaziland –
      Sweden – Switzerland – Syria

T   Tanzania – Thailand – Togo – Tonga – Trinidad & Tobago –
      Tunisia – Turkey

U   Uganda – Ukraine – United Arab Emirates – United Kingdom –
      United States – Uruguay – Uzbekistan

V   Venezuela – Vietnam

Y   Yemen – Yugoslavia

Z   Zambia - Zimbabwe

Appendix B

Archangel: Past and Present

It is my understanding that the Interpol Archangel Program was founded in 1979, an offshoot of an earlier unit that dated to the 1960s and had been designed specifically to hunt those who traffic in children. Archangel's operation was covered under the second of Interpol's loosely worded missions: "To establish and develop all institutions likely to contribute effectively to the prevention and suppression of ordinary law crimes." Of the member countries participating in Interpol—and the many others that did so without official membership—there was a unanimous condemnation of this traffic. By 1988, there was tacit approval of Archangel by some officials who referred to it as a "supranational body to investigate sexual exploitation, pornography, and trafficking in children."

Archangel had successfully been budgeted and organized within the Interpol Special Programs Sub-Directorate. Interpol is the common name for the International Criminal Police Organization (ICPO), also the Organisation Internationale de Police Criminelle (OIPC) located in Lyon, France. The term "INTERPOL" was the telegraph address of the ICPO. In a nod to common usage, the organization changed its official name to "ICPO-Interpol" (alternatively, OIPC-Interpol) in 1956. Today, Interpol is an international criminal police organization that comprises designated national central bureaus (NCB's) from the law enforcement agencies of its 179 member nations. It has two primary missions:

1. To ensure and promote the widest possible mutual assistance between all criminal police authorities within the limits of the laws existing in the different countries and in the spirit of the 'Universal Declaration of Human Rights.'

2. To establish and develop all institutions likely to contribute effectively to the prevention and suppression of ordinary law crimes.

Archangel's role included legitimate law enforcement, such as apprehending a French citizen in Paris who had escaped from a Thai prison while serving time for child molestation or identifying missing children from the Archangel records. It also performed clandestine operations, such as assignments deep in the heart of Romania, Thailand and other countries. Archangel's activities were sometimes successful and sometimes fraught with failure. Later, one official noted that "Previous attempts at monitoring and combating the trafficking of children and their exploitation through pornographic materials have been problematic and tainted by vigilantism and excesses in jurisdictional malfeasance." Archangel was all of these things. Nevertheless, for a little over a decade, it was the world's most effective body for monitoring, tracking and illegally punishing criminals who kidnap, rape, torture and often kill children for the purpose of creating pornography and reselling the materials.

Child pornography is an unprotected visual depiction of a minor child engaged in actual or simulated sexual conduct, including a lewd or lascivious exhibition of the genitals. In the United States in 1996, 18 U.S.C. § 2252A was enacted and § 2256 was amended to include "child pornography" that consists of a visual depiction that "is or appears to be" of an actual minor engaging in sexually explicit conduct. United States federal age of a minor child is under eighteen. The practice not only included buying children as young as one year from willing parents, but also kidnapping others and trading them around the world. In many cases this traffic included unspeakable sexual abuse, murder of the victims, and resulting pornography recording these acts. Other images and tapes were made by individuals abusing their relatives or children in their care, and then sold. This child pornography commanded huge amounts of money on the international market. The overwhelming, global nature of child molestation and pornography forced the creation of a team dedicated to hunting those who produced and traded these materials. Archangel's mission: identify child porn producers who danced around the laws of multiple nations and eliminate—or "clean"—them. Archangel was a clandestine but viable option within international law enforcement.

Archangel officers were recruited from within and without Interpol ranks. A potential Archangel officer that had been courted, coerced or recruited was known as a "Clarence." The name was a reference to the angel who was trying to earn his wings in Frank Capra's internationally renowned film, *It's a Wonderful Life*. Recruits trained and worked from a warehouse in La Verpillere, France, which had been leased indefinitely beginning in 1979 for that purpose by the first and only program director, Commissaire Jacques Defferre. Known within Archangel as "Archie," Defferre worked within Interpol to aggressively and creatively budget the special program. One of his earliest budget maneuvers was to allocate funds for his position—which theoretically didn't exist. A posting was distributed throughout Interpol for an Assistant Director for the Special Programs Management Planning Office in early summer 1980 and it was awarded to Defferre without an interview. He had to be circumspect because budget considerations often lead to hints, documents and public mention of an otherwise highly clandestine program despite aggressive efforts at data protection. The need for money often has that effect, which is undesirable strategically but necessary in allocating funds.

Defferre used the same budget juggle to allocate funds for his recruits, including the author of the present work, who filled a posted position as a Crime Intelligence Officer that was never intended to be anything other than an Archangel member. Creative budgeting was not an entirely new bureaucratic concept, although methods of law enforcement differed in each country. However, according to the terms of the United Nations Convention on the Rights of the Child, the superior interest of the child must take precedence over all other considerations.

Archangel had two sections: an enforcement arm responsible for apprehension or elimination of child sexual abusers, called "cleaners"; and an intelligence gathering arm, known as Rosetta. Rosetta gathered and reviewed evidence and intelligence data on prospective and active targets; then disseminated the information to officers. The primary consideration prior to delivering a target—meaning a subject for assassination—to a cleaner was that there must be irrefutable evidence that the target was "with child." This was a euphemism indicating a target has been identified via photographic and video media, as well as eyewitness accounts, in the act of sexually abusing a child. It also referred to a target attempting to distribute videos and photographs of him or herself sexually abusing a child. Rosetta was responsible for making this final confirmation before assigning a cleaner.

Rosetta provided assessments—detailed analyses of information relating to a particular assignment—and profiles with complete background information on a target. This information was disseminated to the head of Archangel, and those officers or cleaners involved, in "wraps"—internal Archangel envelopes with designated signature(s) that were delivered wrapped in sealed plastic. The sealed plastic protected against the counter-intelligence tradecraft of "French Opening," in which one end of an envelope could be slit open to examine the contents, which was then reinserted and the cut area restored. Those wraps containing assessments of an assassination target were jokingly called "CleanWraps."

Rosetta's role within Archangel warrants special mention as it was resolved to: "Encourage States to establish a national database containing disaggregated criminal data on child trafficking and exploitation with the support of organizations specializing in the field, including Interpol Rosetta Program." Rosetta's information gathering techniques were models for many later programs, including some seemingly unrelated initiatives. For instance, the European Anti-Fraud Office's predecessor, the Anti-Fraud Coordination Unit (UCLAF), created intelligence units some say were patterned on Interpol Rosetta organization charts. The intelligence units were completely modified and attached directly to the Director General by September 2000.

With the expertise of Rosetta working within its structure, Archangel's roles were not always vigilantism. However, as mentioned earlier, the organization adopted any means possible—legal or not—to combat the global problem of child endangerment from sexual predators. Archangel (and Rosetta) worked with the Inter-American Children's Institute to establish a complex information system to assist Pan-American children. The Inter-American Program of Information on Children and the Family (PIINFA) was created in 1987 as a joint program with Interpol. It was approved by the General Assembly of the OAS in 1990 and has the central objective of producing and promoting the use of information systems directed to all those individuals and institutions working on behalf of children, in order to generate spaces of integral information that contribute to creating processes of change in the living conditions of children in the Region, and to always have the principles of the Convention on the Rights of the Child as the main axes of its work. Rosetta's association with Archangel made both organizations bywords for information gathering and technological excellence. Rosetta grew beyond its initial operation with Archangel, and evidence suggests that it was still effectively active as an intelligence gathering organization as late as October 2000.

By the late 1980s, the level and intensity of international crime were increasing. Under Secretary General Andre Bossard, whom foreign nationals called "Inspector Clouseau," sub-organizations like Archangel flourished.

When Recommendation No. R (91) 11 was adopted by the Council of Europe Committee of Ministers on September 9, 1991, it led to Interpol's cutting off of funds and the eventual disbanding of Archangel, at least for a period. The recommendation also outlined a new role for Interpol: "Increase and improve exchanges of information between countries through Interpol, in order to identify and prosecute offenders involved in sexual exploitation, and particularly in trafficking in children and young adults, or those who organize it."

The appeal of the Internet and its mass use throughout the world has led to a new set of problems for international law enforcement. Prior to the Internet, it was more difficult for pedophiles to find child pornography and to link with others who had similar interests. By the late 1980s, Interpol's Archangel program and international police cooperation had cut the flow of child pornography down considerably. The Internet changed all that. ("Innocence Exploited: Child Pornography in the Electronic Age," Canadian Police College, May 1998, p.16).

ECPAT, the network of organizations and individuals working together for the elimination of child prostitution, child pornography and trafficking of children for sexual purposes, hosted the International Consultation on Enforcing the Law Against Sexual Exploitation of Children in Bangkok in January 1996. At the meeting, Bjorn Eriksson, Director of the Swedish National Board of Police and President of Interpol in that country, expressed concern about the volume of child sexual abuse on the Internet: "I have been puzzled by the fact that it has taken such a long time for the law enforcement agencies to realize that the commercial sexual exploitation of children was a problem. I cannot explain the delay, but I do think that until recently there was no understanding of the extent to which it was a problem—the volume of this type of activity. It was looked upon as involving questions of morals, there was denial that it took place, sexual abuse was not discussed openly. It was a matter which was regarded as a question of privacy; people were probably ashamed or perhaps frightened to discuss the questions to which commercial sexual abuse gives rise."

Despite its role—or perhaps because of it—some observers have offered tacit approval of Archangel's methods. It should be noted, however, some are unaware of the actual work performed by Archangel officers. And denial of its existence appears to be the official position of Interpol.

However, to answer the new, even greater threat of child pornography on the Internet, Archangel may have become active again. Evidence is circumstantial at best. Perhaps the most telling allusion to current Archangel activities was in a communication from the Commission of the European Communities to the Council, The European Parliament, the Economic and Social Committee and the Committee of the Regions on 24 January 2001. In it, the Commission used recent operations against child pornography rings, such as Starburst and Cathedral, to display "the value of coordinated international action by law enforcement and judiciary."

During Operation Cathedral, law enforcement agents in fourteen countries raided the property of nearly 200 people suspected of membership in a child pornography ring on the Internet. Over one hundred people worldwide were arrested on suspicion of belonging to the ring known as the Wonderland Club, which took its name from Lewis Carroll, author of *Alice's Adventures in Wonderland*, who had a fetish for photographing slightly clad little girls. United States Customs Service officials reported that investigators found a database of more than 100,000 sexually explicit photographs of children, including graphic acts with adults and toddlers as young as eighteen months. Interpol estimated that as many as 25,000 people were involved worldwide in the production and distribution of images and live child-sex shows related to the Wonderland Club network, Wondernet. Apprehended Wonderland members shared the codes to the Wondernet with authorities. Jacques Defferre, previous head of Archangel, reported that, once collected, "the aggregate total of seizures for all of the countries will... run to huge amounts."

The Commission of the European Communities submitted that Operation Cathedral and other similar efforts suffered major legal and operational difficulties, citing the primary frustration as "the role of intergovernmental organisations dealing with police issues (Interpol and Europol in particular)." Having clearly indicated evidence of the effectiveness of international law enforcement cooperation while, at the same time, also indicating the shortcomings of such cooperation within standard procedure, the Commission cites the World Conference

Against Commercial Sexual Exploitation of Children in Stockholm on August 28, 1996 where "proposals were made to empower Interpol as a supranational body to combat child pornography on the Internet."

As you may imagine, in seeking support documents to expose Rosetta and Archangel, two secret programs of Interpol, I've run into many roadblocks. In sixty years, there has been no exposé on Interpol and I have been told "they" do not want one.

In the fall of 2002, Jacques Defferre, who was coming to Washington, D.C. for a meeting, agreed to see me. In exchange for reading my manuscript, he said he would give me plenty of documentation on the Archangel and Rosetta missions, although he once again reiterated that "'They' do not want your book to see the light of day." Surprised that despite this he was willing to bestow proof upon me, I agreed thinking his offer was due to our past close relationship; so we spent several days together.

However, later when I returned home, I did some digging of my own and found that some of the documents given to me also were available on government and various organization's websites. When I checked the versions I now had against those on the websites, I discovered my documents had been altered and the material on Archangel and Rosetta had been added. I called Jacques who said the documents I found on the Internet must have been edited. Perhaps this is true, but had I utilized the documents given to me, my story would have been discredited. I could not help remembering Jacques' advice to me early in my missions for Interpol: "Don't make too many friends. You may have to betray them in the end. Or lose them."

GLOSSARY

In a small attempt to present a compelling book, I promised myself that I would not burden the long-suffering reader with too much technical detail. Plain language is always preferable when getting to an important point. For example, the phrase "We have diagnosed your unidentified breast masses as benign, based solely on a Fine Needle Aspiration (FNA)" may be informative and accurate, but lacks the stress-relieving simplicity of "You do not have breast cancer." However, terms and descriptions have their place. For readers interested in such details, this glossary presents thorough descriptions of key organizations and terms that were omitted from the text in the name of brevity. Also included are law enforcement and missing person organizations.

The terms listed are presented as a quick reference for the reader that may be unfamiliar with Asian and European organizations, intelligence/espionage terms and some unsavory slang. Readers may be intrigued to learn more about Archangel under such headings as "Rosetta" and "Archie"—bits of information that did not directly relate to the book but illuminate the inner workings of the organization.

Terms change from country to country. For example, a forger is referred to as an "artist" in the United States, a "cobbler" in Russia and simply a "forger" at Archangel. Even more confusing, the same term can have different meanings (even between organizations using the same language or in the same country). The term "nugget," for example, was an Archangel term for information gathered through unofficial means; the same term in British intelligence services referred to bribes and lures offered to defectors. I have attempted to offer brief but inclusive definitions, including as many variants as are relevant to the text.

I have attempted to use terms most familiar to the educated general reader. For example, Britain's intelligence organization is properly referred to as Secret Intelligence Service (SIS), but MI6 is more commonly known to most readers and was used in the book. Similarly, Interpol was used rather than the more correct ICPO, or the even more exact, OIPC—both of which are defined in the introduction and briefly in this glossary.

I also attempted to use only one identifier for any given organization – despite the intelligence community's milieu of changing acronyms in its own Alphabet Spy Soup. An example is the South Korean National Intelligence Service (NIS), mentioned frequently in the text. In 1981, the NIS was established under the name Agency for National Security Planning (ANSP). It was for this fledgling agency that Lee Hyung-Jin was recruited. ANSP went through a few other names before it was finally renamed the NIS on January 22, 1999 with the inauguration of the People's Government. To avoid confusion, I referred to this agency as the NIS throughout the text, although, at times, it would more correctly have been identified as the ANSP. The Met – Scotland Yard is another example where jealously guarded jurisdictions in London require a more exact description of the law enforcement officials involved— all from different agencies and often with conflicting and uncooperative agendas. These political delineators would have burdened the reader within the text but may interest those who choose to read this glossary.

A

Abduction – Kidnapping. *Family Abduction* is by a non-custodial family member, a common and often the least dangerous type of abduction. *Stranger Abduction* is by a non-family member, usually with force and often end up as homicides or – with children – as parts of child porn rings and trafficking in human beings.

Access – Obtaining Archangel classified information via appropriate security clearance.

Accommodation Address – Safe address reserved by officers to communicate with Archangel.

Action Officer – An officer that performed a specific task during a clandestine assignment, usually in a hostile or dangerous area. See Case Officer.

Agent – An agent was a person controlled by Archangel to obtain information – a nice term for a snitch. Agents were recruits working in their native countries, not employees of Archangel. "Warning" agents were used to provide alerts regarding significant changes in their watch areas. See Asset.

Agent-In-Place – An agent that maintained his or her current association, employment or position while providing information to Archangel for identifying targets. See Agent.

Agent Provocateur – An agent who discredited an individual or group via revealing or instigating incriminating information or acts.

All Source Intelligence – Information culled from all available venues. See Open Source (OSINT).

Ambush – When an Archangel officer was observed and arrested while on an assignment.

Angel – A term in intelligence communities that usually denoted a member of an opposing service.

ANSP – Agency for National Security Planning (ANSP), South Korea. Originally named the Korea Central Intelligence Agency (KCIA) in 1961, it changed its name under the direct authority of President Chun Doowhan. Due process and warrants were optional. Alternately called ANSP or NSP for short, the organization served both counterespionage and internal security roles. Working with the military

Defense Security Command (DSC), the civilian NSP was used by the ruling government to arrest and torture political dissidents and opposition politicians. From 1985, the NSP used the National Security Act to suppress student riots. Its reputation marred by the torture and killing of Seoul National University student Pak Chongch'ol in 1987, the organization endured severe internal and international public scrutiny but still managed to make significant contributions in ensuring the security of the 1988 Seoul Olympic Games. In 1994, the ruling and opposition parties reformed the NSP as a politically neutral intelligence/internal security service, assigning an Information Committee to watchdog the organization, and extending its charter to include international crime and terrorism. The following year, the NSP relocated from its dual Seoul sites in Mt. Nam, downtown, and the eastern office in Imun District, combining both offices in a new building in Naegok District, southern Seoul. It was renamed the National Intelligence Service (NIS) on January 22, 1999 with the inauguration of the People's Government. See KCIA, NIS.

Archangel – Archangel was founded in 1979, an offshoot of an earlier Interpol program that dated to the early 1960s that had been designed specifically to hunt those who traffic in children. Archangel's operation was covered under the second of Interpol's loosely worded missions: "To establish and develop all institutions likely to contribute effectively to the prevention and suppression of ordinary law crimes." Of the 170-plus member countries participating in Interpol – and the many others that did so without official membership – there was a unanimous condemnation of this traffic. The practice not only included buying children as young as one year from willing parents, but also kidnapping others and trading them around the world. Invariably this traffic included unspeakable sexual abuse, murder of the victims, and resulting pornography recording these acts. Other images and tapes were made by individuals abusing their relatives or children in their care, and then sold on the market. This kiddie porn commanded huge amounts of money on the international market. The overwhelming, global nature of child molestation and pornography forced the creation of a team dedicated to hunting those who produced and traded these materials. Archangel's mission: Identify child porn producers who danced around the laws of multiple nations and eliminate – or "clean" – them.

Archie – Head of Archangel.

Artist – British term for a forger. See Cobbler.

Assassination – An active policy of Archangel and intelligence services worldwide.

Assassination device – Special weapons, usually concealable and designed to leave no trace, used to assassinate targets.

Assessment – Detailed analysis of information related to Archangel's goals, usually presented in a sealed "Wrap." See Rosetta, Wrap.

Asset – In general terms, any resource, whether a person, a method, or technical device, that is available for an assignment. Most commonly used to refer to an agent.

Assignment – Archangel term for mission or operation.

Audio Surveillance – Eavesdropping with electronic equipment.

B

Babysitter – A bodyguard.

Backstopping – Pre-testing a cover as though it were being challenged by an outside service.

Bang and Burn – Demolition and sabotage.

Basic Intelligence – Information that was unquestioned and fundamental such as physical, social, economic, political and cultural factors. See Open Source (OSINT).

Black – A shorthand term for "black-bag job," breaking and entering to steal information or place illegal surveillance equipment.

Blacklist – Archangel's list of known or suspected child pornography distributors whose actions had not warranted cleaning; in counterintelligence, a list of known collaborators or suspected sympathizers to causes that threaten a nation's security.

Black Ops – Archangel assignments or operations that could not be traced back to Interpol.

Black Propaganda – Propaganda that appeared to originate from a news source or specific country that was actually authored by Archangel.

Black Trainees – Trainees forced to enter Archangel that were unaware of the identities of other officers or the full scope of the organization's operations; a CIA term for foreigners recruited to train undercover at "The Farm."

Blind Date – Archangel officer's term used to indicate a meeting set up by an agent that was considered dangerous due to lack of information.

Blowback – Disinformation "kernels" distributed through obscure sources that would "blow back" to the intended audience. For example, a news story about a South Korean politician's visit to a child brothel in Pakistan would be covered in a small Pakistani paper; months (or even years) later, when the politician's career was under scrutiny, Archangel would tip the investigating reporter to the obscure Pakistani newspaper story. See Kernel.

Blown – An Archangel officer's cover or legend exposed; also an entire network of agents and officers exposed.

Bona Fides – An officer's true affiliation and identity; an intelligence paradox, since most legends were designed specifically to simulate bona fides. See Legend.

Bridge Agent – Agent who carried information between Archangel officers and another agent in a restricted or dangerous area.

Brief Encounter – Brief contact between an officer and an agent known to be under surveillance.

Brush Contact/Pass – A prearranged, brief public contact between officers, agents or handlers at which information or materials were passed.

Bugging – Electronic eavesdropping.

Bureau – The United States Federal Bureau of Investigation (FBI).

Burn – Sacrifice of an agent or officer to protect the identity of a mole or otherwise strengthen an assignment. Usually the agent or officer had already been compromised.

Burned/Burnt – When an officer or agent was compromised; also when they were sacrificed to strengthen an assignment.

C

CAC – FBI Crimes Against Children program designed to track and apprehend Internet online child pornographers, which includes the Innocent Images National Initiative (IINI).

Call Out Signal – Contact signal between an officer and an agent.

Camp Peary – CIA special operations training facility, known as The Farm or Camp Swampy, a 10,000-acre domestic base near Williamsburg, Virginia, USA.

Cannon – Double-cross specialist assigned to steal back whatever bribes Archangel paid an informant.

Carnivore – FBI system for monitoring Internet Service Providers (ISPs), including email; an important tool in tracking Internet child pornographers.

Case – A complete assignment and the record of that assignment.

Case Agent – An agent in charge of a case

Case Officer – An officer that recruited agents and controlled the officers and agents involved in a specific case. See Controller and Handler.

CC&D – Camouflage, Concealment and Deception.

Cell – Lowest rung on the espionage ladder, staffed with expendable agents.

Chart – Small book filled with encoded contact numbers, staggered in sets of threes and fours. Each set contained entries known only to the book's owner. Numbers in a set were to locations in three different countries; with the second number reversed. A set of four numbers immediately followed each set of three, with the first and fourth numbers reversed. For example, the fictitious entry of three numbers "05146378822009201940312819561́4" might represent (051) 463-7882 in Pusan, 04-91-02-90-02 in Marseilles (reversed), and 312-819-5614 in Chicago. See Polyalphabetic substitution.

Chicken Feed – Legitimate but inconsequential information provided to a known agent or mole of the opposition; real enough to convince that the source is valid, small enough to leave them hungry for more.

Child Pornography – An unprotected visual depiction of a minor child engaged in actual or simulated sexual conduct, including a lewd or lascivious exhibition of the genitals. The Child Pornography Act enacted in 1996, 18 U.S.C. § 2252A, 2256, made illegal any visual depiction that "is or appears to be" of a minor (under age eighteen) engaging in sexually explicit conduct. This act was declared unconstitutional in 2002; "virtual" pornography was held to have constitutional protection since real children are not involved.

CIA – The Central Intelligence Agency of the United States of America was formed in 1947 to co-ordinate foreign intelligence gathering and counterintelligence operations abroad. Similar to Britain's MI6.

CIAink – CIA's Intranet.

Cipher – A code in which numbers or letters are substituted within an open text. See Code.

Citizen – Slang for law-abiding citizen. Also, Taxpayer.

Clandestine – Covert and unknown to the target or enemy. Clandestine Service(s) were the part of the CIA responsible for espionage operations, known as the Directorate of Operations (DO) formerly the Directorate of Plans (DP).

Clandestine Assignment – An Archangel assignment designed to remain secret indefinitely.

CLANSIG – Clandestine Signals Intelligence.

Clarence – A potential officer that is being courted or co-erced by Archangel. The name was a reference to the angel who was trying to earn his wings in Frank Capra's internationally renowned *It's a Wonderful Life.*

Classified – Information controlled by Rosetta that, if made public, was deemed harmful to Archangel.

Clean – Assassinate or "eliminate."

Cleaner – Assassin trained and deployed by Archangel.

CleanWrap – Joking slang for an internal Archangel envelope sealed with designated signature(s) that contained the details of a cleaner's assignment. See Wrap.

Cloak – Disguise technique.

Cobbler – Russian term for a forger. See Artist.

Code – System created to hide messages with ciphers, marks, symbols, sounds or any other pre-arranged means. Whereas a cipher substitutes numbers and letters in text messages, codes symbols may represent a sub-message or concept.

Cold Approach – Attempting to coerce or recruit an Archangel officer without prior knowledge of the subject's background and personality.

Collectors – Rosetta's gatherers of raw information.

Combatants – Undercover cleaners. (See Cleaner)

COMINT – Communications Intelligence, gathered via technical or human interception, including breaking and entering. A sub-category of SIGINT.

Commo Plan – Planned communications between a single agent and an Archangel contact.

Company, The – The CIA.

Compromised – When an assignment or officer was uncovered.

COMSEC – Communications Security, designed to block enemy SIGINT.

Concealment Device – Any device designed to store and move materials without detection, such as messages, film, code keys, or poison pills.

Confusion Agent – An agent that placed disinformation and used other confusion tactics, rather than collected intelligence.

Controller – Senior Archangel officer who controlled other officers and agents. See Handler.

Cooking the Books – Deliberate misrepresentation of information to promote a particular agenda. One Rosetta officer guilty of "cooking the books" to implicate his ex-lover in a child pornography ring was surprised to find a "CleanWrap" with his name on it.

Co-Opted Agent – Agent that willingly assists a foreign power.

Cosh – A blackjack; a handheld weapon with a flexible stem and a covered heavy metal end. Archangel cleaners trained in using the cosh as a deterrent and as a lethal weapon.

Counterespionage – Penetrating and disrupting a hostile intelligence service.

Counterintelligence (CI) – Countering the espionage and intelligence operations of foreign, including protecting personnel and installations against espionage and terrorism. See DST.

Counter Surveillance – Detecting and stopping surveillance operations.

Counter Terrorism – Prevention of terrorist activities. Interpol's involvement in the fight against International Terrorism materialized during the 54th General Assembly in Washington in 1985 when Resolution AGN/ 54/RES/1 (Washington, D.C., 1985) was passed calling for the creation of a specialized group within the then Police Division to "..co-ordinate and enhance co-operation in combating international terrorism.." See DST.

Courier – A person used by Archangel to carry secret information between an officer and an agent, often unwittingly or for a fee. Usually this person was a criminal identified by Rosetta as deeply involved in a child pornography ring and was eliminated by a cleaner after the assignment was complete. See Cutout, Mule.

COVCOM – Covert communications.

Cover – A guise used by an individual or organization to hide its true identity and assignment. See Legend.

Covert Action Operation (CA) – Archangel activities that were attributed to other organizations, kept secret for an indefinite period of time, and almost impossible to trace back to Archangel.

Covert Agent/Officer – An officer or agent that carries out covert or secret assignments.

Cracking – Illegal entry into a computer network with malicious intent.

Creds – Credentials

Critical – Referring to Critical Intelligence; information of the utmost importance.

Cryptoanalysis – Breaking a code without access to keys or encryption systems.

Cryptography – Codes and ciphers designed to conceal an original message from anyone without the key or knowledge of the system. See NSA.

Cutout – A person used to create a buffer between officers and agents, enabling personnel to exchange information without meeting. Unlike couriers, cutouts were aware of their role and were not generally cleaned at the end of an assignment. See Courier and Mule.

Cyberwar – Information warfare, whether between countries, terrorists, or criminals (such as Internet child pornographers) and those who track them.

D

DEA – U.S. federal Drug Enforcement Agency.

Dead Drop – A secret, pre-arranged location that allows an officer and agent to exchange information and materials without direct contact. The KGB used a hollow tree trunk in Washington, D.C. In a typical scenario, an agent might drop a microdot into a hidden container attached to a park bench; then attach tape on a signpost a few blocks away (see Signal Site) to indicate there was a message. As much as two or three days later, an officer would retrieve the information. Also known as a dead letter drop. See Petit Louvre.

Dead Telephone – A telephone signal or code passed without speaking. Archangel officers were notoriously adept at vague telephone signals.

Deep Cover Agent – An agent with a permanent and thoroughly prepared legend.

Defector – An intelligence officer who delivers information to a foreign service. Voluntary "walk-in" defectors arrive unannounced, others are recruited and remain loyal to their home country as "defectors in place" supply information as moles. See Mole.

Denied Area – Country where there is no recognition of Interpol.

Development – Section of Archangel assigned to manufacture devices for officers, such as cases with false bottoms or new lock picking materials.

DGSE – *Direction Générale de la Sécurité Extérieure* (General Directorate for External Security). French external intelligence service. Founded in 1982 by President Francois Mitterand to replace the discredited External Documentation and Counter-Espionage Service (SDECE), the DGSE is similar in function to America's CIA and Britain's MI6.

Diplomatic Cover – A fake position associated with a consulate or embassy that protected an officer from prosecution in a foreign country.

Direct Intelligence – Activities that can be confirmed with observation. See With Child.

Dirt Bins – Derisive term used within Archangel for the apartments assigned to cleaners.

Dirty Tricks – Secretive operations designed to discredit and confuse an opposing intelligence service or individuals, media organizations and political parties. False rumors, "blow backs," and cleaners are all part of the bag of dirty tricks.

Discard – An officer or agent betrayed by Archangel to protect an assignment or more valuable officer.

Disinformation – Misleading or false information designed to damage an individual, group or country. See Blowback, Dirty Tricks.

Dissemination – Distributing information.

DMZ – Demilitarized zone between North and South Korea.

Doctor – Archangel and Russian term for the police.

DOJ – Department of Justice, provincial, and federal justice departments in Canada and the United States; such as the USDOJ (U.S. Dept. of Justice [Federal/US]) and the NBDOJ (New Brunswick Dept. of Justice [provincial, Canada]).

Double Agent – An agent controlled by another intelligence service to work against his original service, which does not doubt their loyalty. Different from a Mole.

Drop – Leaving material in a Dead Drop.

Dry Cleaning – Techniques for detecting surveillance while on an assignment.

DST – *Direction de la surveillance du Territoire* (DST – Directorate of Territorial Security). French counterintelligence and internal security service organized in five directorates: counter-espionage, internal security, international terrorism, technical administration and general administration. The DST also had a special office of national and international relations that often crossed paths with Interpol, countering organized crime, drug trade, money laundering, and arms dealing. Similar function to Britain's MI5 or the United States' FBI.

E

Ears Only – Classified material that can only be discussed orally, never committed to print.

Echelon – Multinational surveillance network controlled by America's National Security Agency (NSA) that can intercept nearly all forms of electronic communications. See NSA.

ECM – Electronic countermeasure devices that disrupt an enemy's electronic equipment, used extensively in Counterintelligence.

Elicitation – Gathering information from an individual or group that is unaware of the purpose to which the information will be used.

ELINT – Electronic Intelligence.

Espionage – Spying. Collection of intelligence.

ESR – *Equioes Spécialisées de Reconnaissance* - Specialized Reconnaissance Teams. Belgian ESR units were organized in 1961 to gather intelligence on deep reconnaissance missions. Euphemistically referring to themselves as "Shadow Warriors," ESR teams soon took on other roles, including counter-terrorism. Their existence was sometimes praised, but more frequently denied, by the Belgian government. They worked closely with the Belgian Long-Range Reconnaissance Patrol Detachment (LRRP) commando teams.

Established Source – A source of information that had been used frequently by Interpol and Archangel.

Executive Action – Assassination directed by an intelligence service.

Exfiltration – An operation designed to bring an officer or agent out of a hostile country.

Eyes Only – Information that should be read only and not duplicated or discussed, except in specific restricted situations.

F

Fairgrounds – Geographic locations broken down into sub-classifications for study within the Rosetta department of Archangel; teams assigned to those locations. See Rosetta.

False Flag – An officer that appeared to represent one organization but actually represented a separate organization. False flag recruitment was used to convince an agent or informer that he was working for a child porn ring or a distributor, when actually he was working for Archangel.

FBI – Federal Bureau of Investigation; United States anti-crime, counterintelligence and internal security organization similar to Britain's MI5. Founded in 1924.

Fence – A dealer in stolen goods; also, the Russian term for a country border.

Field – Any location for an assignment; also, the British term for a foreign territory.

Fiber Intelligence – Observations that are not physically verifiable by direct observation, such as fetishes, a target's personal feelings, morale, hearsay, social and economic trends.

FINCEN – Financial Crimes Enforcement Network, the U.S. Treasury Department's intelligence network on money laundering.

Firm, The – The CIA.

Fix – Grift, blackmail, compromise, con or trick.

Flaming – Unplanned or improvised activities during an assignment; referring to the Archangel Michael's mythical flaming sword of justice.

Flaps and Seals – Opening then resealing envelopes and other secured containers without alerting postal carriers or the recipient. The phrase refers to envelope flaps and wax seals. Another method, called "French Opening," slit one end of an envelope then restored the cut area. Archangel documents were wrapped in special sealed plastic to counter this tradecraft.

Flash – High precedence communiqué.

Floater – Freelance agent used for minor assignments.

Foots – Surveillance team members working on foot or as passengers in cars.

Four-Player – A double agent, officer or criminal who is turned back to his or her original loyalties. Also known as a Re-Doubled Agent.

Friends – British term for MI6.

Front – Business created as a legitimate cover for Archangel officers.

Fumigating – Removing surveillance devices.

Fusion – Assessing all known information on a known target. See Rosetta.

G

Gamekeeper – British term for Controller or Handler.

Gardening – Forcing an agent to send a message in code, providing cryptographers with a sample.

Genii – Experts outside of Archangel who were used to review documents or equipment in their field.

GIGN – French Intervention Group of the National Gendarmerie, one of the world's finest counter-terrorist special forces. Formed in 1974, they have participated in over 1250 public and countless covert operations. Famous for HALO (High Altitude Low Opening) jumps and exhaustive training requirements. See Modern Ninja.

Global Organized Crime – Worldwide efforts of criminal organizations to establish via financial and political influence firm communication and cooperation in trafficking in human beings, child pornography, drugs, money laundering, arms smuggling and many other schemes.

Graymail – As compared to blackmail, a threat to expose sensitive information if prosecuted.

GRU – *Glavnoye Razvedyvatelnoye Upravlenie* (Chief Intelligence Directorate of the General Staff); military intelligence service for the former Soviet Union and now the Russian Federation.

H

Han – Korean term loosely translated as "unrequited sorrow"; a sense of grief and misery so deep that in inspires an unanswerable adamant resolve for vengeance.

Handle – A vulnerability such as information, blackmail, or money, than was used by an Archangel officer to control an individual, usually an agent.

Handler – An officer responsible for officers and agents during an assignment. See Controller.

Hapkido – Korean martial art, literally translated as "Way of Coordinated Internal Energy," that uses joint-locks, throws, strikes and kicks to turn an attacker's strength against him or her.

Happy Crappy – Same as SNAFU: Situation Normal, All "Fouled" Up.

Hard-Target Country – A nation that was difficult for spying and uncooperative with Interpol, such as North Korea.

Hello Kitty – Euphemism to confirm that an assignment was thoroughly researched by Rosetta and approved by Archangel.

Honey Trap – Sexual entrapment. See Raven, Swallow.

Horse – A person with longer experience or higher rank in Archangel that helps a new recruit adjust and progress.

Hospital – North Korean (and Russian) intelligence term for a prison.

Hostile – Any individual, group, intelligence service, surveillance, law organization or location that threatens an officer's assignment.

HUMINT – Human intelligence; collection of information by and from human sources (for example, all types of agents) as opposed to data collected using technology. Sometimes known as HUMANT by intelligence services outside the United States, such as the Mossad and NIS.

I

ICPO – International Criminal Police Organization. See Interpol.

Illegal – An officer working in a hostile country without legal or diplomatic protection but with the benefit of a legend. An illegal usually had no direct contact with his or her embassy and was directly controlled by his or her organization.

IMINT – Imagery intelligence.

Immediate – Second-highest urgency for communications.

Impersonal Communications – Secret methods of communicating when physical contact is impossible or unwanted.

Indication and Warning – Detecting and reporting urgent information on terrorist activities.

Infiltration Operation – Infiltrating a given area for a set amount of time without detection.

INII – Innocent Images National Initiative, part of the FBI Crimes Against Children program designed to track and apprehend Internet online child pornographers.

Institute – The Mossad.

Institutional Recruitment – An officer that became "part of the woodwork." A long-time member of Archangel that could be "recruited" for specific assignments beyond the officer's original training.

Intelligence – Term loosely applied to espionage, information gathered via espionage, or the final product.

Intelligence Cycle – Planning, Collection, Processing, Production, Analysis and Dissemination.

Intelligence Estimate – Overview and appraisal of all available information, known as Intelligence Appreciation in Britain.

Intelligence Officer – Professional associated with an intelligence service.

Intelligence Producer – Officer or department that produces intelligence.

Intelligence Requirement – Requirement to gather intelligence on a specific subject or target.

Interception of Oral Communications – Bugging.

Interdepartmental Intelligence – Sharing of intelligence between departments to contribute to a bigger picture.

Interpol – International Criminal Police Organization (ICPO), also the *Organisation Internationale de Police Criminelle* (OIPC). The term "INTERPOL" was the telegraph address of the ICPO. In a nod to common usage, the organization changed its official name to "ICPO-Interpol" (alternatively, OIPC-Interpol) in 1956. Interpol is an international criminal police organization that comprises designated national central bureaus (NCB's) from the law enforcement agencies of its 179 member nations. It has two primary missions:

To ensure and promote the widest possible mutual assistance between all criminal police authorities within the limits of the laws existing in the different countries and in the spirit of the 'Universal Declaration of Human Rights.'

To establish and develop all institutions likely to contribute effectively to the prevention and suppression of ordinary law crimes.

See the *Introduction* for a thorough discussion of Interpol's role in fighting international crime.

K

KCIA – Korean Central Intelligence Agency (KCIA), South Korea. Created in 1961 to supplant the Army Counter-Intelligence Corps (CIC), the organization wielded unlimited power in its intelligence and internal security role and was guilty of gross political suppression. On October 26, 1979, KCIA chief Kim Chaegyu assassinated President Park Chunghee, who was replaced by Major General Chun Doowhan. In 1981 the discredited KCIA was renamed the ANSP. See ANSP, Kwangju Riots, NIS.

Kernel – Disinformation planted in obscure sources to be revealed months or years later as credible "evidence." Many kernels were planted in anticipation of "blow back" operations; then were never used. See Blowback.

KGB – Komitet Gosuderstvennoy Bezopasnosti (Committee of State Security); intelligence and security service of the USSR during the Cold War.

Kiddie Porn – Child Pornography.

Kingdom Come – Recruitment activities of Archangel.

Kwangju Riots – In the springs of 1980 and 1981, South Korean student demonstrations exploded against new president Chun Doowhan's imposing of martial law and the arrest of civic leader Kim Daejong, as enforced by the KCIA, Special Forces and other organizations. The nation-wide riots led to bloody rebellion in Kwangju City that lasted nine days (1980) and three days (1981) and cost nearly 2,000 lives. See KCIA.

L

L-Pill – A lethal ("L") cyanide capsule kept by intelligence officers to be used if captured as an alternative to torture. Both North Korean terrorists involved in bombing KAL 858 carried L-Pills; one succeeded in using it to commit suicide.

Lead – Information from one criminal that incriminates another; also, a person who provides secondhand information.

Legal – An officer protected by diplomatic immunity, usually associated with an consulate or embassy.

Legal Attaché (Legat) – Officer that serves as liaison to law enforcement and intelligence services.

Legend – A complete false identity developed for an officer on assignment, including plausible documentation and a coherent cover story to support the officer's background, living arrangements, job, hobbies, daily life and family. The most effective legends used the identity of a real person, though usually a dead one, to keep the need for fraudulent documents to a minimum. See Cover.

Link Encryption – Total encryption of a communications link using online crypto-security techniques.

Listeners – Archangel surveillance officers who provided information to Rosetta.

Listening Post – Any site that conducted electronic audio surveillance.

LRRP – Belgian Long-Range Reconnaissance Patrol Detachment (LRRP) commando teams. See ESR.

M

Mail Cover – Request made to postal authorities to examine the outside of a piece of mail and report on addresses, postmarks or any other information.

Mail Drop – Accommodation address.

Majors – Principal manufactured documents to support and authenticate a legend. (see Legend.)

MASINT – Measurement and Signature Intelligence.

MATINT – Materials Intelligence.

Measles – Euphemism for a cleaning so skillfully performed that the target's death appeared to be natural, for example, "a case of the measles."

Merch – Merchandise. Slang for smuggled items, whether manufactured, digital or human. See Product.

Meet – Biweekly meeting of in-house Archangel personnel to list current assignments in order of importance.

MI5 – British counterintelligence and internal security; originally an abbreviation for Military Intelligence, Section 5. Founded in 1909, MI5 is a civilian organization that is now officially called the Security Service. Similar to the FBI in the United States.

MI6 – British Secret Intelligence Service (SIS), formerly Section 6 of Military Intelligence. Founded in 1909, it is a civilian organization controlled by the Joint Intelligence Committee and is responsible for foreign intelligence service. Similar to the CIA in the United States and the Mossad in Israel.

MICE – (Money, Ideology, Compromise and Ego). The four primary motivations exploited when recruiting agents. Because Archangel paid so little, officers often joked that their motivations were "handfuls of RICE: Revenge, Idiocy, Crumbs and Eccentricity."

Michael – Euphemism for an Archangel Cleaner, referring to the Michael the Archangel's Biblical role as a protector of children. "And at that time shall Michael stand up, the great prince which standeth for the children of thy people." (Daniel 12:1)

Microdot - Photographic reduction of a message that is so small it can be hidden anywhere, 1mm or smaller in size.

Minaret – NSA program designed to intercept civilian communications, particularly those from foreign nationals to the USA.

Missing Person – A person missing without known or apparent cause, including a Mysterious Disappearance without evidence of runaway or abduction. Critical Missing person is someone whose pre-existing condi-

tions (diabetes, Alzheimer's) may be a health risk, or who may be mentally ill or suicidal.

Missing Persons Organizations in the U.S. and Canada:

CCSC – Child Cyber Search Canada (North America) Also known as the RCMP.

CF – Child Find (Canada).

CMEW – Center For Missing & Exploited Women (USA).

MCHC – Missing Children Help Center (USA) Known by 1-800-USA-KIDS.

MCSC – Missing Children Society of Canada (Canada).

NAMCA – North American Missing Children's Association (North America).

NCMEC – National Center for Missing and Exploited Children (USA).

NMCC – National Missing Children Center (Global).

Pklaas – Polly Klaas Foundation (USA).

Mission – An assignment with details on its task and purpose.

MK-ULTRA – CIA Cold War drug and mind-control program run by Dr. Sidney Gottlieb (1918-99) until his retirement in 1973.

Modern Ninja – A euphemism for Japanese National Police's elite counter-terrorist Special Assault Team. Trained by the French Intervention Group of the National Gendarmerie (GIGN) special operations unit, the Japanese team endured a rigorous schedule of combat shooting, close quarter battle, hostage rescue, counter-espionage and surveillance of known belligerents – such as North Korea. See GIGN.

Mole – An officer or agent that works under a legend within a highly sensitive organization, or a voluntary ("walk-in") or recruited defectors or agents who already worked within the organization.

Mossad – *Ha Mossad, le Modiyn ve le Tafkidim Mayuhadim*, Institute for Intelligence and Special Operations. Known as the Institute. Founded in 1951, the Mossad is Israel's foreign intelligence service, responsible for counter-terrorism, HUMINT gathering and covert operations. It is similar in function to America's CIA and Britain's MI6.

Mule – A knowing or unknowing courier smuggling items through customs; the term is most frequently applied to drug smuggling.

Music Box – Clandestine radio set.

Musician – Radio operator.

N

Naked – Working on an assignment entirely alone, without support or assistance.

Need to Know – Restricted classification of a document or information.

Negative Intelligence – Information that is known by an opposing organization and is therefore compromised and unusable, except when it can be spun into disinformation.

Network – A group of officers working on a particular assignment, in a specific region, or on similar long-term projects. A network is often categorized into smaller teams, called cells.

News – Bad news. See Happy Crappy.

NIC – The National Intelligence Committee of the Central Committee of the Korean Workers Party (NIC); governing body of all North Korean intelligence services. The NIC controlled some 1,500 agents; it was estimated about 200 were in South Korea at any given time. In the 1970s, North Korea began clandestine tunneling operations along the entire Demilitarized Zone (DMZ) between North and South Korea. Three tunnels were discovered by the South Koreans. Twenty-eight more were suspected. See RDEI.

Nightcrawler – Archangel recruiter that trolls bars and clubs looking for prospective agents (such as government employees, law officers, military personnel) that can be exploited via sex, liquor, drugs, or other vices.

NIS – National Intelligence Service (NIS), South Korea. Founded as the KCIA in 1961, and then renamed the ANSP in 1981. Also known as the NSP. South Korea's counterespionage and intelligence service also serves roles in counterintelligence, counter terrorism and internal security. The NIS oversees a vast network of SIGINT sites across the peninsula, with primary listening posts at Taegu, Tongduchon, Oijongbu, Osan, Pyong'aek, Yongsan, as well as on Kangwa and Pyongdong Islands. See ANSP, KCIA.

Nonofficial Cover (NOC) – An officer's fake or real private sector cover job.

NOTELLS – Archangel slang for documents that cannot be shared outside of Archangel, even to other Interpol officers.

Notional Officer – A fictitious officer whose identity is leaked to the media or opposing organization as part of a disinformation strategy.

NSA – National Security Agency. Formed in 1952, NSA is the American SIGINT agency responsible for information security, foreign signals intelligence, and cryptography.

Nugget – (1) Archangel term for information gathered outside official means by Archangel teams, such as unauthorized surveillance, information from informants and agents, and discreet access to classified information provided by intelligence or law enforcement personnel. (2) British intelligence services also use the term in reference to the lures offered to defectors, such as asylum, sex or money.

Nursemaid – Archangel officer traveling with recruits, agents or a skell who rolled on his distribution ring.

O

Offsite – A covert site away from the main Interpol offices, where officers perform such activities as surveillance or undercover operations.

OIPC – *Organisation Internationale de Police Criminelle.* See Interpol.

One-time pad (OTP) – Sheets of paper or silk used only once and printed with a series of random five numbers/letters (sometimes printed on microfilm or microdots). Each cipher is used only once and is therefore almost impossible to break

Open Source (OSINT) – Also referred to as OSCINT; open source intelligence gathered from public records.

Operations Intelligince (OPINTEL) – Information used in planning an assignment.

Operative – An officer on assignment.

OPSEC – Operation Security.

Opposition – Any hostile organization, country or individual.

Overt Intelligence – Open Source information.

OWVL – One-Way-Voice-Link; short wave radio link that transmitted coded messages to an officer on assignment.

P

Padding – Additional digits (letters, words, numbers) inserted in an encoded message to confuse decryption.

Pattern – Daily behavior and routine of an officer or target.

Perimeter Surveillance – Also known as picket surveillance, in which officers are placed in a way that encircles an area being watched.

Pavement Artist – Street surveillance officer.

Personal Meeting – A covert meeting between two officers to share information. See Brush contact.

Petit Louvre – Archangel term for a dead drop.

Photo Intelligence (PHOTOINT) – Also known as Image Intelligence (IMINT).

Piano – Clandestine radio set; a pianist was the radio operator.

Play Back – Known by the Germans as the radio game during WWII. By impersonating a dead or arrested criminal on the phone or via radio communications, an Archangel officer provided disinformation to the skell's distribution ring while obtaining accurate information. Alternatively, an Archangel Nursemaid might monitor while the original skell performed the same role.

Plumber – Officer who plants audio surveillance devices.

PNG – Persona Non Grata, referring to a person exposed as an illegal, an officer without diplomatic or legitimate cover and deported.

Poacher – Hostile officer in the area of an assignment.

Political Intelligence – Information relating to the social and political climate surrounding an assignment.

Positive Vetting – Thorough security check.

Prober – An officer that assesses border security and controls prior to an exfiltration or spy swap.

Product – (1) Term for smuggled items, whether manufactured, digital or human (see Merch); (2) the final result of an assignment.

Profile – Complete background information on a target, provided in a sealed wrap. See Assessment, Wrap.

Provocation/Provocative – Aggressive action intended to expose surveillance.

PsychWrap – Euphemism for a psychological profile provided by Rosetta to Archangel cleaners, delivered in an official "wrap" and sealed envelope with designated signatures.

R

Raven – A male officer who uses romantic/sexual enticements to ensnare a target. See Honey Trap, Swallow.

RCMP – Royal Canadian Mounted Police, the Canadian federal law enforcement agency that also serves as provincial and local police in many areas of the country.

RDEI – Research Department for External Intelligence, North Korea's primary agency for foreign intelligence gathering, working under the NIC. The RDEI had four subsections assigned to as many geographic regions, including North America. The largest subsection was devoted exclusively to South Korea. RDEI officers primarily relied on human source intelligence for gathering of data in South Korea. They had limited capability to intercept communications and electronic transmissions and so depended on intelligence gathered by agents. Usually they recruited agents by appealing to the overwhelming sympathy for reunification between North and South Korea. See NIC.

Receiver – Electronic device that receives signals from surveillance equipment.

Reconnaissance – Assignment designed to provide advance information on a target.

Recruitment – The process of enlisting or coercing an individual to work with Interpol.

Recruitment in Place (RIP) – A foreign official who openly works for his government while covertly providing another country with information of intelligence value.

Repro – Creating false documents.

Ring – Distribution network.

Roll – Give information about one's illegal activities, partners or organization to law officers.

Roll-Out – Sliding two slender poles, such as steel chopsticks, into the slight opening of an envelope, hooking the letter inside, rolling it tightly round the poles, then sliding it out of the envelope without opening it.

Rolled Up – When an officer is exposed, arrested or killed, ending an assignment.

Rosetta – A unit in Archangel that gathered and reviewed evidence and intelligence data on perspective and active targets; then disseminated the information to officers.

Route – Pre-set system of transportation designed to detect if an officer is being tailed.

Runaways – The primary target of child pornographers and those who traffic in human beings. Any person under the age of 18 who intentionally left home. An *Endangered Runaway* either left home in fear of harm, or has become involved in dangerous activity, such as prostitution or drugs. An *Estranged Runaway* was forced to leave home by parents/guardians. Also called throwaways, they often go unreported but live in the same danger as any other runaway.

Runner – A messenger who ran information between Archangel officers and headquarters. See Courier.

S

Safe House – Operational apartment owned or rented by Archangel.

Sanctification – Blackmail.

Sanction – Approval for assassination.

Sanitize – Falsification of information, either by providing fake sources or deleting specific references within reports.

Scalp Hunters – Officers who recruit defectors.

Scotland Yard – Headquarters of the Metropolitan Police, London (The Met), named after a palace given by King Edgar to Kenneth of Scotland to receive the kings of Scotland when they visited England. All public orders to the force come from Scotland Yard.

SDR – Surveillance Detection Run; surreptitious route to expose any surveillance.

SDRA – *Service de Documentation de Recherche et d'Action* (SDRA), the Belgian military security service.

SE – *Surete de l'Etat* (SE) or *Staats Veiligheid* (SV) Belgium security Service or BSS, the internal security service controlled by the Belgian Ministry of Justice.

Secret Writing – Invisible messages sent to accommodation addresses, using microdots or written on innocuous materials, such as secret inks (wet system) or special-treated carbon papers (dry system) that require a reagent to read the message.

Securitate – *Departamentul Securitatii Statului* (Department of State Security); Romania's despised and feared secret police of the Communist Party, responsible for internal security and suppression of dissidents during the Ceausescu regime.

Security Service – Internal counterintelligence service.

Set Up – Surveillance of a target.

Setting Up – Entrapment.

Sheep Dipping – Disguising equipment or persons.

Shoe – Archangel officer that was untrained in assassination but was used to assist a Cleaner on a specific assignment, as in "An extra shoe for stomping bugs." Also, A Russian term for a passport, with matching term, Shoe Maker, a passport forger.

Shopped – Betrayed to an enemy in hopes that the person betrayed will be killed.

Shopworn Goods – Useless information.

Signals – System for signaling, using codes, signs, or other methods.

SIGINT – Signals Intelligence for gathering information via all electronic data transmissions. (Combination of COMINT and ELINT.)

Signal Site – A location to place pre-arranged signals used to communicate with other officers, such as tape on a signpost, which indicated that there a message stored in a Petit Louvre. See Dead Drop, Petit Louvre.

Sijo – Short Korean poetry form that originated in the middle of the Koryo Dynasty (918-1392) and is still alive today.

Silent Clean – Assassination using a silent means, such as poisoning or close quarter combat methods specifically designed for quiet execution, such as certain bladed weapon techniques; also referring to assassination that is "semi-silent," such as using a pistol modified with a silencer, or even a regular Beretta .22, which was known for creating less noise than other similar caliber guns, making it difficult to identify the source of the shot.

SIS – British Secret Intelligence Service. See MI6.

Sister – A bi-sexual or homosexual officer who uses romantic/sexual enticements to ensnare a target. Also known as Ladies or Swallows. See Honey Trap, Raven.

SITREP – Situation Report.

Skell – A criminal.

Sleeper – An agent that lives undercover for years as an ordinary taxpaying citizen in a given country until being "awakened" via pre-arranged signals, usually for terrorist activities. See Mole.

Slick – Any place an officer used to conceal weapons or documents.

Soap – Sodium Pentathol (So-Pe), the infamous "truth serum."

Source – Person providing information, knowing or unknowing, willing or unwilling.

Special Tasks – Assassination, murder and kidnapping.

Sponsor – Whoever is paying for an assignment, such as Archangel or an intelligence service.

Spook – A Spy.

Spy – Any member of an organization, such as an intelligence or security service, that performs activities of a covert nature for that service.

Spy Network/Ring – Centrally-controlled group of spies.

Spy Swap – Exchanging spies between nations or intelligence services. The trade of an exposed Mole by South Korea for an American prisoner held in North Korea was a "spy swap."

Stage Management – Complete management of all deception elements of an assignment as though from the perspective of observers and hostile investigators, including legends and the physical/social/cultural environment.

Station – CIA base of operations in a foreign country.

Step On – Deliberate radio interference.

Sterilize – Remove evidence and materials from the location of an assignment that may implicate Archangel or the cleaner.

Stones – Computer records of the Rosetta department of Archangel.

Stringer – Low-level agent.

Stroller – Officer wearing a covert surveillance microphone, a "wire;" or a handheld radio unit.

Subject – Target of an investigation.

Sucking Dry – Prolonged interrogation.

Support Agent – An agent that supports other agents, often by maintaining a safe house or serving as a cutout.

Sweeper – Technician that checks a location for electronic surveillance.

Swallow – A female officer who uses romantic/sexual enticements to ensnare a target. See Honey Trap, Raven.

T

Tactical Intelligence – Information gathered in preparation for a small unit's assignment.

Takedown – Arrest of suspects via conventional law enforcement procedures; also used for uncovering a network of child pornographers.

Talent Spotter – Recruiter.

Target – A person confirmed by Archangel as the object of a cleaning; generic term for any person or organization that is the object of an assignment.

Target Bonus - An unexpected person that is "*With Child*" during an assignment and cleaned along with the original target.

Taxpayer – Slang for law-abiding citizen. Also, Citizen.

TECHINT – Technical Intelligence (composed of IMINT, MASINT and SIGINT.)

Telephone Tapping – Listening to and recording telephone conversations using electronic surveillance, whether directly attached to the telephone or using "inductive taps" that require no physical connection. Jokingly called Tinkerbell.

Temps – Temporary surveillance devices used by Archangel's Rosetta for gathering information.

Terrorism – Highly organized or just as often disjointed activities designed to use violence to publicize a particular group's bigotry, nationalistic causes, or political agenda. Often funded via international crime activities, such as child pornography, drugs and money laundering.

Timed Drop – Dead drop material that will be removed after a certain period of time.

Tosses – Tossing drops while in motion, whether by hand or from a car, reserved for emergency situations.

Tradecraft – The methods used in covert assignments, specifically intelligence operations.

Traffic – Legitimate, un-coded messages transmitted via an electronic device. Traffic analysis identifies patterns within large volumes of such messages.

Trafficking in Human Beings – The practice of buying and selling humans. Most often children, these horribly abused slaves are acquired legally as indentured servants in countries that allow this practice, or illegally by kidnapping.

Triple Agent – An agent serving three separate services.

Turned Agent – An officer coerced into becoming a double agent.

U

Unsub – Unknown Subject of a criminal investigation.

USNCB – U.S. Department of Justice National Central Bureau of Interpol.

V

Vidocq – Eugène François Vidocq (1775-1857) was the father of modern criminal investigation. A destitute fugitive in 1809, in two years he rose from police informer to the most successful investigator in French history and the first chief of the Sûreté. Vidocq directed a force of 28 detectives, all of whom were also former criminals. Monsieur Vidocq was a master of disguise and surveillance who introduced record keeping, criminology, and the science of ballistics into police work. Vidocq published *Memoires*, a book that became a best-seller in Europe and firmly established him as the world's greatest detective. In a 1935 English translation of Vidocq's memoires, Edwin Gile Rich wrote, "If one were to judge merely from the many bizarre incidents in an extremely picturesque career... none of the incidents in themselves are unbelievable, but that all of the extraordinary happenings could have occurred in one man's life [lead us] to the conclusion that he was an honest man."

Visual Surveillance – Observing using visual means.

W

Walker – An agent recruited to assist an officer in the agent's country.

Walking the Cat – Retracing a rolled-up assignment to see where the flaw occurred.

Washer/Dryer – Post assignment trouble shooter; Archangel officer assigned to monitor the subsequent criminal investigation following a "cleaning."

WATCHCON – Watch Condition for potential hot spots.

Watchers – Archangel officers assigned to visual surveillance and identification of targets.

Watch List – Rosetta's list of potential sources or targets.

Weapons – Officers usually did not carry weapons, but acquired what was necessary at the location of the assignment. Training of cleaners included making use of common materials to eliminate targets, as well as using agents and other officers to provide the needed tools.

Wet Affair – Term for "cleaning."

Wet Squad – Term for a team of cleaners.

Wet Work – Assassination.

White – An Archangel officer who was not involved in cleaning.

Window Dressing – Extra materials, clothing, indirect documents (receipts, ticket stubs, etc.) and other trivial items designed to lend authenticity to a legend.

With Child – Euphemism indicating a target has been identified via photographic and video media, as well as eyewitness accounts, in the act of sexually abusing a child; referring to a target attempting to distribute videos and photographs of him or herself sexually abusing a child. The final confirmation before assigning a cleaner.

Wrap – Internal Archangel envelope with designated signature(s) and wrapped in sealed plastic; also specifically used for a sealed envelope that contained the details of an assignment, jokingly called a "CleanWrap."

Z

Zoo – Police Station.